Business Continuity

# Springer

*Berlin
Heidelberg
New York
Barcelona
Hong Kong
London
Milan
Paris
Tokyo*

Martin Wieczorek
Uwe Naujoks
Bob Bartlett (Eds.)

# Business Continuity

IT Risk Management
for International Corporations

With Contributions of

B. Dellar, K.-P. Gerlach, L. Goecke, T. Guthrie-Harrison,
U. Naujoks, M. Philipp, K. M. Reimann, H. Schettler,
J. Schmuck, J. Sharp, G. Sutherland, U. Veldenz,
E. Wallmüller, F.-J. Weil, M. J. Wieczorek

Dr. Martin J. Wieczorek
SQS Software Quality Systems
Stollwerckstr. 11
51149 Köln
Deutschland

Uwe Naujoks
WestLB, Dept. 001-79250
Herzogstr. 15
40217 Düsseldorf
Deutschland

Bob Bartlett
Managing Director
SIM Group Ltd.
Albion House, Chertsey Road
GU21 1BE Woking, Surrey
United Kingdom

With 44 Figures and 13 Tables

ISBN 3-540-43051-2 Springer-Verlag Berlin Heidelberg New York

*Library of Congress Cataloging-in-Publication Data applied for*

Die Deutsche Bibliothek – CIP-Einheitsaufnahme
Business continuity: it risk management for international corporations / Martin Wieczorek ... (ed.).
With contributions of B. Dellar ... – Berlin; Heidelberg; New York; Barcelona; Hong Kong; London;
Milan; Paris; Tokyo: Springer 2002
ISBN 3-540-43051-2

This work is subject to copyright. All rights are reserved, whether the whole or part of the material is concerned, specifically the rights of translation, reprinting, reuse of illustrations, recitation, broadcasting, reproduction on microfilm or in any other way, and storage in data banks. Duplication of this publication or parts thereof is permitted only under the provisions of the German Copyright Law of September 9, 1965, in its current version, and permission for use must always be obtained from Springer-Verlag. Violations are liable for prosecution under the German Copyright Law.

Springer-Verlag Berlin Heidelberg New York
a member of BertelsmannSpringer Science+Business Media GmbH
http://www.springer.de

© Springer-Verlag Berlin Heidelberg 2002
Printed in Germany

The use of designations, trademarks, etc. in this publication does not imply, even in the absence of a specific statement, that such names are exempt from the relevant protective laws and regulations and therefore free for general use.

*Production:* PRO EDIT GmbH, Heidelberg
*Cover design:* Künkel + Lopka, Heidelberg
*Typesetting:* K. Detzner, Speyer, from author's data
Printed on acid-free paper   SPIN 10862056   33/3142hs   5 4 3 2 1 0

# List of Contributors and Authors

BARRY DELLAR
*Senior Consultant*
*SIM Group Ltd.*
*Systems Integration Management*
*Albion House, Chertsey Road*
*Woking, Surrey GU21 1BE*
*United Kingdom*
*Email: barry.dellar@simgroup.co.uk*
*Web: www.simgroup.com*
*Telephone: +44 1483 73 3150*

KLAUS-PETER GERLACH
*IT-Security Manager*
*DZ Bank International Luxembourg*
*4, rue Thomas Edison, 1445*
*Luxembourg-Strassen, Luxembourg*
*Email: klaus-peter.gerlach@dzi.lu*
*Web: www.dzi.lu*
*Telephone: +352 44903 2418*

LOTHAR GOECKE
*Senior Consultant*
*Heine & Partner GmbH*
*Stadtplatz 2, 85368 Moosburg, Germany*
*Email: lothar.goecke@heine-partner.de*
*Web: www.heine-partner.de*
*Telephone: +49 8761 6677 0*

TIM GUTHRIE-HARRISON
*Wiremead, East Cholderton*
*Near Andover*
*Hampshire SP11 8LR, United Kingdom*

*Email: tgh@primex.co.uk*
*Web: www.heine-partner.de*
*Telephone: +44 7971 574928*

UWE NAUJOKS
*Assistant Vice President*
*Business Continuity Coordinator*
*for WestLB Banking Group*
*Westdeutsche Landesbank Girozentrale*
*Department 001-79250*
*Herzogstr. 15, 40217 Düsseldorf*
*Germany*
*Email: uwe.naujoks@westlb.de*
*Web: www.westlb.de*
*Telephone: +49 211 826 8432*

MICHAEL PHILIPP
*Consultant*
*SQS Software Quality Systems AG*
*Stollwerckstr. 11, 51149 Köln, Germany*
*Email: michael.philipp@sqs.de*
*Web: www.sqs.de*
*Telephone: +49 2203 9154 1344*

KONRAD M. REIMANN
*K-M-R Unternehmens-*
*und Personalberatung GmbH*
*Neunkircher Str. 152 b*
*66113 Saarbrücken, Germany*
*Email: bridge@pt.lu*
*Web: www.k-m-r-gmbh.de*
*Telephone: +352 35 52 81*

HEINRICH SCHETTLER
*Senior Consultant*
*SQS Software Quality Systems AG*
*Stollwerckstr. 11, 51149 Köln, Germany*
*Email: heinrich.schettler@sqs.de*
*Web: www.sqs.de*
*Telephone: +49 2203 9154 381*

JOACHIM SCHMUCK
*Senior Consultant*
*T-Systems GEI GmbH*
*Goebelstr. 1–3, 64293 Darmstadt*
*Germany*
*Email: joachim.schmuck@t-systems.de*
*Web: www.t-systems.de*
*Telephone: +49 6151 820 3400*

JOHN SHARP
*Chief Executive Officer*
*The Business Continuity Institute*
*PO Box 4474, Worcester WR6 5YA*
*United Kingdom*
*Email: TheBCI@btinternet.com*
*Web: www.thebci.org*
*Telephone: +44 870 603 8783;*
*+44 1886 833 555*

GARY SUTHERLAND
*Business Unit Manager*
*SIM Group Ltd.*
*Systems Integration Management*
*Albion House, Chertsey Road*
*Woking, Surrey GU21 1BE*
*United Kingdom*
*Email: gary@simgroup.co.uk*
*Web: www.simgroup.com*
*Telephone: +44 1483 73 3170*

ULRICH VELDENZ
*General Manager Banking Services*
*WestLB International S.A.*
*32–34 Bd. G.D. Charlotte*
*2010 Luxembourg, Luxembourg*
*Email: ulrich.veldenz@westlb.lu*
*Web: www.westlb.lu*
*Telephone: +352 44741 640*

ERNEST WALLMÜLLER, DR.
*Managing Director*
*Qualität und Informatik*
*Haslemstr. 14, 8954 Geroldswil*
*Switzerland*
*Email: wallmueller@itq.ch*
*Web: www.itq.ch*
*Telephone: +41 1 748 52 56*

FRANZ-JOSEF WEIL
*Operations Manager Banking*
*WestLB International S.A.*
*32–34 Bd. G.D. Charlotte*
*2010 Luxembourg, Luxembourg*
*Email: franz-josef.weil@westlb.lu*
*Web: www.westlb.lu*
*Telephone: +352 44741 315*

MARTIN J. WIECZOREK, DR.
*Head of Departments of*
*Telecommunication/Public and Care*
*SQS Software Quality Systems AG*
*Stollwerckstr. 11, 51149 Köln, Germany*
*Email: martin.wieczorek@sqs.de*
*Web: www.sqs.de*
*Telephone: +49 2203 9154 356*

# Preface

In its daily business, the IT industry makes mistakes that other industries have known about for 10 years or more. For example, two-thirds of the companies in the IT industry do not apply any risk management methods in their IT projects. They do not analyse the risks: not the project risks, nor the technology risks, nor the business risks. Another number: 75% of all e-business projects do not reach their original goals because of a lack of strategic preparation, i.e. their risk management or their project management fails.[1]

In nine European countries 43% of 450 managers in high and middle management state that they are completely dependent on stable hardware and software, a further 34% of them state that they are in some sense dependent. This means that if IT systems fail 92% of such managers lose time in conducting their daily business. This, in fact, is about one hour per week.[2]

In addition, most of the risks might not be mitigated or even understood. This is true for example for a single banking department, a computer centre, or an individual software supplier. Problems and risks are not isolated but rather are interdependent by nature. As such, understanding and mitigating operational risks means having an integrated look at all areas dependent upon IT systems. In this sense, the articles in this book are meant to bridge the gap between IT software system suppliers, system operators, and system users. In a time in which globalisation, reduction of time to market, and cost efficiency are well-known goals for the IT industry and in which the Internet, electronic mailing, B2B (business to business) or, in general, X2Y are meant to save time and costs, the above-mentioned situations are counterproductive. This serves as enough motivation to compile such a book as this one.

This book is divided into three parts. The first part gives an overview of the topic and addresses general aspects. The fundamental background are laws and regulations formulated by countries and supranational institutions of the banking business such as the Bank for International Settlement. The bank's internal auditing department has to play its role in monitoring the fulfilment of such regulations, but there are also opportunities to support activities towards business continuity. On the practical level the most important framework for business continuity is crisis management, which

---

[1] Computer Zeitung, No. 3, January 14, 2002.
[2] Computer Zeitung, No. 4, January 21, 2002.

enables a bank to react in an optimal way in case of an accident or disaster. In a sense, this can be seen as a last firewall for business.

Part two concentrates on special activities in banking departments to shelter their processes from operational risks. The most important tool for this are business continuity plans (BCP). To demonstrate the application of BCP an example of a global bank with its headquarters in Germany is provided. Experiences from initial implementation in a cross-sectional project and quality assurance on a regular basis are discussed. An example tool demonstrates usage in BCP documentation, workflow support and monitoring. Business continuity does not only rely on business continuity plans but also on the appropriate infrastructure. This is exemplified by a disaster recovery site, which is commonly operated by several Luxembourg banks. Last but not least, an early warning technique for controlling operational risks is considered: the children's illnesses of new or redesigned IT systems in the time period after roll-out. This can be achieved by an intensified kind of monitoring.

The third and last part of this book focuses on the role and processes of the software supplier. The wide field of project risks with their various impacts on business processes as well as their necessary mitigation at the project level are discussed. Furthermore, an example demonstrates risk and cost reduction for business and project by adapting and designing engineering procedures to the specific task. The quality assurance part of the development process has the challenge to align its efforts with the risks for business processes, caused by possible software failures.

This book, as part of the Springer series software.quality@xpert.press, addresses decision makers and practitioners in business processes of the financial sector, IT system operations, and software development especially if they are challenged with the task of preventing problems and accidents in their part of the business.

We hope that the examples given will help to implement a practical end-to-end view in the supply chain from systems and software development to business services and products, explicitly focusing on operational risks.

Last but not least we should not forget to thank several people. Firstly, many thanks go to all the authors for their interest and contribution to this book and for their outstanding support in its realisation. Without them, it would have been impossible to compile this collection of highly practical examples from crisis management, business continuity planning and risk management in and through software and quality engineering. Secondly, we would like to thank Heinrich Schettler for his commitment and support during all stages of the production of this book.

| Martin Wieczorek | Uwe Naujoks | Bob Bartlett |
|---|---|---|
| *SQS Software Quality Systems AG* | *Westdeutsche Landesbank* | *SIM Group Ltd.* |
| *(Germany)* | *(Germany)* | *(United Kingdom)* |

# Introduction

The importance of risk and business continuity management has been driven to the fore following the terrorist attacks in the USA on 11 September 2001. Organisations throughout the world are now revising their assessment of terrorist risks and struggling to understand how they could survive such attacks. Whilst some businesses associated with the World Trade Center in New York will fail, many will survive and rebuild. These survivors will have used the principles and practices enshrined in business continuity management (BCM) to start their recovery from the disaster.

As the worldwide crises over the past 12 months have demonstrated, it is not possible to predict events that can seriously affect an organisations ability to maintain continuity of business. Because the unexpected will always occur there is a clear need to protect organisations by forward planning. business continuity management is seen as a vital tool to assist the finance sector in the management of risk and to achieve regulatory compliance.

This book seeks to share with the reader the current best practice and to stimulate the thinking and actions of those responsible for delivering risk and business continuity management in the finance sector.

## 1 The Development of Risk Management

Until recently risk management was seen mainly as an insurance-based discipline. Using historical data and experience, assessments were made of the likelihood of an occurrence of predictable events. It was principally based around the financial loss of life or capital assets. Using actuarial techniques the probability of occurrence was calculated, thus enabling a premium to be established for insurance purposes.

Whilst insurance was seen as the first choice in the management of risks, alternative strategies have been adopted to mitigate failure. These have included the modification or cessation of practices that are considered risky. This has led to a risk adverse approach being adopted by managers within organisations who take precautionary measures adding to the cost base of the company rather than be found wanting at some date in the future. This occurs through a fear of risk that is linked to the unforgiving attitude of managers toward employee failure. It is also about senior managers only being interested in "good news" rather than the truth.

In recent times there have been some major corporate failures and examples of poor or non-existent risk management practices have come to light. Notable amongst these have been the UK Maxwell Pensions fraud and the Barings Bank collapse. The result of these and other similar events led to demands for improvement in Corporate Governance. The principles of good corporate governance have spread throughout commercial companies worldwide. In the UK this was outlined in the Turnbull Report, published in 1999, and entitled: *Guidance for Directors on Internal Controls for Risk Management.* This calls for directors of UK stock exchange listed companies to clearly state in their published reports and accounts what they consider to be their key risks and how effective their internal controls are in managing these risks.

In the last two to three years there has been a shift away from the traditional insurance-based risk management to one closely linked to the operations of the organisation. Risk management is now progressing from a purely actuary-based insurance approach to incorporate any occurrence, internal or external, that can disrupt the organisation's ability to operate. The term operational risk management is increasingly being adopted by major organisations. It is accepted that it is impossible to predict what these occurrences might be and that it is better to understand how a loss of capabilities will impact the achievement of the organisation's mission.

## 2 The Development of Business Continuity Management

**Disaster Recovery**

Until the early 1970s most companies had no serious form of continuity planning. Major disasters were rare and companies relied on insurance to protect them against asset loss and loss of profits. Business complacency was shattered, however, by the OPEC oil embargo; this showed US corporations they were vulnerable to external events beyond their control. Dealing with the rest of the world suddenly became riskier with the emergence of terrorism and global cultural conflict.

At the same time the US financial sector realised they were becoming more and more dependent upon new computer technology and the catastrophic impact that non-availability might have on a financial institution's ability to function. The regulators put considerable pressure on the financial sector to develop contingency plans to protect clients' funds. The computer industry saw this as an opportunity to sell more equipment. If loss of a data centre could put the survival of the business at risk then surely it would be a good idea to duplicate it in a location that could not be affected by the same disaster. For the computer suppliers, disaster recovery became an ideal complementary business and it gave their clients who could not afford duplicate sites the opportunity to participate in a shared service with minimal risk.

Disaster recovery developed to encompass the replacement of facilities and property lost due to fire, flood, earthquake or other disasters. The escalation of terrorist activities in Europe in the 1980s further heightened the need for contingency plans.

**The Emergence of Business Continuity Management**

In the late 1980s the concept of business continuity was established as a new way of managing risks within a business, viewing the continuation of business functionality in all circumstances as the key responsibility of the Board. Recovery of computer systems was simply part of the technical implementation of the overall business strategy. Unlike disaster recovery planning business continuity is about anticipating that things are beginning to go wrong and taking planned and rehearsed steps to protect the business and hence the stakeholders' interests. It is about co-ordinating and integrating all the planning processes across departments and presenting a confident image to the outside world.

Business continuity management has progressively developed to a point where today it takes a holistic view of an organisation, and is defined by the Business Continuity Institute (BCI), *"as the act of anticipating incidents which will affect mission critical functions and processes for the organisation and ensuring that it responds to any incident in a planned and rehearsed manner whilst the business recovers"*.

The term incident is used rather than disaster. Directors of organisations do not accept that their companies will be subject to disasters. 'It will never happen to us' is the retort still heard from directors. This leads to an ill-prepared organisation unable to respond at critical times.

Research in the mid-1990s undertaken by Knight and Pretty of Templeton College, Oxford in the UK has shown that the effect of disasters on shareholder value can be serious. They discovered that it is the lack of confidence in the ability of senior managers and directors to act quickly and professionally at the time of disaster that drives down share values. Knight and Pretty quote various examples of organisations that have lost the confidence of shareholders at critical times. The classic example is Perrier who, at the time of the benzene contamination of their product, failed to respond adequately to the concerns of the market. Their market share was dramatically reduced and the value of the Perrier shares fell so seriously that the company became vulnerable and was eventually taken over by Nestlé.

Examination into the causes of most major disasters has found that there are several incidents or circumstances that combine together which lead to the eventual disaster. BCM is about prevention, not cure. It is about being able to deal with incidents as and when they occur thus preventing disasters. It has been found that this concept is more acceptable to directors.

The BCI definition calls for the identification of those incidents that will affect the mission critical functions and processes of an organisation. Until the critical areas have been identified, work should not commence on the business continuity plans.

BCM requires that effective plans be established to ensure an organisation can respond to any incident. But the process does not stop at the planning stage. Plans are worthless unless they are rehearsed. In the Knight and Pretty study, five of the organisations investigated had suffered serious consequences as a result of poor disaster management. Some of these companies had business continuity plans in place but they failed because they had not rehearsed them. The rehearsal of plans is essential. There is not a plan created that will work the first time; rehearsing ensures that disconnections with the plan and omissions are fixed before it is used in reality.

In the BCI definition the term business continuity management is used rather than business continuity planning. This is deliberate as planning implies that there is a start and end to the process. BCM is a continuum; plans must be kept up to date as the organisation changes. External environments and influences are constantly in a state of flux and so the process, to be valid, must continue throughout the life of the organisation.

# 3 Key Drivers

It is becoming essential for organisations to introduce BCM. There are several key drivers that determine this. The most important is about delivering confidence to all stakeholders. Stakeholders are not only the investors. The list includes customers and employees, suppliers, the community, the environment and frequently, protest groups.

Industry regulations and legal requirements are having an increasing influence upon organisations. There is an increased awareness by the regulators that organisations should have effective BCM in place for the protection of customers and critical infrastructures. The Risk Management Group of the Basel Committee on Banking Supervision has shown that they consider effective continuity plans essential for the banking sector and extends this to include outsourcing suppliers to the sector.

Frequently directors turn to the insurance industry to help them manage business risk. It is not the physical loss that causes the greatest pain for any organisation but the loss of customers. Business interruption insurance is seen as a way of covering the revenue lost whilst the facilities are rebuilt. Insurance companies will have greater confidence in the management's ability to rebuild, and hence be more inclined to provide adequate cover, if they can see evidence that effective BCM is in place.

Just as major customers have insisted that their suppliers have quality and project management processes in place they are now demanding that BCM be established to ensure continuity of supply. This is driven, not only by their need to achieve corporate governance compliance, but also by the need to maintain their market share.

The speed of business has changed and there is very often little time to allow a gradual recovery. The emergence of e-banking and the lack of loyalty amongst customers has changed the need for recovery to one of availability. Organisations for whom this is key have to ensure that their services are available 24×365. The BCM process includes an assessment of availability and how the BC plan should be structured to meet customers' expectations.

An internal survey carried out by a German financial company over the past three years has found a changing view of why BCM is important. Initially the need was to ensure compliance with regulatory requirements; it then changed to one of protecting their customers' interests. Today it is about ensuring that corporate value is maintained. Without that value, underpinned by the confidence of their investors, the company would be vulnerable in their highly competitive market.

**The Future of Business Continuity Management**

As BCM has evolved, an underlying model of best practice around the world has emerged. Driven by the global financial industry and the professional BCM practitioners a methodology has been developed based on the ten certification standards of the Business Continuity Institute. The BCI is pleased to be associated with this publication as many of the chapters in this book reflect that methodology.

All departments and functions have a role to play in the overall BCM process, yet in most organisations their actions are not coordinated. The Board can assist this process by appointing a BCM manager at the senior level whose role it is to draw together, under a matrix team approach, representatives from the various functions, together with key business heads, to ensure a coordinated approach to BCM.

Each major crisis raises the awareness of organisations to their vulnerability. Businesses have become more exposed to threats, both internal and external. The adoption of lean supply chains, just in time manufacture and flatter organisations has removed the resilience essential to absorb failures. The focus on business activities by the media and protest groups expose and exploit any weakness or mistake very quickly to the wider world. Investors are looking closely at the performance of board directors and regulation is forcing organisations to introduce risk management.

Since the terrorist activities in the US on 11 September 2001 BCM has gained a much higher profile around the world. Organisations that were delaying the introduction of the process are now approving previously blocked proposals. Governments are beginning to demand that BCM processes should be established across their own departments and agencies. More importantly, the demands of the regulators to establish effective risk management has highlighted the need to manage those risks that cannot be eliminated. BCM is now seen as an effective tool to assist the management of these risks.

JOHN SHARP
*Chief Executive Officer*
*The Business Continuity Institute*

# Table of Contents

## Part I  Overview and General Aspects

*Heinrich Schettler, Martin J. Wieczorek, Michael Philipp:*
Operational Risks and Business Continuity: An Essayistic Overview ...... 1

*Klaus-Peter Gerlach:*
The Role of States and of International and National Organisations
as Super-Risk managers .................................................. 32

*Konrad M. Reimann:*
Position of the "Internal Audit Department" in a BCP Project .......... 64

*Tim Guthrie-Harrison:*
Crisis Management for a New Century ................................... 80

## Part II  Business and System Operation

*Uwe Naujoks:*
Business Continuity Planning (BCP) in a Globalised Bank ............... 97

*Uwe Naujoks:*
Verification/Testing and Monitoring of Business Continuity Plans ...... 118

*Lothar Goecke:*
The Benefits of BCP Tools, with Special Reference to CAPT® and CM® .... 127

*Ulrich Veldenz, Franz-Josef Weil:*
Creating the Complete Environment for the Survival of a Bank ......... 139

*Barry Dellar:*
Robustness Provided by Internet Monitoring Systems ................... 156

## Part III  Software and System Supply

*Ernest Wallmüller:*
Risk Management for IT and Software Projects ......................... 163

*Gary Sutherland:*
**The Control of IT Risk by Means of Risk-Based Testing** . . . . . . . . . . . . . . . 179

*Joachim Schmuck:*
**Software Reengineering for Mission-Critical Applications –
Minimizing Business Risks and Reducing Maintenance Costs** . . . . . . . . . . . 189

**References and Links** . . . . . . . . . . . . . . . . . . . . . . . . . . . . . . . . . 210

Part I

**Overview and General Aspects**

# Operational Risks and Business Continuity: An Essayistic Overview

Heinrich Schettler, Martin J. Wieczorek, Michael Philipp
SQS Software Quality Systems AG (Germany)

**Abstract:** This article is intended to give a comprehensible introduction to operational risks and business continuity to an interested reader who is not necessarily an expert. Nowadays, business has become complex because of many factors: globalisation, distribution of services, new technologies and so on. Such factors lead to risks which are sometimes not used to dealing with. However, none of those factors may be considered in isolation. They are, to a certain extent, always present and they have to be considered in their context. This is also necessary from the viewpoint of time, budget, and the quality of the corresponding activities.

After some historical examples of risk management, mainly in the context of trading and banking, the notion of robustness is introduced in an informal way and the driving forces in the field of operational risks today are discussed. An overview of strategies to control the risks to business processes is presented. Here the roles of business owners and of system and software suppliers are described, emphasising the issue of co-operation. In addition to the opportunities arising from risk management and business continuity planning, some limitations and open questions are sketched, indicating that there is no final patent remedy. As a conclusion, the needs for the balancing of risk control against other business activities and for its integration with those activities are outlined.

**Keywords:** Operational risks, Robustness, Risk management, Business continuity planning, Crisis management, Software and project risks, Benefits and costs, Risk map, Basel II

## 1 Introduction

While this article was being written, on September 11th 2001, the terrorist attacks on the World Trade Center and the Pentagon occurred. This catastrophe had many immediate political and economic effects. The other, more long-term effects cannot be predicted with today's knowledge and experience. Besides the human catastrophe this terrible event also highlights the enormous amount of interaction and interdependencies between business, technology and other kinds of infrastructure and their sensitivity to disturbances. This event has shown, in a horrible manner, the practical importance of operational risks and reminded us of the principal limitations of risk control.

Though the 11th of September is a striking example of a new quality of risk, we are used to dealing with risks. The glance at evolution and history in the next section will show this. Section 3 discusses current operational risks in the context of globalisation and internationalisation, and Section 4 introduces the idea of robustness. Possibilities for dealing with operational risks will be discussed in Section 5 from two different viewpoints, namely the business process and the supplying of IT systems which support the business process. Section 6 will take a closer look at the problem of balancing all activities against operational risks with respect to benefits and costs, as well as opportunities and risks.

## 2 Examples of Risk Management in History

As a vivid example of risk management, observe a bird in the garden. How does the bird behave? Normally it is picking for worms or drinking water. That is its business process. When it is alarmed by strange, sometimes very small changes in its sensual field, the bird concentrates on the spot in which the changes have occurred (continuously operating early-warning system) and decides very quickly whether to escape (business continuity plan to shelter from substantial damage, e.g. by a cat), to continue observation of the spot or to continue exploiting its opportunities (worms). This comprises risk management behaviour, coded in DNA by biological evolution. In this way the bird achieves a certain amount of protection from dangers, e.g. cats. That is robustness of its "business process".

Today we envision evolution as an optimisation process with the preservation of species as one of its goals. This optimisation process produces a certain amount of short-term inefficiency. Our bird does not use all of its time to pick worms, to drink water or to reproduce. If it did, the bird would have been eaten by a cat long ago, so that we would not observe it today.

In the following we give some historical examples of operational risks and their management from the field of trading, banking and insurance and consider the business system as a whole.

### 2.1 Trading

In addition to risk management by evolution, there is also a long tradition of conscious human risk management. One obvious step is reflected in the birth of the idea of risk in the 17th century [Broc96]. The Italian word *ris(i)co* meant "to sail around a rock", which was a typical risk in those days in the business of trading with India.

In 1599 a trading company in the Netherlands sent four ships to India to buy pepper. Only two of the ships returned in 1601, demonstrating the risky side of trading. On the other hand, documents report profits of up to 300% [Brau86]. This resembles figures for successful start-up enterprises not so long ago.

What was the nature of the operational risks of trading? Rocks, bad weather, inaccurate maps, navigational mistakes and absence of information on what to sell or buy and where to do so. These risks mostly affected a single ship or a single trade, and in rare cases a small fleet, but they did not affect the worldwide trading system as a whole. To cope with their individual business risks, traders distributed their merchandise among several ships and diversified into different trades and locations. There were technological and procedural developments which increased the robustness of shipping. Copper hulls, simplification of steering and navigation, and differentiation and specialisation of work by centralising control of the ship in the hands of specially trained experts on the one hand, and leaving operational activities to semiskilled people, on the other hand, are only a few examples. The last feature allowed not only for better and quicker reaction in case of trouble (crisis management) but also the manning of many ships with people who had not previously worked on ships (efficiency and flexibility).

Another practice has had obvious consequences that have continued to the present day. As predecessors of our joint-stock companies, traders used to own and operate ships through shares, taking business opportunities and risks in common.

## 2.2 Banking and Insurance

Early forms of banking can be found in the Bible. Its medieval big-business form, for example as practised by the Fuggers, began by concentrating on financing the activities of kings and rulers such as conquests and wars. The careers of these bankers began to end when they overestimated the possibilities of a Spanish king and bid on a single horse.

A big opportunity arose in the context of trading in the form of a multiple function: on the one hand credit allowed traders to undertake expensive, long-term trading trips and reduced their financial risk, and on the other hand it allowed participants or investors to participate in the opportunities of trading and distributed the associated risks.

Financial risks were mitigated by comparatively small banking and insurance companies. In the beginning often a single company or businessman acted as trader, banker and insurer in one. The impacts of the bankruptcy of one such institution were also restricted.

A large operational risk, not only for banking, lay in the production of sound accounts, especially when the business was distributed over several locations and independent business transactions took place to a certain extent. Methods such as double-entry accounting (used for the first time by the Fuggers and in Upper Italy) and procedures for saving data and transferring information were used to prevent wrong accounting. These appear to be predecessors of practices such as two-phase commit protocols, re-routing and encryption techniques, which are nowadays used in computer networks to control similar risks. In addition, these risks accelerated the development of mathematics as a key technology and of banking as the "engineering" discipline par excellence.

Probably the best known example of an early insurance business is Lloyds of London (which originated at the end of the 17th century), a co-operation of companies which originally insured ships. As one important part of its business, Lloyd's operated an early warning system, which allowed the London headquarters to monitor as exactly and as quickly as possible the position and state of the insured ships. It is reported that Lloyd's was even better informed than the ships' owners. This knowledge protected Lloyd's from insurance fraud and provided data to assess future claims by means of probability theory.

## 2.3 Business Network

Most of the operational risks of the 17th and 18th century arose from comparatively small, independent, isolated causes which affected single trades, ships or business partners. These risks did not affect the business network as a whole, which behaved in a stable and robust manner even under the conditions of the wars that were usual at that time.

One feature of this network was the great amount of flexibility and fault tolerance among the business partners regarding delays. Delays were a fact of life: delays in journeys by ship, delays in the transport of information and delays in the transport of bills of exchange between different branches. This indicated an inherent credit opportunity for the business partners, reflected in their business ethics, which were based to a great extent on mutual confidence. Prolongation of credit, time buffers and buffers for goods (warehouses) were basic measures to tackle the risks. As a framework, there evolved a stable and sufficiently effective but not very quick information network between business participants, which announced opportunities and risks.

However, there arose threats to the business system. Vital points, which controlled the business system and made it vulnerable to chain reactions, developed. From the 17th to the 18th century, the city of Amsterdam in the Netherlands developed into the central European trade centre and storeroom – a warehouse and banking place in one. For a long time, there were no real threats to this location in spite of various wars.

A decline of the Netherlands and Amsterdam took place in the second half of the 18th century, accompanied by crises in the credit business, which had Amsterdam as its centre. These crises were induced by an increase in bills without sufficient underlying value. The crises ended in the occupation of Amsterdam by foreign troops and a revolution in 1787, which was the first major predecessor of the French Revolution in 1789. These impacts were not anticipated by the important businessmen in Amsterdam. These businessmen furthered the crises by initiating and multiplying the uncontrolled use of excessively large amounts of paper.

Today globalisation and internationalisation are sometimes identified as new sources of operational risks. But in the 17th and 18th centuries there was already a business network which spanned the world. Until then its density had increased at a modest velocity. Globalisation and internationalisation are thus old but ongoing processes.

## 3 Operational Risks Today

On February 10, 2001, a German newspaper [FAZ101] reported an incident concerning an underwater cable which connects China with North America. This cable is used for Internet traffic and had been damaged near Shanghai, probably by a fishing net. The interruption lasted about half a day and caused a lot of trouble for businesses and private users, even after the traffic had been re-routed to a second cable. This example shows the need to look for interactions that are not obvious but nevertheless possible. It shows the need to look at the sometimes hidden vital or critical points upon which a great deal of business depends. The Y2K activities reminded us of the importance of the supply of energy, water and communication services.

On May 16, 2001 the same German newspaper [FAZ201] reported that the second largest daily loss ever recorded, measured in absolute figures, had occurred on the London Stock Exchange on May 15th. Somebody had entered the wrong input into a computer program and "suddenly" released a series of very quick selling orders for British stocks. A typical chain reaction. The impacts were obvious. The reasons why – as usual in such cases – were not published. London Stock Exchange officials announced that the security precautions of one member would have to be checked. This example is only one of many examples and shows what can happen if only a short reaction time is available. This situation, perhaps in combination with panic, allows only Pavlov-like, formal reaction schemes. It is remarkable that the subsequent sellers tried to reduce their clients' risks, but by doing so only achieved the contrary.[1] Efficiency- or time-optimised processes tend to react very sensitively to small, unpredicted variations in their inputs and their environment.

To get an overview of the vast number of possible risks, we need some ordering scheme. The Basel Committee on Banking Supervision, for instance, proposes the risk areas listed in Table for the banking industry [BASE]. We shall use this table in our overview of operational risks as an example of how to structure risks for the purpose of understanding their causes and of facilitating risk control.

---

[1] The residual risk from the measures to control risk was greater than the initial risk.

Table 1: Risk areas according to the Basel Committee on Banking Supervision

| Risk area | Description |
|---|---|
| External factors | External factors summarise all interactions of a banking enterprise with its clients, external business partners and environment. |
| Processes | All internal business, management and service processes performed by the organisation to fulfil its tasks including their internal interactions (e.g. by "material flow"). |
| Systems | This area addresses the technical infrastructure to perform the banking processes; especially<br>IT and Telecommunication (TC) infrastructure<br>facilities such as business premises, buildings and associated technology.<br>We interpret "Systems" not only in the sense of IT but in a wider sense. |
| People | This area addresses all the persons performing the business of the banking organisation, from senior management to the operational level. |

## 3.1 External Factors

Obviously, the above-mentioned example of the trawler that cut an Internet cable fits into the field of environmental interactions, which has an enormous potential for dangers that are not so easy to predict.

In general, within the area of external factors, risks might be associated with:

- material flow with banking partners (e.g. in the context of international payment transactions)
- supply and services provided by external partners (e.g. supply of business data, as in the case of Reuters; supply of parts of banking services such as credit card management; IT operations; facility supply; and energy supply)
- criminal activities, for example by external defrauders, hackers or terrorists (new opportunities are presented, for example, by new client interfaces)
- political developments
- natural disasters such as earthquakes, hurricanes and so on.

The only item in this list for which there seems to be no increase of risk is the field of natural disasters. Such risks are traditionally mitigated by the appropriate engineering of buildings and by insurance. Risks (or more exactly the knowledge of them) can possibly be increased or decreased through new scientific insights, for example, about the danger presented to locations by earthquakes. The relevance of risks from criminal activities is obvious. The stability of the political environment varies from country to country. But at the moment we believe that the probability of unpredictable developments is increasing.

In today's business world there is a tendency to outsource business parts or services as separate enterprises. This obviously increases the number of business interfaces which have to perform properly. The robustness of an external partner is not so easily judged as the robustness of an internal department. Figure 1 presents our view of the relevant interfaces in the context of financial business.

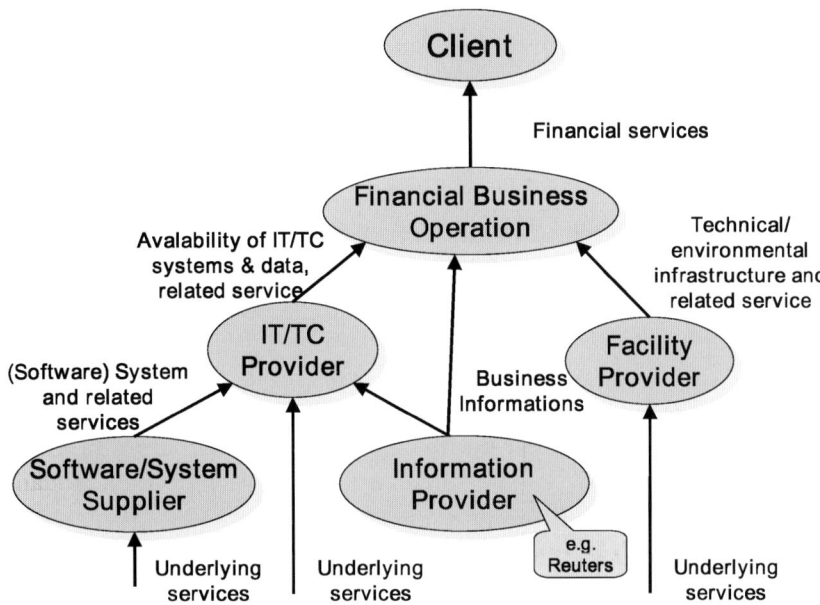

Figure 1: Differentiation of work between business process and suppliers

As an additional effect, an external partner will provide its services to several customers. The coincidence of high-volume service needs by several customers, for example, might influence each of these customers in a sometimes unpredictable way.

Often, internal service departments have informal knowledge about the usage of their service and direct contacts people in the business processes. This knowledge and these contacts help such departments to react properly and quickly in disturbances or crises.

The patent remedy in this situation is a service-level agreement (SLA). This is an appropriate form for such needs but does not prescribe the content of the service in a comprehensive manner. Rather, SLAs tend to concentrate on normal business, and there might be a considerable residual risk resulting from the specifics of this type of co-operation.

## 3.2 Processes

This area addresses the internal business, management and service processes performed by the bank to fulfil its tasks, including their internal interactions, e.g. by "material" and/or service flow. A characteristic feature of banking is the worldwide distribution of interacting branches. Along with this, there is an increasing coupling of banking processes between those branches, e.g. for the purpose of international payment transactions or worldwide stock trading. Activities such as these are subject to the continuous control of a central office, with sometimes very short reaction times. This coupling is intensified by the desire to shorten and streamline transaction workflow for reasons of efficiency and competitive advantage. Looking at risks, there is a higher sensitivity to disturbances of all kinds and a growing potential of chain-reaction-like failures, as in the stock-trading example at the beginning of this section.

Another interesting feature of today's world is the accelerated concentration of business through mergers and acquisitions. If these efforts reach the level of operational business they often result in a restructuring of the operational processes. This can sometimes change the work of a lot of people in a comparably short time, thus temporarily increasing the potential of operational risks owing to a lack of synchronisation or co-ordination of work. For instance, restructuring tends to cut off informal workarounds practised in the case of disturbances, thus impairing robustness. This effect might be intensified if change management is not actively performed. Internal restructuring efforts, most often performed with the aim of raising efficiency, can have similar impacts.

The remedy in this situation is called "standardisation of normal business", most often by means of a large amount of documentation. Apart from the sometimes underestimated cost, which is a operational risk in itself, the standardisation paradigm ignores fluctuations in the environment and, especially, in the individual and time-dependent variations of the strengths and weaknesses of human resources.

## 3.3 Systems

Systems are the main technical resources of business. The risk associated with them depends upon two factors. The first is their vital nature for business or, to put it differently, their potential to cause damage to business. The second is the probability of failures, which correlates with the error-proneness of the system.

Obviously, the vital nature of IT and TK systems is high in banking. A bank's ledger, for example, seems today to be practically impossible to maintain without the support of IT systems. Moreover, business processes in a spatially distributed environment are difficult to perform without IT systems. This difficulty is strengthened by the growing velocity and amount of interaction. Consequently, the potential damage is increasing.

In addition, the error-proneness appears to be increasing.[2] First – as a very rough indicator – there is the growth in system volume. This is induced, especially, by growth in functionality, in the number and velocity of interactions with partner systems and users and, last not least, in the requirements for robustness.

The functional interdependency of a bank's systems suggests that we should no longer view them as a collection of (independent) systems but as a single, large system with many subsystems and components. A special case is the integration of IT "dinosaur" systems which have behaved well for decades in stand-alone operation but display strange behaviour if integrated.

The second factor which increases error-proneness is that the engineering abilities and capacities to develop and operate such systems are still not as mature as those for their smaller, more independent predecessors. This results in a lower quality of work and products.

The third factor is the widespread use of new technologies. Products based on new technologies are naturally not as robust as those based on well-known technologies and reveal a greater error-proneness.

A further risk-relevant effect today is indicated by the common failures of local area networks and intranets caused by bottleneck situations, which have an impact on many application systems.

In areas of technical infrastructure such as air conditioning, fire protection and access control systems, there is also a tendency towards more widespread integration and automation, thus increasing not only opportunities but also operational risks.

In his description of experiences in the field of large-scale, technically supported businesses, Perrow [Perr99] analysed accidents resulting from unexpected interactions in complex systems such as nuclear and chemical plants and aircraft and shipping logistics, within their organisational and environmental contexts. These disciplines have a long tradition and experience in the normal operation and risk engineering of huge, complex technical systems and business procedures. However, "regularly" occurring accidents such as the ICE train catastrophe in Germany in 1999, the fire at Düsseldorf airport, the explosion in a chemical plant near Toulouse in September 2001, the Kursk disaster, the explosion of a firework plant in the Netherlands, the crash of Concorde near Paris in 2000, the collision between a US atomic submarine and a Japanese trawler in 2000, and other events show the inherent limitations of risk management in spite of our experience and more mature knowledge.

---

[2] Not on the level of single components but on the level of complete systems.

## 3.4 People

The field of operational risks caused by people can be further divided into the area of general human error and the area of conscious violation of rules. Important examples of the violation of rules are fraud, theft and sabotage. In addition, internal enterprise rules have to be obeyed. A well-known example is the case of Nick Leeson. Owing to the variety of possible situations, rules of all kinds must to some extent include discretionary powers that allow appropriate actions for a specific situation. But we are not perfect; we cannot guarantee that the use of these power will always be appropriate. But how do we regard such risks in daily business?

In the London Stock Exchange example given at the beginning of this section, it is plausible to assume that time pressure played an important role. Time pressure might be a normal problem faced by professionals in stock trading, but that doesn't change the fact that traders share the usual human limitations and that there is an individual variation in capabilities too. Time pressure seems to be spreading and intensifying mainly as a result of the use of IT systems to accelerate business. This, for example, affects the operators of interconnected IT systems with very short overall transaction times, high throughput and enormous vitality for perhaps worldwide distributed business processes. Systematic examinations, as cited by Masing [Masi88], confirm the common-sense knowledge of a super-linear increase in the probability of human error with the time available.

Short reaction times are not such a problem when events of this type can be predicted through experience and prepared for in sufficient detail, and when the participants master the routines to tackle them (this especially applies to the field of business continuity plans). But in the case of new businesses and technology, a certain number of events will arise which we cannot yet predict, and we must not forget the rare events with high damage potential waiting to occur with the currently used technology. In such cases a risk component lies in the element of surprise followed by panic or an otherwise wrong reaction, as in the classic *Titanic* accident.[3]

The growing interdependency within business, its spatial distribution and the growing technical dependencies make it more and more difficult for us to see the complicated and partially "hidden" cause–effect chains in sufficient detail, especially when only a short time is available. The ability to react properly depends mainly on the skills and qualifications of the people involved.

The voluminous and complex interactions in normal business are usually managed by use of more and more detailed standards, which govern the activities of the business process participants. Possible negative effects of standardisation are boredom, "over-

---

[3] When the iceberg was seen, the commanding officer tried to get the ship out of its way. Most probably, he unintentionally caused the sinking of the *Titanic* in this way.

routine" and an awareness oriented towards only the standardised rules. This weakens the robustness on the individual level and increases the sensitivity of business to disturbances.

## 3.5 Coincidental Risks

Even the best scheme for the classification of risks cannot prevent events from occurring that cross the borders of predefined risk areas such as those defined in Table 1. The possibility of such coincidences must be considered.

To show this, we shall take an example from the airport area. Someone placed an oversized piece of luggage on the baggage transport system of an airport. Such systems are very large, interconnecting almost all operational areas of an airport. On its way through the system, the piece ripped away one "head" of a sprinkler system. The sprinkler system did what it should do under these circumstances: it sprinkled. Some distance below, a LAN router was installed; it was not vital for the core business of the airport but was important for the airport's internal processes in a large area. The water destroyed the router, which in turn greatly disturbed the internal processes. This problem lasted more than a day before complete recovery. Clearly a coincidence, but what were the causes? The baggage transport system was designed to transport oversized luggage. But this special oversize item seems to have been new on this path. Because of the baggage system's size and complexity, no luggage operator can ever know all possible paths. The engineer planning the router did not take account of the fact that there was a sprinkler a few dozen metres above the position of the router and the possibility of interaction with water. Besides the coincidental aspect, this event highlights the problem of maintaining an overview of huge, complex, expanding systems.

Examples such as this show the growing potential of coincidence. Driven by potential business opportunities, with new clients and products, the operational business processes and their underlying infrastructure are sometimes changed on the basis of a technology which is not yet mature and, especially, not robust enough. The speed-up of business transactions and business changes challenges the abilities of the stakeholders, as does the increasing linking of technical and business process components, resulting in an increase of operational risks that cannot be ignored. Obviously, this development is amplified by threats external to the operational business.

# 4 Robustness

Robustness is the ability of business processes, organisations or technical systems to continue business and to protect their substance effectively from damage in the case of disturbances, incidents and accidents. Roughly speaking, robustness is the ability to survive in the case of trouble. Therefore robustness is the goal of risk management.

The historical examples given in Section 2 indicate that the following strategies and general "tools" were used to maintain and improve robustness:

- early warning and awareness
- skill and practice in coping with risks
- flexibility and fault tolerance
- diversification in all levels of business
- fallback resources and procedures (e.g. "business continuity plans" and resources)
- abstract resources such as buffers of time (e.g. the buffers provided simply by the slowness of processes) and buffers of credit or budget
- process improvements (e.g. double-entry accounting)
- technological improvements (e.g. in shipping).

Today we use the same strategies and tools to control risks, but they have a more up-to-date look.

The historical examples indicate loose coupling to be an important feature of robust systems. The development of vital points, however, increased the vulnerability of the business system.

The look at operational risks today in Section 3 reveals coincidences as indicators of a new quality of operational risks. The possibility of coincidences is due to the complexity of the business system and, especially, the complex technical infrastructure. Complexity enables an enormous amount of dangerous interaction, which did not have time to occur before now. Thus, complexity is the opposite of loose coupling, which for a long time helped the business system to be robust.

The effects of complexity are intensified by the increasing lack of transparency of the business system. There may be not only obvious vital points but also, perhaps, hidden vital points, which will be revealed only by the occurrence of a disaster.

The historical examples indicate that there was some slowness in business processes, which gave time to control undesired developments. The speeding up of processes today cuts down the most important resource of risk management: time.

## 5 What Can Be Done?

The general answer is easy to give and well known from risk management. To achieve robustness you must prevent risks from influencing your business and/or limit the damage to a tolerable residual risk level if the former is not possible. This is most often done by the introduction of redundancies in the form of fallback procedures and resources into business. But the problem is that these redundancies have to fit your risks, the environment you are working in and your operational possibilities.

The most important prerequisite for controlling risks is knowing them. You must have a sound map of your risks, which includes all of the "devils in the detail" arising from the specifics of the business operation and environment.

The task has to be shared by business processes and IT suppliers, whose different roles are discussed in the following sections.

## 5.1 From the Viewpoint of the Business Process

What does robustness mean in the case of a business process?

1. The process must protect people from injuries in all cases. This goal is required not only by business but also by ethics and, most often, by law.
2. The process must protect its substantial resources from damage; in particular it allow for the recovery of business activities. The main resources are people, essential business data and documents, the process infrastructure, and, last but not least, the company's reputation.
3. The process must deliver its intended output, e.g. banking services or products, even in the presence of disturbances such as the breakdown of IT systems.

The fulfilment of these goals guarantees business continuity. The first and the second goal focus mainly on risks to the substance of the business process, the third focuses mainly on risks to its operational results.

In order to reach these goals, you must be able to manage a crisis and to reduce the extent and frequency of crises through the specific preparation of business continuity measures and a sound knowledge of the underlying risks.

### 5.1.1 Crisis Management Capability

The capability to manage crises is the basic part of business continuity and a prerequisite for all its components. Roughly speaking, it is the ability to act whatever happens. If there is an event which has not been specially prepared for, the company is able to act appropriately as an organisation. Put in greater detail, it is able to inform all people involved in the crisis, especially those who are not aware of it but could suffer from it or have a role in coping with it. Someone can get an overview of the situation and can direct the resources and act in an effective, efficient manner, directed by the goals mentioned above. The company can do all of this as fast as necessary or, more correctly, as fast as possible, because at the beginning of the crisis you will not (completely) know what has happened, what can happen and what is necessary. This speed can only be achieved through the thorough preparation of an information and decision network which spans the business process, its business partners in the workflow and its IT and facility providers.

Since crises are rare, the routine of daily business does not suffice as preparation. To achieve and maintain a bit of routine, simulations and training should be performed with all people who could possibly be involved. A classical example is an evacuation exercise. The WTC accident showed that this was not a superfluous game. But some abilities cannot be trained. There are people who have a natural ability to perform this kind of job; this ability is especially valuable if it is combined with profound knowledge and experience of processes and infrastructure. These people are chosen to become real crisis managers.

An important precondition for crisis management is an appropriate infrastructure, especially the means to communicate with those involved wherever they might be, even if the standard means of communication no longer works.

In addition to a general capability to perform troubleshooting, crisis management provides the organisational, informational and decision framework for the more specialised components of business continuity.

### 5.1.2 Business Continuity Capability

You can achieve business continuity capability if you prepare for specific risky events by planning in advance. The benefits of this preparation, namely the reduction of risks, should balance the costs.

A simple, fictitious example: if a bank (or a bank department) is exposed to the risk that the payment transaction system might break down for a considerable amount of time, the bank can prepare, train and practise manual procedures to handle these situations in such a way that business continues and the business impacts of the risk are minimised.

If the payment transaction system recovers, the preparation allows the bank to update the payment transaction database and to return to normal business. Sometimes, however, the system recovery takes too long. In this case the bank is prepared to shut the business down completely and to inform and pacify its clients. If the bank were not to inform them, their anger would in most cases be even greater. If, finally, the system recovery is completed, the bank is prepared to recover its business from the state it was in at the time of business shutdown.

In addition, the bank is prepared to continue business, if need be, with reduced capacity. In a similar way it is able to handle all the risks relevant to the goals presented above. As a main issue here, the bank is prepared to protect people and business assets such as its data and documents, business infrastructure and reputation from damage.

To be prepared implies the availability of sufficient fallback manpower (in the simplest case, hours of overtime) and the appropriate technical and organisational fallback infrastructure has to be guaranteed. This can range from the provision of paper forms not used in normal operation, up to disaster recovery sites where business continues if the business premises are no longer available. The business continuity plans should fit the abilities of all participants.

As with crisis management, the aspect of training is very important, especially if the underlying risks imply a large damage potential but are rare. Similarly, periodic checks ensure the existence and availability of the fallback infrastructure.

The most important prerequisite for preparation through business continuity plans is a sufficient amount of time, followed by the availability of appropriate resources. But the preparation can only be performed if there is concrete, sound, current knowledge of the risks to which your business is exposed.

### 5.1.3 Risk Awareness Capability

You can only handle your operational risks if you know them. A map of the current risks which provides all of the information needed to judge risks and to decide on the appropriate action, has to be worked out. To keep the map up to date, some kind of early warning and supervisory system should be operated to observe all areas in which short- and long-term problems might arise.

The knowledge about risks (the map) should be organised to support the localisation of the causes of risk and thus give hints about the starting points of well-directed risk control. Because there might be many risks to consider in detail, the map should be structured by risk areas as shown in Section 3. An important means of calibrating this map is to evaluate the experiences of problems (occurrences of risks) in the company.

In order to obtain an overview of the risks and for the purpose of prioritisation, the "greatness" of each risk should be determined by evaluating the probability of harmful business impact and the size of this impact. In many cases, however, you might not evaluate these factors explicitly. In such case risk indicators or qualitative evaluations which correlate to some extent, on their own or in combination, with the "greatness" of the risk may help.

On the basis of the risk map, the company decides on the necessity of actions to improve its business continuity capability, and the company uses the map to judge the success of actions already taken. In particular the risk map supports the balancing of the costs of business continuity measures against the amount of risk reduction achieved by them. The activities towards business continuity start with the most urgent and important risks in the map.

Which sources of information should be used in the early warning system? Some heuristics:

- The company investigates possible fields of risk in a systematic way, whenever it is not sufficiently sure of them. It looks especially at signs of unexpected interactions with "long-distance effects".
- It analyses changes, especially the entry of innovations into the risk areas, not when they are carried out but when they are planned.
- It investigates problems in daily business, especially peculiar events and disturbances without any obvious explanation. By looking at variations of their cause–effect chains, you might discover variants associated with very big risks.
- Technical monitoring devices are used to collect indications of risks.
- Not only the documented or explicit knowledge of all people involved in the process but also their "feeling" about risks are taken into account.
- External sources of risk are taken into account.

To finish the description of risk awareness capability, a very important feature must be mentioned. There has to be an awareness of the limits of knowledge about risk. This knowledge will never be as sound as the knowledge about things which did happen.

A specific limit is caused by the restricted risk scope of a company. From the viewpoint of a single bank, for example, it is difficult to map the risks for the entire area of worldwide banking business or for business in general. This task is attempted by legislative authorities supported by organisations such as the above-mentioned Basel Committee on Banking Supervision (see [BIS] and [BASE]), which prepares worldwide risk assessments and general measures to control risks for the worldwide banking systems. Owing to a broader statistical basis, those institutions are able to detect risks that a single bank would never perceive. Considerations of risks beyond the scope of a single bank have resulted in laws such as the German KontraG (Gesetz zur Kontrolle und Transparenz im Unternehmensbereich) and MaH (Mindestanforderungen an das Betreiben von Handelsgeschäften).

In the area of operational risks we are still far away from over-engineering. But too much preparation also seems not to be good, and not only because of cost reasons. There should be a tolerated level of risk background noise. This offers the best opportunity for real-life practice in handling risks. That's why the fire brigade is not unhappy to carry out some limited operations regularly.

## 5.2  From the Viewpoint of the Software System Supplier

As indicated in Section 3.3, the supplier of software and IT systems provides a basis for business opportunities, but at the same time operational business risks.

The region of risks with respect to an IT system can be broken down according to the localisation of possible faults. Risks can be caused by

- faulty interaction within the system (e.g. risks induced by faulty components)
- faulty interaction between the system and its partner systems through interfaces (e.g. risks induced by the increase of interactions in worldwide networks)
- faulty interaction between persons and the system (e.g. qualitative and quantitative changes in the context of new types of end-users in e-business)
- faulty system behaviour as a result of disturbances in its environment or in its underlying services (which may be widely distributed systems with reduced control of the environment, e.g. heterogeneous Internet clients of end-users).

The furthest evolved techniques to handle risks by means of the development process concentrate on the first item in this list. With the other three items, there is an increase in risk. The development of appropriate means is ongoing but not yet completed.

In addition, this increase is mixed up with a growing pressure of time on software development. You have to develop faster than usual and, in parallel, you have to discover a significant amount of operational and technical virgin soil. As a not too rare result, there are fewer opportunities carried out than expected and some very poor compromises for example in the case of Internet/Intranet portals.

As a background for the following discussion, Figure 2 depicts the main structure of the software development process and its main interaction paths with a business process.

The development process consists of a construction part and a quality assurance part. The development is triggered by a request from a business process for improved

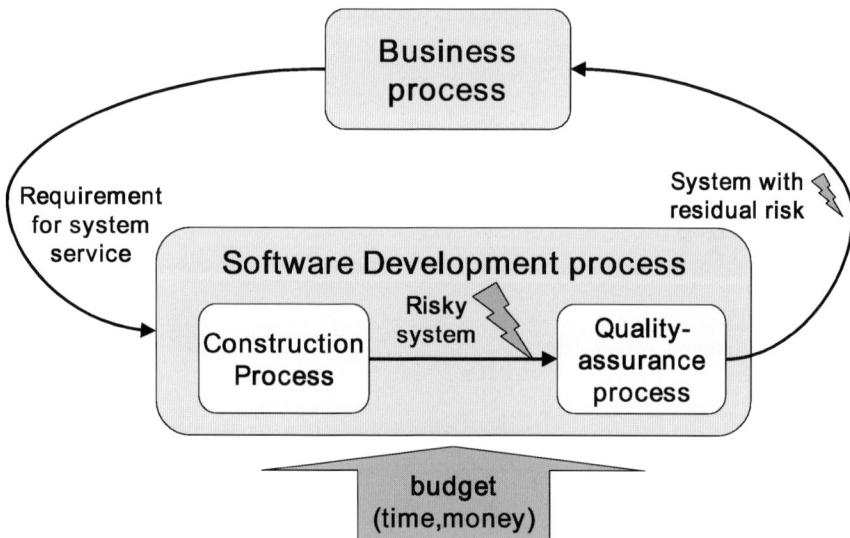

Figure 2: Structure of development process

support. This is often the first source of risk, owing to potential failings in the transfer of understanding and knowledge of requirements, technical/economical feasibility and associated imponderables between the client and the development process. This is especially relevant if there only is an abstract vision of a business opportunity that has not yet been broken down to the operational, procedural level and the specific tasks the system is to fulfil. If a breakdown exists, it is expected to be unstable, because it has not yet been proved and improved by practice. This, combined with the (naturally) lower maturity of new technologies and techniques, is often unsuccessfully handled as a "normal" project. The amounts of practical research and learning necessary on the business process and supplier sides are not considered.

The construction part of the development process produces the software system, which – in addition to the initial faults caused by mutual misunderstanding – is extremely likely to contain faults added during the construction process. The main factor influencing the quality and quantity of risks is the abilities of the developers and their managers, as individuals and as teams. But even in the best case there always will be some considerable residual risks.

The extreme likeliness of faults in construction is the basis of quality assurance's livelihood. Quality assurance acts as a sensor for faults, which, in combination with a defined threshold, helps to control a software delivery valve that allows systems to pass to the business process. Naturally, even when the valve opens there is sometimes a considerable amount of residual risk. There are, in principle, the following reasons for risk:

- the human counterparts of sensors and valves and their constraints ("Nobody is perfect")
- statistical errors induced by checking the behaviour of the system only in comparatively small samples
- the level of risk the business process is prepared for and willing to accept.

If necessary, these residual risks must be explicitly controlled by business continuity measures within the business process. This is often omitted, and that is one reason why the period after roll-out is sometimes accompanied by a feeling of subliminal horror.

### 5.2.1 Robustness of Systems

A special challenge of software development is to improve the robustness of software systems. Traditionally this is interpreted as some appropriate behaviour in the case of false operation by a typical experienced user. For example, the system should not break down if the user enters a syntactically wrong input.

Today, this topic is enriched by new groups of users who only occasionally work with the system, have no training, are less patient and have – from the developers' viewpoint – fantastic ideas for bringing the system down or corrupting its data.

A further aspect is that the interfaces with partner systems, for example in a worldwide network, tend to be less well known and reliable than they used to be in the smaller LAN context. This often comes along with the increasing rate of change of interconnected systems. There appears to be a development comparable to the above-mentioned new groups of users, as indicated by everyday test engineering experience.

Furthermore, increasing variation in software and hardware platforms and associated services, which is emerging especially in e-business, may give rise to more risks. To conclude this summary, we should mention the widely discussed topic of system misuse (e.g. viruses and hacking).

Therefore, an expanded catalogue of robustness maxims for software development should include:

- Protect the system, especially its data, from wrong inputs.
- Protect the system from misuse.
- Let the system run as long as possible to perform its task (if necessary only partially), even if some interfaces have temporarily broken down or behave strangely and/or some parts of the platform behave (temporarily) strangely or don't work. This is especially important in the case of requirements for high availability.
- Let the system monitor for and detect peculiar behaviour that could involve intolerable risk potential, and if necessary let the system cry for help or even shut down (early warning).
- Minimise the irritation of users and operators in cases of disturbance (in such cases there is reason enough for irritation).
- Construct the robustness features such that their reliability is appropriate to the situations in which they are used.
- Be sure that the robustness features are not a reason for additional failures. Their reliability must be even better than that of the system in a state of normal operation.

Now, which opportunities does the software supplier have in order to improve the robustness of a system?

### 5.2.2 Software Construction

The common background of software development is characterised by increasing limitations on time, budget and/or resources. This requires aids for a more exact prioritisation of the various tasks. These aids should focus on the expected error-proneness of the system that is being developed which controls the probability of failures, and on the vitality or damage potential of the parts and features of the system when it is used in business processes. In other words, this prioritisation should depend upon the risks which might arise from system or software failures in the business process.

As an illustration: a small, simple module within a process control system had the task of enabling the communication between all of the programs of the system. The task of programming the module was given to an inexperienced newcomer. So the error-proneness of the module was high in spite of the simplicity of the task. Naturally the module contained some faults; still, the newcomer had performed his work comparatively well. The failures did not occur during normal operation but only in a few rare but practically relevant stress situations with considerable damage potential (high vitality). The faults were discovered by chance before the system went into operation. Whether the usual standard test procedure on the system level would have discovered the faults was not certain.

In this example, the risk was not seen by the team leader, owing to the module's simplicity.[4] He did not consider in detail the relevance of the module within the system and for production; the module should at least have been intensively checked or, even better, programmed by a more experienced programmer. Why didn't the team leader consider this?

The example highlights a lack of understanding of the system's use in the business process as one source of risk. The example also suggests that faults "like" to concentrate on interfaces. So there is a considerable error-proneness in the coupling of programs in particular. This includes all types of shared use of static data (databases and files), online interfaces between programs and systems, the synchronisation of programs and the effects of temporarily unavailable platform/network resources. This is very similar to phenomena in and between organisations.

A detailed risk map can serve as an aid to enhancing the mutual comprehension of system use in the business process and the practical awareness of associated risks. The risk mapping should be integrated into the process of specification of requirements and functionality to supplement the usual attitude of looking for and believing in opportunities. This image of the risks which the business process might incur in the case of system misbehaviour can help to focus the construction processes according to the relevance and error-proneness of the system and to protect it better from its own weaknesses.

### 5.2.3 Quality Assurance

Quality assurance processes have to improve the accuracy of quality assurance efforts. Thus, they have to incorporate more explicitly and in more detail the risks to business processes from system misbehaviour. To do this, the understanding of the business process and its context must also be improved.

---

[4] This module is another example of a vital point.

A software system's "right to exist" depends upon its support of business processes. So quality goals depend mainly on the amount of software induced risk the business process is able to tolerate or to handle. The testing and quality assurance measures must be directed towards reducing risk to this tolerable level. As mentioned above, one factor of this risk is the damage potential within the business process, the other factor is the error-proneness of the software delivered by software construction. This second factor controls the probability of system failures. It depends, on the one hand, on the amount of software delivered and, on the other hand, on the quality of the construction work. So the strengths and weaknesses of the construction process, of its suppliers and of its environment influence the risk to a large extent.

So – as a means of synchronising the joint efforts of construction and quality assurance to deliver a system with tolerable risks – there is a need for the above-mentioned map of risks to be shared with the construction process. Experiences from test consulting confirm the importance of this need.

One result of quality assurance should be a specification of the residual risks for business after roll-out, in addition to the usual quality declaration. This specification should address, in particular, the system's "teething troubles" following roll-out, and risks with low probability or frequency but high damage potential. Information such as this would allow business processes to improve the accuracy and cost-effectiveness of their business continuity measures.

There is one considerable limitation to testing which arises from the tighter coupling of systems within the production network: the increasing difficulty in simulating the totality of widespread, interconnected operational systems in testing laboratories. However, it seems to be possible to improve the strategies for the selection of test targets according to the associated risks. The rate of change of systems does not allow a complete integration test whenever one of the partner systems is updated.

In the previous sections we discussed the benefits of risk control, especially through quality assurance as a reduction of business process operational risks. Today it is more or less a standard task, supported by an appropriate controlling infrastructure, to calculate the costs with sufficient precision and timeliness. Reductions in risks and residual risks will, most often, be estimated not explicitly, but by rules of thumb or by guessing. If done by experts, this is not the worst way to act, but this does not work as reliably and efficiently as is necessary.

### 5.2.4 Operational Risks of IT Projects

From our experience – with no claim to completeness – the following are currently the main elements in the operational risk of IT projects:

- Difficult time constraints, sometimes caused by a predefined market entrance, might result in best-case planning that leads to significant delays.

- Quality deficits in deliveries, resulting in unexpected, significant problems in the business process. Time constraints are not the only possible source, others are indicated below.
- "Virgin soil" in business practices and the manner of using systems for business (e.g. e-business), resulting in necessary but not sufficiently predictable trial-and-error work on the side of the business process and within development.
- "Virgin soil" in system and development platforms and tools, at least from the viewpoint of the available development resources. Sometimes, even technological innovations without any engineering expertise.
- An increasing number of co-operation partners external to the project, accompanied by spatially distributed work. This is often a direct result of the above-mentioned increasing number of technical interfaces in the systems and, in addition, the tendency towards outsourcing. Owing to the project's sensitivity to disturbances at its interfaces, the project risks increase. Self-organisational practices may no longer work, and existing project standards sometimes do not fit the new situation.
- Intercultural, sometimes worldwide co-operation within project teams.
- Even if there is a sufficient budget, too few or insufficiently qualified people.

Clearly the basic ideas for managing the operational risks of IT projects are the same as for business processes. However, IT projects are most often structured according a particular process model containing several phases, e.g. requirements analysis, architecture and design, implementation, test, and roll-out, including initial operation. Each phase is more or less subject to its special kinds of risks, which must be considered thoroughly. The phases finish with milestones, which contain a fundamental decision on schedule, budget and resources that is concentrated on the subsequent phase (forecast). The most important of these decisions is obviously the decision on the initial plan. Therefore the decisions incorporate a significant damage potential, which should be examined through risk assessments as a part of the project's early warning system. Furthermore, the project management should be integrated with a component of continuous risk and problem management to protect it from problems and risks which are relevant during the project's duration.

Explicit project continuity plans – as the project counterpart of business continuity plans – and appropriate crisis management might be necessary for phases and activities with high, time-stressed interactions with a large number of project partners, especially during integration testing, roll-out and initial operation. The project continuity plan dedicated to roll-out has to match the business continuity plans for system operation and the business process on the side of the business holder. Emergency services provided by the software supplier should be a part of the system support for the business process after the project has finished, for example as part of a service-level agreement between the software supplier and the business process. This becomes especially important if the quality goals of the project are to be relaxed owing to time constraints or, equivalently, the residual risks to the business processes from software and system failures are to be systematically increased.

A similar kind of coupling between a project and a business process (in latter being partially simulated) takes place during testing activities, especially integration testing. These activities might require a specialised continuity plan, which can be a predecessor of the plan used during operation after roll-out. The integration test phase also presents an opportunity to check and improve this plan in advance of operation.

To protect its own business, the software supplier should perform one risk management shared by all projects. The people involved in each project should thoroughly analyse all the problems and risks encountered during its duration and recommend measures to protect future projects from problems and risks. This input should be systematically evaluated by the management to obtain a complete, consistent risk map, which includes all projects, and to define the appropriate risk control measures, considering synergy effects between projects.

### 5.2.5 A "Cultural" Factor in the Background

We see a general "cultural" factor which tends to de-integrate the necessary team play between the business process and IT development as the root of many problems and risks.

This can be sketched in extreme fashion as follows. Often developers do not know and understand the odds and ends of the business process in sufficient detail to construct an appropriate system or to test it. "I only have to build the system. What the user will do with it is none of my business!" In addition, they tend to assume that everybody knows the abilities and limitations of the technologies used, even if they are new. Fascinated by new technologies, the developers tend to overestimate their technical opportunities.

In contrast, the representatives of the business process tend to take for granted that everybody, including developers, knows and understands all of the odds and ends of the business. In addition, they do not believe that there might be odds and ends in the technical field too, though these are especially possible in view of the new fascinating technologies. On this basis, both sides come to an operational consensus, whose gaps do not become obvious in detail.

The initial trigger for an operational risk is often a simple misunderstanding, sometimes enhanced by an overestimation of technological opportunities and/or time pressure.

The engineers of development processes concentrate on formally nice, consistent frameworks. But such frameworks do not take sufficiently into account the fact that the developers and business representatives involved did not learn effective communication with the goal of mutual understanding. This – the problem of different languages and social interaction – is not unique to software development and its clients. However, other engineering disciplines have already gained more experience in neutralising its effects. One concept used here is called "Simultaneous Engineering" (see [KaBr95] for a short description). The basic strategies are to involve all the stakeholders of a development project from its beginning and to enable interdisciplinary teamwork.

## 5.3 Which Risks Remain?

The previous sections have indicated that a lot can be done to control risks. But which risks remain after one has taken these measures to control risks? Clearly, there are the residual risks in the risk map, which the company does not want to mitigate. The company is sure that it can tolerate their impacts if they occur.

Many of these residual risks and the initially identified risks are well known, in the sense that they have occurred in the way identified or a comparable way, such that they could be studied in reality, modelled and prepared for. We learn to prevent a disaster from the experience of the disaster.

We observe that, in addition to those well-known risks, risks with very low probability but very high damage potential remain, for instance in the context of business and technological innovations and/or in a dependency upon environmental influences. We can think of the London Stock Exchange example (see Section 3) as a comparably small event and September 11th 2001 as a big one. How should they be tackled?

The general goal should be to offer protection from these risks, at least to the extent that some limits of damage are impossible to cross. A traditional example here is the famous four-eye principle, used not only in banking but also elsewhere as a business equivalent of an emergency brake. Sometimes the emergency brake might even imply the abandonment of possible technologies, if they are not robust enough for business or their impacts on business processes are not definitely controllable or sufficiently known.

To some extent it is helpful to systematise risk assessment techniques for the examination of limited areas with a high potential for risks. This will work if there are practicable models. An example of specialised risk assessments is the Y2K activities, which not only controlled the risk addressed but, in addition, increased the knowledge of interdependencies and revealed many possibly risky interactions in the neighbourhood of Y2K problems.

When the risks are not exactly known but they announce themselves in a timely way through perceivable harbingers, it is possible to adjust the early warning systems to look for them. The operator of a worldwide early warning system could be a supranational banking institution such as the Basel Committee (see above). In co-operation with the individual banks, such an institution could perceive signs of risks (e.g. by statistical means) that an individual bank or an individual state would rarely see. In addition, the institution would also have an opportunity to examine the net interactions between the individual banks. Such institutions, in co-operation with states, would be able to establish limits for tolerable residual risks.

One approach of risk management is to consider some worst-case scenario in order to study the causes and impacts linked to it and to define useful measures for control. It would be very useful to know such a worst-case scenario for the operational risks of a bank or of the banking system as a whole. Is it similar to the WTC attack? Might it be even worse, owing to a small software error which spreads undiscovered in a very short time across a worldwide banking network and causes uncontrollable damage? If the WTC was not the single "heart" in the "middle" of the banking system, is there such a "heart" which could be hit? All of this is unknown to us. What seems to be clear is that a Super MCA (Maximum Credible Accident) must have greater dimensions than the WTC attack.

In spite of all the possible technical, scientific, organisational and method-related tools, the most important device for discovering "new" risks is our brain, which can be triggered first by our gut feeling (as with opportunities) on the basis of experiences which have not yet been systematised and scientifically formalised. We should train our most valuable tools on the target.[5]

Concluding this section we say in summary that there is no guaranteed way to have no risks but that there is a usable possible way to have fewer risks.

## 6 Balancing

As indicated in the previous sections, there is a need to balance the benefits against the costs for each risk control measure. Benefit is gained through risk reduction; cost is incurred through the corresponding activities. This balancing might imply that some well-known risks will not be mitigated.

But there are some more general balancing tasks: the integrated consideration and balancing of robustness against other components the goals of business processes and, especially, integrated consideration and balancing against business opportunities.

---

[5] At this point, however, we do not favour uncontrolled Murphy-like thinking or superstition. Such an approach misleads and produces so many risk scenarios that nobody ever will be able to judge them.

## 6.1 Balancing of Goals

Clearly, risk management, including business continuity planning for the purpose of robustness, is not the only goal of a business process.[6] This is evident in the concept of "business continuity" itself, which implicitly refers to normal business.

Figure 3 depicts an abstract scheme for the various components of the goals which have to be considered and balanced in an overall examination. The priorities given to those factors seem to be reasonable in many cases and situations.

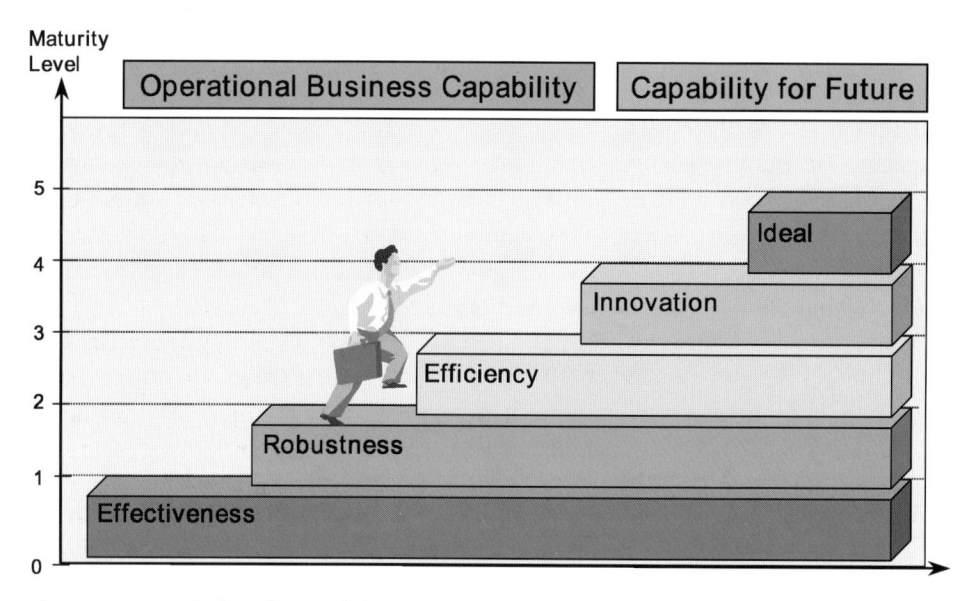

Figure 3: Factors in benefit–cost balancing

The first component of the goals of a business process is that the process should perform under normal circumstances in an effective and sufficiently efficient way. The second goal is to achieve robustness. The third is to be effective and robust in the most efficient manner, and the last two components refer to the process's ability to take advantage of opportunities arising from innovation. The totality of the components reflects the business process's interest in its short- and long-term life.

Normal business, and restricted business in the case of incidents and accidents generate the cash flows to finance normal, robust, efficient business and its future, as well as to make a profit. The relative importance of the business goals varies depending on the particular situation of an enterprise and with time. In recent years there has some-

---

[6] The following remarks refer, accordingly, to support and supply processes.

times been a general emphasis on innovation alone. Today the focus seems to be shifting towards robustness, in reaction to the developments in the field of the operational risks mentioned above.

However, neither of those factors should be considered in isolation. They are always both present in business and influence each other, at the very least because there is only one budget to sponsor them.

## 6.2 Balancing of Opportunity Against Risk

As a typical example of balancing opportunity against risk, let us consider an IT system which is to be developed to automate a manual banking operation, i.e. to increase the efficiency of work. In the business process, each individual case in which the system is used will offer some benefit in terms of cost reduction. The amount of cost reduction varies depending on the specifics of the situation, but clearly there is some upper boundary to the amount. Owing to the nature of the banking process, the IT system must modify the contents of some very important databases (e.g. accounts, assets or clients), which are substantial in the context of the bank as a whole.

Of course, nobody is perfect, including the managers, architects, developers, quality assurers and component suppliers of the IT system. Therefore software errors which cause malfunctions, thus inducing financial losses in business processes, must be taken into account. These losses might be small if only a small amount of work has to be repeated, as might happen if the software is used wrongly, but they might be enormous if the above-mentioned databases are corrupted. From the bank's viewpoint, the permanent corruption of the databases might be equivalent to bankruptcy and an infinite loss.

To obtain an overview of the individual benefits and losses, we may represent them together in one figure. The combined distribution of benefits and losses for the various possible cases in which the IT system is used might possibly look like that in Figure 4.

The asymmetry of the distribution is obvious. Its most remarkable features are a concentration of probability on the benefit or opportunity side, in combination with practically infinitely large values with very low probability on the loss or risk side. We presume that distributions of comparable shape[7] and behaviour represent many situations, perhaps even the overall operational opportunity and risk of a bank.

In decision situations, e.g. a decision on the use of the above IT system, we are used to considering mainly the expectation value of such a distribution. This we assume to be located near the peak on the benefit side and to be clearly positive, so the decision seems to be clear and easy. An almost imperceptible increase on the loss side, however, might cause the expectation value to become negative. So we tend to ignore the varia-

---

[7] However, we think that it is possible to have more than one peak.

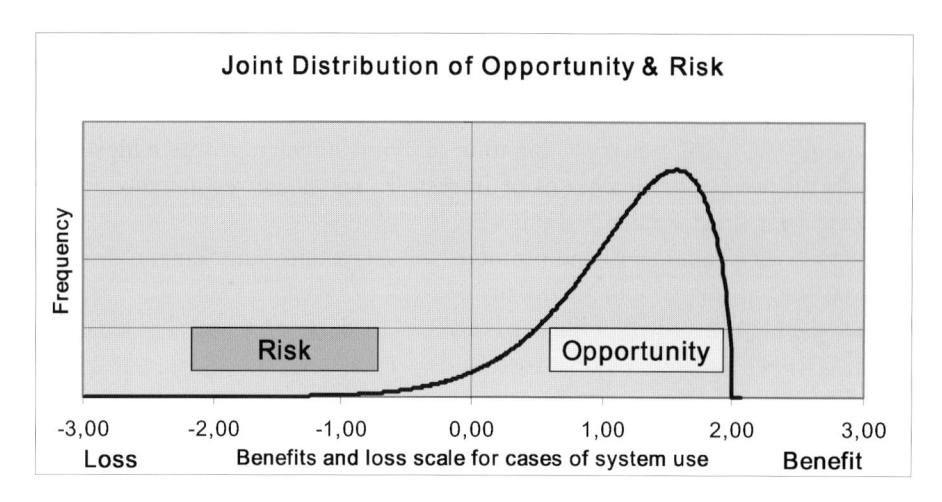

Figure 4: Distribution of opportunity and risk

tion of the distribution. Mostly we do not even try to calculate such figures or to gather the underlying qualitative and quantitative information.

The opportunity side of the distribution is comparably easy to fit because there is much empirical background data. This side reflects successful, normal daily business. On the side of very large losses or great damage, it is practically impossible to predict or calculate the probabilities with sufficient accuracy if there is a lack of empirical data and practicable modelling techniques (see also Section 5.3). Examples are cases of new technologies or business architectures. There is therefore a diffuse grey area of ignorance, which might be interpreted as a high risk in itself. As one example of the relevance of this potential, remember the accident at the Three Mile Island nuclear power plant in Pennsylvania, which occurred after years of nuclear power plant operation in the US; and we should not forget the 11th of September 2001.

How do we behave in such situations? We tend to "think positive" and to ignore our ignorance. So we end up again with the relevance of the "human factor".

# 7 Concluding Remarks

Systematic risk management and business continuity planning help to achieve robustness to a large extent. But the risk potential of rare events remains, revealing itself from time to time in unexpected and enormous catastrophes. This risk potential is continuously being replenished by new technologies and new engineering of business processes; in summary, mainly in the context of technological and/or organisational innovations.

One possible way to tackle these risks would be to structure the business in such a way that its worst-case scenario would imply only a restricted impact. To give a rather simple idea of what we mean: the attack on the WTC and its aftermath were possible only because the WTC contained a combination of many innocent people, a high level of business traffic; and a great amount of infrastructure and investments, and, we should not forget, it had an enormous symbolic value, and all at a single location.

To finish, let's return to history. One prototype of protection from danger is represented by the clumsy medieval knight with his heavy armour, which didn't allow him to get out of the way. The other prototype is the mobile bowman with only his weapons, whose mobility was his most efficient protection and who conquered the knight. The main prerequisite for his efficacy was his room to manoeuvre.

Either way has its drawbacks, but in the interest of long-term survival and efficiency we think that we need more room to perceive existing risks, to control them and perhaps to discover the opportunity in them.

# The Role of States and of International and National Organisations as Super-Risk Managers

KLAUS-PETER GERLACH
*DZ Bank International Luxembourg, Audit/IT Security*

**Abstract:** In recent years, the necessity and importance of contingency plans have been stressed continuously by supranational organisations, banking supervisory authorities, audit companies and associations and even law courts. The driving forces for this development are, for example, Y2K, the increasing outsourcing of services, and the development of the Internet, including new business channels and products such as e-banking.

This chapter will show how regulators, auditors and standardisation institutions are keeping pace with this development. The focus will be laid upon the regulations in Germany, Luxembourg and the United States.

**Keywords:** Contingency planning, Risk management, Internet, Business continuity, Continuity of operations, Business resumption planning, Disaster recovery, Outsourcing, Supranational organisations, OECD, BIS, Basel Committee, EU, ECB, Standardisation institutions, ISO, NIST, IFAC, Supervisory regulations, National audit standards, IDW, IRE

## 1 Definitions

As the OECD stated in 1992 [OECD92] "security of information systems is the protection of availability, confidentiality and integrity. *Availability* is the characteristic of information systems being accessible and usable on a timely basis in the required manner."

"A computer security contingency is an event with the potential to disrupt computer operations, thereby disrupting critical mission and business functions. Such an event could be a power outage, hardware failure, fire, or storm. If the event is very destructive, it is often called a disaster. To avert potential contingencies and disasters or minimize the damage they cause organizations can take steps early to control the event. Generally called *contingency planning*, this activity is closely related to incident handling, which primarily addresses malicious technical threats such as hackers and viruses. *Other names include disaster recovery, business continuity, continuity of operations, or business resumption planning*" [NIST1].

For reasons of clearness, all of these terms, which will appear in the various rules and regulations quoted in this chapter, will be used as synonyms for "contingency plans".

Financial institutions are subject to extensive regulation; they are obliged to take possible risks very carefully into account. Generally speaking, financial institutions should have a risk management process to enable them to identify, measure, monitor, and control their risk exposure. In the following, "risk management" means the exposure to operational risks.

In recent years, the necessity and importance of contingency plans have been stressed continuously by supranational organisations, banking supervisory authorities, audit companies and associations and even law courts.

Besides the Y2K computer glitch, the following main reasons for this development can be identified:

- the "traditional" principles of proper accounting
- the increasing outsourcing of services, and
- the development of the Internet, including new business channels and products such as e-banking.

I shall try to show how regulators, auditors and standardisation institutions are keeping pace with this development. The focus will be laid upon the regulations in Germany, Luxembourg and the United States.

According to my knowledge there is at the moment no law requiring business continuity directly; the requirements are derived from administrative or supervisory decrees.

For example the German Securities Trading Act of 1998 defines in article 33, certain organisational duties. These duties are put in concrete form only by a directive of the Federal Security Trading Supervisory Office on the specification of the organisational duties. This directive demands in Section 2.2 that trading companies must have the means and procedures available and are capable of using them to carry out trading services in a proper way. These means and procedures include, in particular measures to avoid any delay in executing or processing orders In the case of a system breakdown or failure.

# 2  The Principles of Proper Accounting and Internal Controls

## 2.1  Federal Department of Finance, Germany

The principles of proper IT-based accounting systems (GoBS) [GoBS95] require the security of data:

- The dependence of a company on its stored information makes a detailed back-up concept essential for fulfilling the GoBS requirements. The company must be aware that data security can be achieved and maintained only if it is known what, against what, how and how long data have to be stored and protected.

- Not only is the information relevant for accounting purposes and stored on data media to be filed and protected, but also other information in whose protection the company has an interest or that the company is obliged to secure by law. "Information" in this sense is software (operating system and applications), historical data, master data, transaction data and other records. Vouchers and other records which are stored on paper also have to be secured and protected.
- The information has to be protected against loss and unauthorised changes. Beyond the requirements of GoBS, confidential information must be protected against unauthorised gaining of knowledge.
- Information relevant for accounting has to be filed and protected at least until the end of the legally required retention period. The company has to decide if, and for which information, a longer retention period should be applied. To comply with the requirement to make accounting information legible at any time during the retention period, not only the availability of data and software but also that of hardware must be guaranteed. Therefore the back-up concept must cover also the back-up of the technical equipment (hardware, lines, etc.).
- How the company achieves data security and maintains it permanently depends on the technical conditions and the resulting capabilities.
  - Information can be protected against unauthorised changes by access controls and admission supervision. Access controls must guarantee that only authorised personnel can access programs and data, and only within the scope of their functions. Admission controls must prevent unauthorised persons from gaining admission to data carriers, especially to rooms in which back-up media are stored.
  - To protect information against loss, firstly, back-up procedures for applications and data have to be performed. The performance of back-up procedures is obligatory. Besides periodical back-ups, "ad hoc" back-ups are suitable if, between two back-ups, programs and/or data have been changed in an unusual way. For relevant to accounting, information and other sensitive data and programs, additional copies of the back-ups should be produced and stored in another security area or outside of the company's premises. Secondly measures have to be taken to protect information against the risks of data being not traceable, and of deletion and theft. The risk of lacking traceability can be mitigated by a systematic inventory of backed-up data and programs. For each back-up medium the inventory should contain information about location, content, date of back-up and the earliest allowed date of erasure. The risk of deletion of data carriers should be mitigated by adequate protection of the storage rooms against fire, temperature changes, humidity, magnetic fields etc. The risk of theft should be mitigated by retention in adequately protected rooms or safes. To guarantee the legibility of data carriers during the retention period, the legibility itself has to be checked regularly, depending on the storage technique used.

- As the data security depends on the available technique, the company has to adjust its data security concept to the actual requirements and facilities.
- The back-up concept must be documented, especially the procedures for back-ups.

## 2.2 Basel Committee on Banking Supervision

The Basel Committee, established by the central-bank governors of the Group of Ten countries at the end of 1974, meets regularly four times a year. It has about thirty technical working groups and task forces which also meet regularly. The Committee does not possess any formal supranational supervisory authority, and its conclusions do not, and were never intended to, have legal force. Rather, it formulates broad supervisory standards and guidelines and recommends statements of best practice in the expectation that individual authorities will take steps to implement them through detailed arrangements –statutory or otherwise - which are best suited to their own national systems. In this way, the Committee encourages convergence towards common approaches and common standards without attempting detailed harmonisation of member countries' supervisory techniques.

*Principle 8* of the Framework for Internal Control Systems in Banking Organisations [Base98] declares:

"An effective internal control system requires that there are reliable information systems in place that cover all significant activities of the bank. These systems, including those that hold and use data in an electronic form, must be secure, monitored independently and *supported by adequate contingency arrangements*."

The Committee explains this principle as follows:

A critical component of a bank's activities is the establishment and maintenance of management information systems that cover the full range of its activities. This information is usually provided through both electronic and non-electronic means. Banks must be particularly aware of the organisational and internal control requirements related to processing information in an electronic form and the necessity to have an adequate audit trail. Management decision-making could be adversely affected by unreliable or misleading information provided by systems that are poorly designed and controlled.

Electronic information systems and the use of information technology have risks that must be effectively controlled by banks in order to avoid disruptions to business and potential losses. Since transaction processing and business applications have expanded beyond the use of mainframe computer environments to distributed systems for mission-critical business functions, the magnitude of risks also has expanded. Controls over information systems and technology should include both general and application controls.

General controls are controls over computer systems (for example, mainframe, client/server and end-user workstations) and ensure their continued, proper operation. General controls include in-house back-up and recovery procedures, software development and acquisition policies, maintenance (change control) procedures, and physical/logical access security controls. Application controls are computerised steps within software applications and other manual procedures that control the processing of transactions and business activities. Application controls include, for example, edit checks and specific logical access controls unique to a business system. Without adequate controls over information systems and technology, including systems that are under development, banks could experience loss of data and programs due to inadequate physical and electronic security arrangements, equipment or systems failures, and inadequate in-house back-up and recovery procedures.

In addition to the risks and controls above, inherent risks exist that are associated with the loss or extended disruption of services caused by factors beyond the bank's control.

In extreme cases, since the delivery of corporate and customer services represents key strategic and reputational issues, such problems could cause serious difficulties for banks and even jeopardise their ability to conduct key business activities. This potential requires the bank to establish business resumption and contingency plans using an alternate off-site facility, including the recovery of critical systems supported by an external service provider. The potential for loss or extended disruption of critical business operations requires an institution-wide effort on contingency planning, involving business management, and not focused on centralised computer operations. Business resumption plans must be periodically tested to ensure the plan's functionality in the event of an unexpected disaster.

## 2.3 Financial Services Authority (FSA)

The Financial Services Authority (FSA) is an independent non-governmental body, given statutory powers by the Financial Services and Markets Act of 2000. The FSA is a company limited by guarantee and financed by the financial services industry, and regulates the financial services industry in the UK.

In relation to the discussions concerning capital adequacy, the FSA says about the various risk calculation models [FSA01]:

"A model is any formalised and systematic method of analysing risk, and the programme used to carry out that analysis. Models are primarily used for assessing credit and market risk, but can themselves be a source of risk if they make unrealistic assumptions. In assessing whether the model is implemented with integrity, the FSA considers the systems used to run the model and associated calculations.

As an important part of its model recognition process, therefore, The Research Department (TRD) examines the integrity and robustness of these systems. In particular, the FSA considers:

- feeder systems (for material risks);
- risk aggregation systems; the time series database(s);
- the value at risk system itself; stress testing system(s);
- the backtesting system(s), including Profit and Lost (P&L) cleaning system(s) where appropriate;
- data quality, reconciliations and checks on completeness of capture;
- system development, change control and documentation;
- security and audit trails;
- system availability and contingency procedures;
- network adequacy; and
- operational statistics relating to the Value at Risk (VaR) production process.

These statistics include timeliness, number of reruns required, reliability of data feeds etc. Interruption. The components of electronic systems are vulnerable to interruption and failure; without adequate contingency arrangements this can lead to serious operational difficulty and/or financial loss."

## 2.4 Audit Standards

### 2.4.1 German Institute of Accountants (IDW)

In a draft [IDWd01] the German Institute of Accountants (IDW) required that b*ack-up and external storage procedures* must ensure that the data and information are available and legible at all times. Suitable procedures are sufficiently staggered daily, monthly and annual back-ups, inventories of all back-up media, including cataloguing of data carriers, and storing important back-ups outside the computer area.

A transparently documented back-up system requires systematic catalogues of the data, information and program back-ups to be kept to ensure the orderly storage and retrieval of back-ups.

Generally, regular data back-ups are needed to

- reconstruct historical programs, data and information;
- provide evidence of the version status of the different programs; and
- reconstruct current software and data in case of hardware malfunctions.

As part of the back-up procedure to ensure the recoverability of the IT system, the number and regularity of recurrence of back-ups (generation concept), the back-up media used and the type of storage for the back-ups must be defined.

The operation of IT encompasses procedures both for the orderly standard operation of IT applications and for emergency operations. The *orderly standard operation* of IT applications requires documented procedures for work preparation, program planning, the operation of IT applications and networks, and follow-up work. In this connection, the use of program versions, processing sequences and access to files and databases must be defined. Procedures for *emergency operation* comprise organisational arrangements for restoring operability and range from action to be taken in the case of system malfunctions (restart concepts) to concepts for use when the IT system fails completely (contingency concepts).

Constant availability of the IT system is essential for the continuation of business operations. Precautions must therefore be taken to enable *emergency operation*. The failure of key IT applications when no alternative is available at short notice can cause material and immaterial damage and constitutes a significant deficiency in the bookkeeping.

*Measures to safeguard operability* can be divided into measures that are aimed at replacing individual system components at short notice and so-called contingency concepts which are designed to enable a restart if an enterprise's entire IT system fails completely (e.g. owing to fire, water, earthquake damage or acts of violence).

In order to compensate for the *failure of individual system components*, fault-tolerant systems are generally used in conjunction with partly redundant system components in all important areas. Typical examples of this are mirrored servers and hard disk technologies in which a back-up system does the work of the failed system.

*Contingency concepts* range from computer centres in other locations that can accommodate each other's full computing load and back-up computers inside or outside the enterprise, to service agreements between enterprises and special back-up service providers or hardware manufacturers and suppliers. An enterprise's choice of a specific concept is determined by its dependence on the availability of IT applications and the type of technology it uses.

If, having analysed the risk situation, an enterprise comes to the conclusion that its business can be continued manually for a limited period of time, such measures may, in certain cases, not need to be taken if the costs outweigh the benefits. But in any case, back-ups are required so that programs and data can be reconstructed and rendered legible within a reasonable period of time.

In accordance with IAS 401, *Auditing in a Computer Information Systems Environment*, the IDW says [IDW01]:

"Measures to secure the state of readiness comprise the employment of single system components and so-called disaster scenarios. The measures are necessary to secure the availability of IT functions and completeness and verifiability during the retention periods of data.

Within the audit of the structure, the procedures against failures of IT have to be assessed as to whether they take into account enterprise-related risks and the dependence of the enterprise on the functioning of its IT adequately. The organisational procedures (disaster manual) and the technical measures taken (e.g. redundancy of hardware, back-up agreements and back-up computer centres) must guarantee adequately that the period of time within which in the case of an emergency, the program functions and processes should be recovered is not exceeded. In particular, the plausibility of the disaster scenarios supposed by management and their effects on business continuity have to be assessed critically, on the basis of the documentation of the measures.

Enterprises depending strongly on IT systems (e.g. banks and telecommunication companies) have to meet special requirements regarding the quality of risk precautions and detailed contingency planning. It must be investigated, whether and how far the planned measures are suited to allowing the enterprise restart processes following the failure of a single hardware component or to recover functions in the case of a disaster within a period of time specified by management. It must also be investigated, whether escalation procedures are organised in a proper way and whether the effectiveness of recovery and disaster procedures is verified by regular tests.

The auditor may omit its own tests of the effectiveness and efficiency of these measures if the success of testing can be assessed properly by means of test documents."

### 2.4.2 Commission de Surveillance du Secteur Financiere (CSSF), Luxembourg

The CSSF is the Luxembourg authority for supervising banks, other professionals in the financial sector, investment companies, pension funds, the stock exchange, payment systems, fund management companies and security-trading companies. In its circular 01/27, the CSSF describes the following obligations for year-end auditors [Cir101]:

"The global plan that the bank has created for a disaster in its premises or in case its premises cannot be entered has to be described and assessed (group solution, specialised company, regular testing and security measures). For IT security and back-up, refer to Section 3.4.5 of the audit report.

*3.4 IT Systems*
Here the IT systems and the processes are described, and their reliability and the security of processed data have to be assessed. The auditor has especially to check whether the bank meets the requirements of the principles concerning data processing as laid down in IML circular 96/126, 4.5.2. The result of this checking is to be documented in the annex using the IRE questionnaire "Fulfilment of IML circular 96/126".

*3.4.3 Risk Analysis*
The following issues have to be taken into account:

- Data security: criteria of confidentiality, integrity and continuity (IT security policy, procedures and follow-ups; physical and logical security).
- Development and maintenance of systems (quality control, taking into production, documentation).
- Operating (execution of batch jobs, back-ups, producing of listings, planning, execution and control; control procedures for results and plausibility, recovery and filing procedures).
- Technical support (system software maintenance, maintenance and administration of databases, maintenance and check-up of network, user support and support of peripheral devices).

*3.4.5 IT Back-up*
The business continuity plan is to provide a rough description. This plan must enable the bank to perform its activities and services in the case of failures of the IT systems, including Internet-based services."

# 3 Outsourcing of Services

Material outsourcing is the use of third parties to provide services to a bank which are of such importance to the bank that:

- a weakness or failure in any of the activities outsourced would cast into serious doubt the bank's continuing compliance with the minimum legal criteria for authorisation; or
- the outsourcing is done by business units which are *significant units*.

## 3.1 Federal Banking Supervisory Office (BAKRED)

The Federal Banking Supervisory Office (Bundesaufsichtsamt für das Kreditwesen – BAKRED) is a federal government agency. It has a statutory mandate to regulate banks and other financial services institutions in Germany.

In regulating the case of branches of American banks processing their data in the US, the BAKRED required, as early as 1992 [Anno92]:

- Files with relevant accounting information must be transmitted back to the bank in an actualised form within 24 hours after transmission of the original transac-

tion information to guarantee complete, timely, orderly and traceable (by a competent third party if given adequate time) accounting in accordance with the law and with the standards of proper accounting.
- The processing must be fail proof; this include an adequate back-up system and technical and operational recovery procedures outside the computer centre. In the case of failure of the production centre, these procedures must allow at any time the continuation of computer processing according to the regulations of this announcement (off-site disaster recovery facilities). Deleted files must be recovered in such a time that information relevant to accounting can be transmitted to the German bank within 24 hours in an actualised form. An exception to the 24-hour rule can be conceded under certain circumstances; this extension must not exceed 48 hours. Generally, this exception can be conceded only in the case of total disaster. Any extension of the 24-hour rule has to be reported in detail and immediately to the banking supervision authority.

In December 2001, the BAKRED required in a circular l [Cir201], that

- an outsourcing financial institution and the service company have to determine and lay down in writing the security requirements that the service company has to meet. The bank has to monitor the adherence to these requirements at all times.
- The outsourcing bank has to guarantee proper continuation of business *at any time* in the case of an emergency. It has to be determined who will guarantee the continuance of the outsourced processes if the outsourcing service company is not able to perform its services. The risk that the service company cannot be replaced has to be taken into account by adequate procedures. The bank and the outsourcing company have to guarantee the data protection requirements and take care of the confidentiality, availability and correctness of data. Customer data have to be protected by adequate technical and organisational procedures against unauthorised access. In particular the systems have to be protected against unauthorised or accidental deletion, accidental loss, technical faults, falsification, theft, illegal use, unauthorised modification, unauthorised duplication, unauthorised access and any other unauthorised processing.

## 3.2 Institut Monétaire Luxembourgeois (IML)[1]

In its circular 96/126, the Banking Supervisory Authority of Luxembourg came to the same conclusions:

---

[1] Now known as the Commission de Surveillance du Secteur Financiere (CSSF).

If a financial institution calls for IT services from a service company,

- any use of such services must be the subject of a written specification;
- the usage of such services may not lead to a transfer of accounting functions to the service company.

To enable the financial institution to control the reliability and completeness of data processing and to comply with the accounting regulations the following are required:

- Any access by a third party, especially any change of applications, must be allowed by the financial institution before the access happens.
- The financial institution must have at least one staff member who is able to understand the effects of the applications on the accounting system.
- The financial institution must have adequate documentation of the applications at its disposal.
- For reasons of data protection and confidentiality, no third party is allowed to have access to documents containing confidential data.
- This prohibition applies also to service companies running the IT systems of the financial institution. If, in the case of larger repairs, access to such data is unavoidable, the staff of the service company have to be accompanied by staff of the financial institution.
- Each financial institution has to nominate an employee who is responsible for the administration of access to confidential data.
- The third parties are allowed only to work on test systems; any access needs explicit consent from the financial institution.
- If services use telecommunication lines the financial institution has to take precautions against unauthorised access. In particular, the data transferred must be encrypted or protected by equivalent techniques.

Besides these measures, the financial institution must be capable of functioning normally in the case of a breakdown or failure of the telecommunication links for a prolonged period.

The IML regulates even more strictly the case in which a financial institution has its data processed by an computer centre that it does not own or of which it is only a co-owner. In this case, the institution must be capable of functioning normally even in exceptional circumstances such as a breakdown in the communication link with the processing centre or the malfunctioning of the centre for prolonged periods.

The input of customer names in a system to which a third party has access is not allowed.

## 3.3 Swiss Federal Banking Commission (SFBC)

The Swiss Federal Banking Commission (SFBC) is an administrative authority of the Confederation; it is independent of the individual directives of the Federal Council and is not a part of central government administration. Administratively, however, it is simply integrated within the Federal Department of Finance. The supervision of those parts of the financial sector over which it has authority is assumed by the SFBC on an independent basis.

In its circular letter concerning the outsourcing of business activities [Circ99], the Swiss banking commission states a Principle 4, Security:

The outsourcing company and the service company determine security requirements and create a security disposal.

The outsourcing company and the service company have to determine the security requirements the service company has to meet. These have to be laid down in a contract, whose fulfilment the outsourcing company has to control. Both parties have to create a common security disposal which allows in all cases for the continuance of the outsourced services if the service company is not able to perform its services. The outsourcing company must be able to maintain its activities properly at all times.

Customer information must be protected, by adequate technical and organisational procedures, against unauthorised treatment.

Both the outsourcing and the service company are responsible for data protection and have to guarantee the confidentiality, availability and correctness of information. In particular, they have to protect the systems against unauthorised or accidental deletion, accidental loss, technical failures, forgery, theft or illegal use, change, copying, access and other unauthorised processing.

Concerning the technical and organisational procedures, the following criteria must be taken into account:

- the purpose of the data processing,
- the type and extent of processing,
- evaluation of possible risks for the customers concerned, and
- the state of the available techniques.

These procedures have to be controlled regularly. For the processing of customer data, the service company has to take technical and organisational measures to meet the requirements of adequate controls on admission, privacy, transport- publication, storage, user, access and input- (see Article 7 of the Federal Data Protection Act and Articles 8 and 9 of the regulation of June 14th, 1993, related to this act).

## 3.4 Financial Services Authority (FSA)

In June 1999 the British FSA published its "Principles of Outsourcing" [Guid99]. The principles affect contingency planning: a bank must have and regularly review contingency plans to enable it to set up new arrangements as quickly as possible, with minimum disruption to business, if the contract is suddenly terminated or the supplier fails. The level of detail in such plans may vary. For example, if there are large numbers of possible alternative suppliers the outsourcer may simply be able to use one of the alternative suppliers. However, this may still be a complex and time-consuming process, and a bank must consider how it would deal with the handover process. If, on the other hand, the only option is for the bank to resume the activity itself the plan should be far more detailed. As a contract with an intra-group supplier is highly unlikely to be terminated through the actions of the supplier, the only significant risk is that the service will be interrupted by another, unrelated event. Such events should be covered by the supplier's business continuity plan, and therefore a separate contingency plan for the bank may not be appropriate.

# 4 The Internet

In an unstable, volatile economic and financial environment, risk control must be a primary objective for all authorities, central banks and supervisors. In this respect, new technologies –notably online banking – are considerably modifying the framework of the banking business and generating new risks.

## 4.1 Supranational Authorities

### 4.1.1 European Central Bank

The European System of Central Banks (ESCB) is composed of the European Central Bank (ECB) and the national central banks (NCB) of all 15 EU Member States. The "Eurosystem" is the term used to refer to the ECB and the NCBs of the Member States which have adopted the euro. In its statement on the effects of technology on the EU banking system [Effe99] the ECB said about operational risks:

"The increasing ability to manage information is improving transparency within banks and making banks' management information systems (MIS) and risk control systems more efficient as the amount and timeliness of information improve (e.g. real-time account balances). However, banks are at the same time becoming more subject to the operational risk of technological failures. Moreover, open systems such as the Internet expose banks' systems to an increasing degree towards external intrusion. As IT disruptions can be very costly, banks need to have extensive back-up facilities."

### 4.1.2 Basel Committee on Banking Supervision

The Basel Committee on Banking Supervision expects risks resulting from e-banking to be recognised, addressed and managed by banking institutions in a prudent manner in accordance with the fundamental characteristics and challenges of e-banking services. To facilitate these developments, the Committee has identified [Risk01] fourteen *Risk Management Principles for Electronic Banking* to help banking institutions expand their existing risk oversight policies and processes to cover their e-banking activities. These *Risk Management Principles* are not put forth as absolute requirements or even "best practice". The Committee believes that setting detailed risk management requirements in the area of e-banking might be counterproductive, if only because these would be likely to become rapidly outdated because of the speed of change related to technological and customer service innovation. The Committee has therefore preferred to express supervisory expectations and guidance in the form of *Risk Management Principles* in order to promote safety and soundness in e-banking activities, while preserving the necessary flexibility in implementation that derives in part from the speed of change in this area. Further, the Committee recognises that each bank's risk profile is different and requires a tailored risk mitigation approach appropriate to the scale of the e-banking operations, the materiality of the risks present, and the willingness and ability of the institution to manage these risks. This implies that a "one size fits all" approach to e-banking risk management issues may not be appropriate. For a similar reason, the *Risk Management Principles* issued by the Committee do not attempt to set out specific technical solutions or standards relating to e-banking. Technical solutions are to be addressed by institutions and standard-setting bodies as technology evolves. These solutions are considered further in Section 5.

Concerning legal and reputational risk management, the Basel Committee continues:

"To protect banks against business, legal and reputation risk, e-banking services must be delivered on a consistent and timely basis in accordance with high customer expectations of constant and rapid availability and potentially high transaction demand. The bank must have the ability to deliver e-banking services to all end-users and be able to maintain such availability in all circumstances. Effective incident response mechanisms are also critical to minimise operational, legal and reputational risks arising from unexpected events, including internal and external attacks, that may affect the provision of e-banking systems and services. To meet customers' expectations, banks should therefore have effective capacity, business continuity and contingency planning. Banks should also develop appropriate incident response plans, including communication strategies, that ensure business continuity, control reputation risk and limit liability associated with disruptions in their e-banking services."

The principles concerning legal and reputational risks (principles 11 to 14 of the Risk Management Principles), according to the Committee, are:

11. Appropriate disclosures for e-banking services.
12. Privacy of customer information.
13. Capacity, business continuity and contingency planning to ensure availability of e-banking systems and services.
14. Incident response planning.

Each of the above issues is discussed more specifically in the subsequent sections of the Committee's report, as they relate to e-banking and the underlying risk management principles that should be considered by banks to address these issues. Where appropriate, sound practices that may be considered as effective ways to address these risks are also offered in a referenced appendix. In the following, only principles 13 and 14 will be described.

*Principle 13: Banks should have effective capacity, business continuity and contingency planning processes to help ensure the availability of e-banking systems and services.*

To protect banks against business, legal and reputation risk, e-banking services must be delivered on a consistent and timely basis in accordance with customer expectations. To achieve this, the bank must have the ability to deliver e-banking services to end-users from either primary (e.g. internal bank systems and applications) or secondary (e.g. systems and applications of service providers) sources. The maintenance of adequate availability is also dependent upon the ability of contingency back-up systems to mitigate denial-of-service attacks or other events that may potentially cause business disruption. The challenge of maintaining continued availability of e-banking systems and applications can be considerable, given the potential for high transaction demand, especially during peak time periods. In addition, high customer expectations regarding short transaction-processing cycle times and constant availability (24 x 7) have also increased the importance of sound capacity, business continuity and contingency planning. To provide customers with the continuity of e-banking services that they expect, banks need to ensure that:

- Current e-banking system capacity and future scalability are analysed in the light of the overall market dynamics for e-commerce and the projected rate of customer acceptance of e-banking products and services.
- E-banking transaction-processing capacity estimates are established, stress tested and periodically reviewed.
- Appropriate business continuity and contingency plans for critical e-banking processing and delivery systems are in place and regularly tested.

In Appendix VI of the report several sound capacity, business continuity and contingency planning practices are identified.

*Principle 14: Banks should develop appropriate incident response plans to manage, contain and minimise problems arising from unexpected events, including internal and external attacks, that may hamper the provision of e-banking systems and services.*

Effective incident response mechanisms are critical to minimise operational, legal and reputational risks arising from unexpected events such as internal and external attacks that may affect the provision of e-banking systems and services. Banks should develop appropriate incident response plans, including communication strategies, that ensure business continuity, control reputation risk and limit liability associated with disruptions in their e-banking services, including those originating from outsourced systems and operations. The current and future capacity of critical e-banking delivery systems should be assessed on an ongoing basis.

To ensure effective response to unforeseen incidents, banks should develop:

- Incident response plans to address recovery of e-banking systems and services under various scenarios, and in various businesses and geographic locations. Scenario analysis should include consideration of the likelihood of the risk occurring and its impact on the bank. E-banking systems that are outsourced to third-party service providers should be an integral part of these plans.
- Mechanisms to identify an incident or crisis as soon as it occurs, assess materiality and control the reputation risk associated with any disruption in service.
- A communication strategy to adequately address external market and media concerns that may arise in the event of security breaches, online attacks and/or failures of e-banking systems.
- A clear process for alerting the appropriate regulatory authorities in the event of material security breaches or disruptive incidents.
- Incident response teams with the authority to act in an emergency and sufficiently trained in analysing incident detection/response systems and in interpreting the significance of the output.
- A clear chain of command, encompassing both internal and outsourced operations, to ensure that prompt action appropriate to the significance of the incident is taken. In addition, escalation and internal communication procedures should be developed and should include notification of the Board where appropriate.
- A process to ensure all relevant external parties, including bank customers, counterparts and the media, are informed in a timely and appropriate manner of material e-banking disruptions and of developments in business resumption.
- A process for collecting and preserving forensic evidence to facilitate appropriate post-mortem reviews of any e-banking incidents as well as to assist in the prosecution of attackers. Monitoring of help desk and customer support activities and a regular review of customer complaints may help to identify gaps in information being detected and reported through established security controls versus actual intrusion activities.

## 4.2 National Authorities

### 4.2.1 Deutsche Bundesbank

The Deutsche Bundesbank, the central bank of the Federal Republic of Germany, is an integral part of the ESCB. The Bundesbank participates in the fulfilment of the ESCB's tasks, with the primary objective of maintaining the stability of the euro, and it ensures the orderly execution of domestic and foreign payments. In its monthly report of December 1999 [Deut99] the Deutsche Bundesbank wrote:

"In a narrow sense, operational risks are risks resulting directly from operations. The main reasons are technical or human failures, IT problems, fraud and inadequate organisational structures. If operational risks are not managed efficiently, besides financial losses, restrictions to banking operations may result in addition, e.g. unavailability of a call centre or failure of a host system."

Operational risks are not entirely new, but come to the fore because of the increased employment of IT. The functioning of the security infrastructure as part of the operational risk, especially for e-banking, is of crucial importance for banking supervision. There is a danger of someone monitoring, spying on, falsifying, deleting or misusing data. Another source of risk is so-called "denial of service" attacks. Here servers are flooded with a multitude of falsified entries, causing overstrain on the system and preventing authorized users from executing their transactions. The dangers of aimed virus attacks by hackers are illustrated every week. Capacity bottlenecks have emerged in the course of big new issues in late spring, the call centres and IT systems of several banks were not able to process the multitude of transaction requests. Because of this unavailability, several Internet banks were requested by the German securities supervision authority to ensure that their systems will be able to process peak loads (at the time of writing, the systems were oversized). In the meantime, the security supervision authority has declared that the availability of Internet banks has increased considerably and that they have fulfilled their obligations to carry out their services correctly.

### 4.2.2 Federal Banking Supervisory Office (BAKRED)

In a report concerning the minimum requirements of trading activities the BAKRED pointed out, in relation to operational risks:

"The performance of the systems used must correspond to the size and mode of the trading activities. Prices, volatilities, etc. held in databases have to be checked for plausibility on a regular basis. If several databases are used, their consistency has to be guaranteed.

If the technical equipment necessary for the trading activities fails, provision must be made for back-up solutions, available at short notice; in a written business continuity plan. Provision has to be made also for software failures or unforeseen shortages of human resources.

The procedures, documentation, systems and business continuity plans applied to trading activities have to be checked regularly."

### 4.2.3 Office of the Comptroller of the Currency (OCC)

The Office of the Comptroller of the Currency (OCC) charters, regulates and supervises all national banks. It also supervises the federal branches and agencies of foreign banks. The OCC published in 1999 the *Comptroller's Handbook on Internet Banking* [OCC] which is intended to provide guidance to bankers and examiners about identifying and controlling the risks associated with Internet banking activities.

According to the OCC, contingency and business resumption planning is necessary for banks to be sure that they can deliver products and services in the event of adverse circumstances. Internet banking products connected to a robust network may actually make this easier because back-up capabilities can be spread over a wide geographic area. For example, if the main server is inoperable, the network could automatically reroute traffic to a back-up server in a different geographical location. Security issues should be considered when the institution develops its contingency and business resumption plans. In such situations, the security and internal controls at the back-up location should be as sophisticated as those at the primary processing site. High levels of system availability will be a key expectation of customers and will likely differentiate success levels among financial institutions on the Internet.

National banks that offer bill presentation and payment will need a process to settle transactions between the bank, its customers and external parties. In addition to transaction risk, settlement failures could adversely affect reputation, liquidity and credit risk.

The following checklist gives an overview. More detailed information may be found in the document itself.

**Business Resumption and Contingency Planning**

1. Determine whether there is an adequate process to develop and review the bank's business impact analysis. Consider whether:
   - Internet banking is viewed as a critical business or product line.
   - Management has reviewed the impact on the bank's reputation if its Internet banking products and services are not operable.
2. Determine whether the bank has an adequate process to develop and test the contingency and business resumption plans for Internet banking products and services, including whether:

- The contingency and business resumption plans provide adequately for recovery.
- The contingency and business resumption plans are appropriately tested on a regular basis.
3. Determine whether the bank has an adequate process in place for Internet banking recovery, including whether:
- Internet banking contingency and business resumption plans are reviewed and updated regularly.
- Specific personnel and staff are responsible for initiating and managing Internet banking recovery plans.
- The plan ensures that single points of failure for critical network points are adequately addressed.
- The plan establishes strategies to recover hardware, software, communication links, and data files.
- Adequate back-up agreements and contracts are in place for external vendors or critical suppliers and whether these back-up arrangements are tested fully.
- The response process ensures that senior management and the board of directors are made aware of adverse events, as dictated by the severity of damage and monetary loss.
- Outreach strategies are adequate to inform the media and customers of corrective measures.
- Legal liability issues are contemplated and addressed as part of the response processes.
- Procedures are in place to bring security breaches to the attention of appropriate management and external entities (e.g. the Computer Emergency Response Team (CERT), FBI, OCC, etc.).
4. Determine whether the bank has an adequate process to review the results of the most recent testing of the contingency and recovery plan, including whether management:
- Requires annual testing of recovery processes and systems.
- Addresses adverse test results in a timely manner.
- Informs the board or executive management of test results.

# 5 Solutions

In the following, two guidelines from standard-setting bodies are described in more detail. They give a very good idea of what is to be considered in developing contingency plans.

## 5.1 National Institute of Standards and Technology (NIST)

Founded in 1901, NIST is a non-regulatory federal agency within the US Commerce Department's Technology Administration. NIST's mission is to develop and promote measurements, standards and technology to enhance productivity, facilitate trade and improve the quality of life. NIST gives the following guidelines for preparing for contingencies and disasters [NIST95]:

"**Chapter 11**
**PREPARING FOR CONTINGENCIES AND DISASTERS**"
A *computer security contingency* is an event with the potential to disrupt computer operations, thereby disrupting critical mission and business functions. Such an event could be a power outage, hardware failure, fire, or storm. If the event is very destructive, it is often called a disaster.

To avert potential contingencies and disasters or minimise the damage they cause organisations can take steps early to control the event. Generally called *contingency planning*, this activity is closely related to incident handling, which primarily addresses malicious technical threats such as hackers and viruses.

Contingency planning involves more than planning for a move offsite after a disaster destroys a data centre. It also addresses how to keep an organisation's critical functions operating in the event of disruptions, both large and small. This broader perspective on contingency planning is based on the distribution of computer support throughout an organisation."

This chapter presents the contingency planning process in six steps:

1. Identifying the mission- or business-critical functions.
2. Identifying the resources that support the critical functions.
3. Anticipating potential contingencies or disasters.
4. Selecting contingency planning strategies.
5. Implementing the contingency strategies.
6. Testing and revising the strategy.

**11.1 Step 1: Identifying the Mission- or Business-Critical Functions**

Protecting the continuity of an organisation's mission or business is very difficult if it is not clearly identified. Managers need to understand the organisation from a point of view that usually extends beyond the area they control. The definition of an organisation's critical mission or business functions is often called a *business plan*.

Since the development of a business plan will be used to support contingency planning, it is necessary not only to identify critical missions and businesses, but also to *set priorities for* them. A fully redundant capability for each function is prohibitively expensive for most organisations. In the event of a disaster, certain functions will not be performed. If appropriate priorities have been set (and approved by senior management), it could mean the difference in the organisation's ability to survive a disaster.

## 11.2 Step 2: Identifying the Resources That Support Critical Functions

After identifying critical missions and business functions, it is necessary to identify the supporting resources, the time frames in which each resource is used (e.g., is the resource needed constantly or only at the end of the month?), and the effect on the mission or business of the unavailability of the resource. In identifying resources, a traditional problem has been that different managers oversee different resources. They may not realise how resources interact to support the organisation's mission or business. Many of these resources are *not* computer resources. Contingency planning should address all the resources needed to perform a function, regardless whether they directly relate to a computer.

*Resources That Support Critical Functions*
- Human Resources
- Processing Capability
- Computer-Based Services
- Data and Applications
- Physical Infrastructure
- Documents and Papers

*Contingency Planning Teams*
To understand what resources are needed from each of the six resource categories and to understand how the resources support critical functions, it is often necessary to establish a contingency planning team. A typical team contains representatives from various organisational elements, and is often headed by a contingency planning co-ordinator. It has representatives from the following three groups:

1. business-oriented groups, such as representatives from functional areas;
2. facilities management; and
3. technology management.

Various other groups are called on as needed including financial management, personnel, training, safety, computer security, physical security, and public affairs.

The analysis of needed resources should be conducted by those who understand how the function is performed and the dependencies of various resources on other resources and other critical relationships. This will allow an organisation to *assign priorities* to resources since not all elements of all resources are crucial to the critical functions.

### 11.2.1 Human Resources

People are perhaps an organisation's most obvious resource. Some functions require the effort of specific individuals, some require specialised expertise, and some only require individuals who can be trained to perform a specific task. Within the information technology field, human resources include both operators (such as technicians or system programmers) and users (such as data entry clerks or information analysts).

### 11.2.2 Processing Capability

Traditionally contingency planning has focused on processing power (i.e., if the data center is down, how can applications dependent on it continue to be processed?). Although the need for data center backup remains vital, today's other processing alternatives are also important. Local area networks (LANs), minicomputers, workstations, and personal computers in all forms of centralised and distributed processing may be performing critical tasks.

### 11.2.3 Automated Applications and Data

Computer systems run applications that process data. Without current electronic versions of both applications and data, computerised processing may not be possible. If the processing is being performed on alternate hardware, the applications must be compatible with the alternate hardware, operating systems and other software (including version and configuration), and numerous other technical factors. Because of the complexity, it is normally necessary to periodically verify compatibility. (See Step 6, Testing and Revising.)

### 11.2.4 Computer-Based Services

An organisation uses many different kinds of computer-based services to perform its functions. The two most important are normally communications services and information services. Communications can be further categorised as data and voice communications; however, in many organisations these are managed by the same service. Information services include any source of information outside of the organisation. Many of these sources are becoming automated, including on-line government and private databases, news services, and bulletin boards.

### 11.2.5 Physical Infrastructure

For people to work effectively, they need a safe working environment and appropriate equipment and utilities. This can include office space, heating, cooling, venting, power, water, sewage, other utilities, desks, telephones, fax machines, personal computers, terminals, courier services, file cabinets, and many other items. In addition, computers also need space and utilities, such as electricity. Electronic and paper media used to store applications and data also have physical requirements.

*11.2.6 Documents and Papers*
Many functions rely on vital records and various documents, papers, or forms. These records could be important because of a legal need (such as being able to produce a signed copy of a loan) or because they are the only record of the information. Records can be maintained on paper, microfiche, microfilm, magnetic media, or optical disk.

**11.3 Step 3: Anticipating Potential Contingencies or Disasters**

Although it is impossible to think of *all* the things that can go wrong, the next step is to identify a likely range of problems. The development of scenarios will help an organisation develop a plan to address the wide range of things that can go wrong. Scenarios should include small and large contingencies. While some general classes of contingency scenarios are obvious, imagination and creativity, as well as research, can point to other possible, but less obvious, contingencies. The contingency scenarios should address each of the resources described above. The following are *examples* of some of the types of questions that contingency scenarios may address:

*Examples of Some Less Obvious Contingencies*
1. A computer center in the basement of a building had a minor problem with rats. Exterminators killed the rats, but the bodies were not retrieved because they were hidden under the raised flooring and in the pipe conduits. Employees could only enter the data center with gas masks because of the decomposing rats.
2. After the World Trade Center explosion [this guideline was written after the first terrorist strike in 1993] when people reentered the building, they turned on their computer systems to check for problems. Dust and smoke damaged many systems when they were turned on. If the systems had been cleaned *first*, there would not have been significant damage.

- *Human Resources:*
    - Can people get to work? Are key personnel willing to cross a picketline?
    - Are there critical skills and knowledge possessed by one person? Can people easily get to an alternative site?
- *Processing Capability:*
    - Are the computers harmed?
    - What happens if some of the computers are inoperable, but not all?
- *Automated Applications and Data:*
    - Has data integrity been affected? Is an application sabotaged? Can an application run on a different processing platform?
- *Computer-Based Services:*
    - Can the computers communicate? To where?
    - Can people communicate?
    - Are information services down? For how long?

- *Infrastructure:*
  - Do people have a place to sit?
  - Do they have equipment to do their jobs? Can they occupy the building?
  - *Documents/Paper:*
  - Can needed records be found? Are they readable?

**11.4 Step 4: Selecting Contingency Planning Strategies**

The next step is to plan how to recover needed resources. In evaluating alternatives, it is necessary to consider what controls are in place to prevent and minimise contingencies. Since no set of controls can cost-effectively prevent all contingencies, it is necessary to coordinate prevention and recovery efforts. A contingency planning strategy normally consists of three parts: emergency response, recovery, and resumption.

*Emergency response* encompasses the initial actions taken to protect lives and limit damage.

*Recovery* refers to the steps that are taken to continue support for critical functions.

*Resumption* is the return to normal operations. The relationship between recovery and resumption is important. The longer it takes to resume normal operations, the longer the organisation will have to operate in the recovery mode.

*Example #1:* If the system administrator for a LAN has to be out of the office for a long time (due to illness or an accident), arrangements are made for the system administrator of another LAN to perform the duties. Anticipating this, the absent administrator should have taken steps beforehand to keep documentation current. This strategy is inexpensive, but service will probably be significantly reduced on both LANs which may prompt the manager of the loaned administrator to partially renege on the agreement.

*Example #2:* An organisation depends on an on-line information service provided by a commercial vendor. The organisation is no longer able to obtain the information manually (e.g., from a reference book) within acceptable time limits and there are no other comparable services. In this case, the organisation relies on the contingency plan of the service provider. The organisation pays a premium to obtain priority service in case the service provider has to operate at reduced capacity.

*Example #3:* A large mainframe data center has a contract with a hot site vendor, has a contract with the telecommunications carrier to reroute communications to the hot site, has plans to move people, and stores up-to-date copies of data, applications and needed paper records off-site. The contingency plan is expensive, but management has decided that the expense is fully justified.

*Example #4.* An organisation distributes its processing among two major sites, each of which includes small to medium processors (personal computers and minicomputers). If one site is lost, the other can carry the critical load until more equipment is purchased. Routing of data and voice communications can be performed transparently to redirect traffic. Backup copies are stored at the other site. This plan requires tight control over the architectures used and types of applications that are developed to ensure compatibility. In addition, personnel at both sites must be cross-trained to perform all functions.

The selection of a strategy needs to be based on practical considerations, including feasibility and cost. The different categories of resources should each be considered. Risk assessment can be used to help estimate the cost of options to decide on an optimal strategy. For example, is it more expensive to purchase and maintain a generator or to move processing to an alternate site, considering the likelihood of losing electrical power for various lengths of time? Are the consequences of a loss of computer-related resources sufficiently high to warrant the cost of various recovery strategies? The risk assessment should focus on areas where it is not clear which strategy is the best.

In developing contingency planning strategies, there are many factors to consider in addressing each of the resources that support critical functions. Some examples are presented in the sidebars.

*11.4.1 Human Resources*
To ensure an organisation has access to workers with the right skills and knowledge, training and documentation of knowledge are needed. During a major contingency, people will be under significant stress and may panic.
If the contingency is a regional disaster, their first concerns will probably be their family and property. In addition, many people will be either unwilling or unable to come to work. Additional hiring or temporary services can be used.
The use of additional personnel may introduce security vulnerabilities. The need for computer security does not go away when an organisation is processing in a contingency mode. In some cases, the need may increase due to sharing processing facilities, concentrating resources in fewer sites, or using additional contractors and consultants. Security should be an important consideration when selecting contingency strategies. Contingency planning, especially for emergency response, normally places the highest emphasis on the protection of human life.

*11.4.2 Processing Capability*
Strategies for processing capability are normally grouped into five categories: hot site; cold site; redundancy; reciprocal agreements; and hybrids. These terms originated with recovery strategies for data centers but can be applied to other platforms.

1. *Hot site* A building already equipped with processing capability and other services.
2. *Cold site* A building for housing processors that can be easily adapted for use.
3. *Redundant site* A site equipped and configured exactly like the primary site. (Some organisations plan on having reduced processing capability after a disaster and use

partial redundancy. The stocking of spare personal computers or LAN servers also provides some redundancy.)
4. *Reciprocal agreement* An agreement that allows two organisations to back each other up. (While this approach often sounds desirable, contingency planning experts note that this alternative has the greatest chance of failure due to problems keeping agreements and plans up-to-date as systems and personnel change.)
5. *Hybrids* Any combinations of the above such as using having a hot site as a backup in case a redundant or reciprocal agreement site is damaged by a separate contingency. Recovery may include several stages, perhaps marked by increasing availability of processing capability. Resumption planning may include contracts or the ability to place contracts to replace equipment.

### *11.4.3 Automated Applications and Data*
Normally, the primary contingency strategy for applications and data is *regular backup* and secure *offsite storage*. Important decisions to be addressed include how often the backup is performed, how often it is stored off-site, and how it is transported (to storage, to an alternate processing site, or to support the resumption of normal operations).

### *11.4.4 Computer-Based Services*
Service providers may offer contingency services. Voice communications carriers often can reroute calls (transparently to the user) to a new location. Data communications carriers can also reroute traffic. Hot sites are usually capable of receiving data and voice communications. If one service provider is down, it may be possible to use another. However, the type of communications carrier lost, either local or long distance, is important. Local voice service may be carried on cellular. Local data communications, especially for large volumes, is normally more difficult. In addition, resuming normal operations may require another rerouting of communications services.

### *11.4.5 Physical Infrastructure*
Hot sites and cold sites may also offer office space in addition to processing capability support. Other types of contractual arrangements can be made for office space, security services, furniture, and more in the event of a contingency. If the contingency plan calls for moving offsite, procedures need to be developed to ensure a smooth transition back to the primary operating facility or to a new facility. Protection of the physical infrastructure is normally an important part of the emergency response plan, such as use of fire extinguishers or protecting equipment from water damage.

### *11.4.6 Documents and Papers*
The primary contingency strategy is usually backup onto magnetic, optical, microfiche, paper, or other medium and offsite storage. Paper documents are generally hard-

er to backup than electronic ones. A supply of forms and other needed papers can be stored offsite.

## 11.5 Step 5: Implementing the Contingency Strategies

Once the contingency planning strategies have been selected, it is necessary to make appropriate preparations, document the strategies, and train employees. Many of these tasks are ongoing.

### *11.5.1 Implementation*

Much preparation is needed to implement the strategies for protecting critical functions and their supporting resources. For example, one common preparation is to establish procedures for backing up files and applications. Another is to establish contracts and agreements, *if* the contingency strategy calls for them. Existing service contracts may need to be renegotiated to add contingency services. Another preparation may be to purchase equipment, especially to support a redundant capability. Backing up data files and applications is a critical part of virtually every contingency plan. Backups are used, for example, to restore files after a personal computer virus corrupts the files or after a hurricane destroys a data processing centre.

*Relationship Between Contingency Plans and Computer Security Plans*
For small or less complex systems, the contingency plan may be a part of the computer security plan. For larger or more complex systems, the computer security plan could contain a brief synopsis of the contingency plan, which would be a separate document. It is important to keep preparations, including documentation, up-to-date. Computer systems change rapidly and so should backup services and redundant equipment. Contracts and agreements may also need to reflect the changes. If additional equipment is needed, it must be maintained and periodically replaced when it is no longer dependable or no longer fits the organisation's architecture.

Preparation should also include formally designating people who are responsible for various tasks in the event of a contingency. These people are often referred to as the contingency response team. This team is often composed of people who were a part of the contingency planning team.

There are many important implementation issues for an organisation. Two of the most important are 1) how many plans should be developed? and 2) who prepares each plan? Both of these questions revolve around the organisation's overall strategy for contingency planning. The answers should be documented in organisation policy and procedures.

*How Many Plans?*
Some organisations have just one plan for the entire organisation, and others have a plan for every distinct computer system, application, or other resource. Other ap-

proaches recommend a plan for each business or mission function, with separate plans, as needed, for critical resources. The answer to the question, therefore, depends upon the unique circumstances for each organisation. But it is critical to co-ordinate between resource managers and functional managers who are responsible for the mission or business.

*Who Prepares the Plan?*
If an organisation decides on a centralised approach to contingency planning, it may be best to name a *contingency planning co-ordinator*. The co-ordinator prepares the plans in co-operation with various functional and resource managers. Some organisations place responsibility directly with the functional and resource managers. Contingency plan maintenance can be incorporated into procedures for change management so that upgrades to hardware and software are reflected in the plan.

*11.5.2 Documenting*
The contingency plan needs to be written, kept up-to-date as the system and other factors change, and stored in a safe place. A written plan is critical during a contingency, especially if the person who developed the plan is unavailable. It should clearly state in simple language the sequence of tasks to be performed in the event of a contingency so that someone with minimal knowledge could immediately begin to execute the plan. It is generally helpful to store up-to-date copies of the contingency plan in several locations, including any off-site locations, such as alternate processing sites or backup data storage facilities.

*11.5.3 Training*
All personnel should be trained in their contingency-related duties. New personnel should be trained as they join the organisation, refresher training may be needed, and personnel will need to practice their skills. Training is particularly important for effective employee response during emergencies. There is no time to check a manual to determine correct procedures if there is a fire. Depending on the nature of the emergency, there may or may not be time to protect equipment and other assets. Practice is necessary in order to react correctly, especially when human safety is involved.

## 11.6 Step 6: Testing and Revising

A contingency plan should be tested periodically because there will undoubtedly be flaws in the plan and in its implementation. The plan will become dated as time passes and as the resources used to support critical functions change. Responsibility for keeping the contingency plan current should be specifically assigned. The extent and frequency of testing will vary between organisations and among systems. There are several types of testing, including reviews, analyses, and simulations of disasters. A *review* can be a simple test to check the accuracy of contingency plan documentation. For instance, a reviewer could check if individuals listed are still in the organisation and still have the responsibilities that caused them to be included in the plan. This test can check home and work telephone numbers, organisational codes, and building and room numbers. The review can determine if files can be restored from backup tapes or if employees know emergency procedures. The results of a "test" often implies a grade assigned for a specific level of performance, or simply pass or fail. However, in the case of contingency planning, a test should be used to improve the plan. If organisations do not use this approach, flaws in the plan may remain hidden and uncorrected.

An *analysis* may be performed on the entire plan or portions of it, such as emergency response procedures. It is beneficial if the analysis is performed by someone who did *not* help develop the contingency plan but has a good working knowledge of the critical function and supporting resources. The analyst(s) may mentally follow the strategies in the contingency plan, looking for flaws in the logic or process used by the plan's developers. The analyst may also interview functional managers, resource managers, and their staff to uncover missing or unworkable pieces of the plan. Organisations may also arrange *disaster simulations*. These tests provide valuable information about flaws in the contingency plan and provide practice for a real emergency. While they can be expensive, these tests can also provide critical information that can be used to ensure the continuity of important functions. In general, the more critical the functions and the resources addressed in the contingency plan, the more cost-beneficial it is to perform a disaster simulation.

## 11.7 Interdependencies

Since all controls help to prevent contingencies, there is an interdependency with all of the controls in the handbook.

*Risk Management* provides a tool for analysing the security costs and benefits of various contingency planning options. In addition, a risk management effort can be used to help identify critical resources needed to support the organisation and the likely threat to those resources. It is not necessary, however, to perform a risk assessment prior to contingency planning, since the identification of critical resources can be performed during the contingency planning process itself.

*Physical and Environmental Controls* help prevent contingencies. Although many of the other controls, such as logical access controls, also prevent contingencies, the major threats that a contingency plan addresses are physical and environmental threats, such as fires, loss of power, plumbing breaks, or natural disasters.

*Incident Handling* can be viewed as a subset of contingency planning. It is the emergency response capability for various technical threats. Incident handling can also help an organisation prevent future incidents.

*Support and Operations* in most organisations includes the periodic backing up of files. It also includes the prevention and recovery from more common contingencies, such as a disk failure or corrupted data files.

*Policy* is needed to create and document the organisation's approach to contingency planning. The policy should explicitly assign responsibilities.

### 11.8 Cost Considerations

The cost of developing and implementing contingency planning strategies can be significant, especially if the strategy includes contracts for backup services or duplicate equipment. There are too many options to discuss cost considerations for each type. One contingency cost that is often overlooked is the cost of testing a plan. Testing provides many benefits and should be performed, although some of the less expensive methods (such as a review) may be sufficient for less critical resources.

## 5.2 International Organisation for Standardisation (ISO)

The International Organisation for Standardisation (ISO) is a worldwide federation of national standards bodies from some 140 countries, one from each country.

ISO is a non-governmental organisation established in 1947. The mission of ISO is to promote the development of standardisation and related activities in the world with a view to facilitating the international exchange of goods and services, and to developing co-operation in the spheres of intellectual, scientific, technological and economic activity. ISO's work results in international agreements, which are published as International Standards. In the International Standard ISO 17799 [ISO00] Chapter 11, the standards for business continuity management are defined.

The objective of business continuity management is to counteract interruptions to business activities and to protect critical business processes from the effects of major failures or disasters.

A business continuity management process should be implemented to reduce the disruption caused by disasters and security failures (which may be the result of, for example, natural disasters, accidents, equipment failures or deliberate actions) to an acceptable level through a combination of preventative and recovery controls.

The consequences of disaster, security failures and loss of service should be analysed. Contingency plans should be developed and implemented to ensure that business processes can be restored within the required timescales. Such plans should be maintained and practised so as to become an integral part of all other management processes.

Business continuity management should include controls to identify and reduce risks, limit the consequences of damaging incidents, and ensure the timely resumption of essential operations.

The several steps the standard describes are:

- 11.1.1 Business continuity management process
- 11.1.2 Business continuity and impact analysis
- 11.1.3 Writing and implementing continuity plans
- 11.1.4 Business continuity planning framework
- 11.1.5 Testing, maintaining and reassessing business continuity plans
    - 11.1.5.1 Testing the plans
    - 11.1.5.2 Maintaining and reassessing the plans

The standard as a whole can be ordered from ISO for a fee. Copyright prohibits further quotation.

There have been a lot of complaints made regarding "irregularities" surrounding approval of ISO 17799, because it was adopted over the objections of some member organisations. The national bodies of Germany, France and Canada have even lodged strong official protests with the ISO central authorities. The US national body considered lodging a similar protest but did not do so; instead, it supported the other protests.

The main point of concern was that there were, at the time no compelling reasons for an International Standard in the difficult-to-quantify area of a computer security "code of practice". While ISO 17799 could be valuable as a self-assessment and improvement tool, it is not acceptable as a standard because it does not have the necessary measurement precision of a technical standard. Discussion is continuing at the time of writing.

## 5.3 Other Sources

The following Web links give further very detailed information about business continuity planning:

- The Federal Financial Institutions Examination Council has published an Information System (IS) examination handbook in two volumes, which gives an exhaustive overview: [FFIE] http://www.ncua.gov/ref/ffiec/ffiec_handbook.html
- The Federal Reserve Board published in 1996 a *Commercial Bank Examination Manual*, whose Section 4060 describes information technology risks
- NIST has published the following special publications, all of which can be downloaded from [NIST2] http://csrc.nist.gov/publications/nistpubs/index.html
    - SP 800-27, *Engineering Principles for Information Technology Security (A Baseline for Achieving Security)*, June 2001

- SP 800-18, *Guide for Developing Security Plans for Information Technology Systems*, December 1998
- SP 800-14, *Generally Accepted Principles and Practices for Securing Information Technology Systems*, September 1996
- A very recent overview (December 2001) of further sources may be found on the Web site of NIST in the document [NIST01] http://csrc.nist.gov/publications/secpubs/otherpubs/reviso-faq.pdf

Concerning the risks of electronic banking, the Banque de France, together with the Commission Bancaire, published in January 2001 a White Paper, *Internet: the Prudential Consequences*, which can be ordered from the Banque de France. The German and Lluxembourg banking supervisory authorities have announced regulations related to electronic banking for the beginning of 2002.

# 6 Conclusion

The justification for the regulations discussed above was shown on September 11, 2001: a basic tenet of corporations is that they survive from generation to generation, transcending the lives of even the most critical employees.

The destruction of the World Trade Center in New York on 11 September has caused many of the most prominent financial institutions in the world to lose not only a shocking number of their employees, but also the technological infrastructure on which their business relied. Despite that tragic loss, the integrity of the business was preserved. Much was made of the ability of the US markets to get up and running so soon after 11 September. While this was mainly due to a fierce determination not to be beaten, the existence of recovery procedures greatly contributed.

The information systems have been accessible and usable on a timely basis in the required manner. The contributing procedures were also a consequence of the heavy regulation of the financial sector.

# Position of the "Internal Audit Department" in a BCP Project

Konrad M. Reimann

*K-M-R GmbH (previously manager of an audit department)*

**Abstract:** The internal auditing department no longer only "audits the past" in an enterprise by just "ticking the box". It has developed into a consultant of the management and the executives while retaining the concept of neutrality. Therefore the auditing department has an essential and inalienable role in the conception of a business continuity plan.

A business continuity plan which feigns security and safety causes confusion in reality revented by an Internal Audit immediately.

This article describes the most relevant conflicts and is therefore a valuable contribution to the successful implementation of a BCP project.

**Keywords:** Business continuity plan, Internal auditing, Assessment procedures

## 1 Introduction

So much has been written about business continuity plans (BCPs) in other places and, especially, in this book, that I should like in this article to deal with the subject from the perspective of internal auditing only.

The internal auditing department is concerned with, or perhaps one should say – on the basis of my experience – ought to be concerned with the BCP before it is even devised. The internal auditing department can find just as much fault with the fact that a business continuity plan has been developed and drawn up as it can with the fact that no plan has been devised. But the internal auditing department's greatest cause for complaint is a BCP which pretends to provide security but, rather than protecting the company, creates terrible confusion in a crisis. So the internal auditing department's tasks with regard to the BCP are as follows:

- it must be involved in the project even before a business continuity plan is drawn up;
- it must also assess the completeness, the up to dateness and certain economic aspects of any existing BCP;

- its audit plan must also include tests to check whether all processes are consistent and all systems are compatible (and I don't mean only IT systems, but also all communication systems, supply systems, etc.);
- in a risk-oriented or value-oriented audit, particular attention must also be paid to the internal auditing system during the BCP-based activities;
- and the last point, but the one which is most often forgotten, is that the resumption of "normal" operating conditions, with "normal" responsibilities, etc., has to be included in the audit plan.

The audit intervals and the degree of detail of each audit – *here I am not referring to involvement in the BCP project* – should be determined using a risk- and value-oriented assessment procedure.

Such assessment procedures include not only the amount of loss, but also the actual probability of occurrence and the probability of occurrence in certain, predefined periods (usually one business year).

Many companies are currently preparing such models: a good example is displayed under KIR at www.k-m-r-gmbh.de. Whether the subject is a company operating locally or internationally plays no role in whether it is included in the audit plan. Such factors will affect only the composition of the audit team.

# 2 The Internal Auditing Department's Involvement in the Business Continuity Plan Project

One complaint I often hear during my audits is that an audit employee is not allowed to work on a project. The idea behind this statement is easy to comprehend and also ensures the neutrality and impartiality of the internal auditing department. However, in this case, as with many other activities in a company, consideration must be given to the exclusiveness of the statement.

For some time now, the internal auditing department has no longer simply been tracking events in a company, but has developed – *whilst retaining the concept of neutrality* – into a consultant for the managing directors and the section and department managers. And, for my part as an auditor, I can say that that was the only step possible. Apart from the presentation of weaknesses, deficiencies and remarks (or whatever terms your company uses to distinguish the major sins from the pardonable ones), this role in the company brings the individual audited areas economic success. Since the internal auditing department's role in the devising of a BCP is so essential and indispensable, allow me to go into more detail.

Work on a project, as the term "project" implies, is extensive, cost-intensive and extremely important for the company. Part of this work is to define projects – that is to say, to create the prerequisites for starting a project on the basis of a task. If such key steps are planned in your company, doesn't it make sense or isn't it natural that the auditing department should be involved in a supporting role during the project? Otherwise, the cost and the additional work needed can quickly assume considerable dimensions. In order to guarantee neutrality, an auditor, who will not participate in the subsequent plan audits, should be selected as part of the auditing department's support for or involvement in the project (see the following figure).

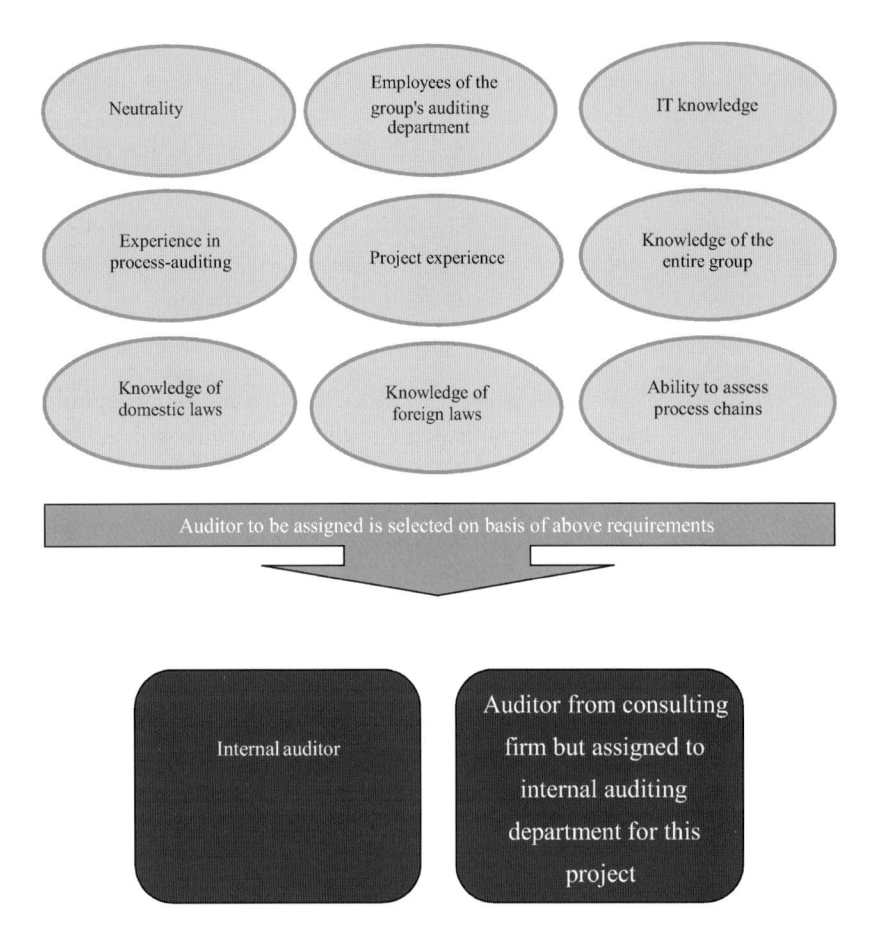

In a company operating on a global scale, this will be possible in many cases. If the management of the internal auditing department has concerns about this too, I suggest that an auditor from a consulting firm perform this task. However, I consider this solution the second-best possibility. Otherwise, significant knowledge of details, gained in a variety of individual audits, is not directly available on the project.

Auditing employees assigned to such a product should also have experience of project work or, better still, of project management, knowledge of the company's IT landscape, knowledge of process analysis and extensive experience in procedure auditing. Companies and groups operating globally should ensure that the work on or support for the project is done by an auditor from the parent company's audit department. This is the only way to make sure that important group-wide aspects are taken into account. This does not mean that an employee assigned to the project cannot or should not utilize the knowledge of his or her local auditing colleagues. Having said that, such involvement of local auditors should be limited to isolated cases and not occur over the entire course of the project work.

It is also possible for an external auditor to assume a supporting function (particularly in situations where the company has no *local* auditing team of its own) in order to carry out the project work.

For an auditor dealing with the business continuity plan for the first time, there are a whole host of factors confronting the employee assigned, which demand a lot of the employee – even in the case of experienced project managers. Attention must be paid to two items in project work, i.e.

- some risks are unknown at the time when the BCP is drawn up and great effort must be made to identify *all* risks; and
- many of the risks identified are outside the project team's or the company's sphere of influence, making an adequate reaction difficult, perhaps even impossible.

One of the internal auditing department's tasks in project work is to report on this and to indicate the limits of the BCP, on an up to date basis, to the management and thus to point out open risks. When I say "point out", I mean "inform", not "criticize". I also believe that the project team should write joint project reports and, where possible, make unanimous decisions. Only in cases where the auditor is unable to reach agreement with the project team should he or she produce a normal audit report and distribute it in accordance with the usual procedure in the company.

The auditor should also participate, with a critical stance, in the composition of the project team and the selection of the project sponsor. As has been made clear, a BCP is a key, cross-section and transnational task for a group with a global presence. The general management has to be 100% behind it and see itself as the "sponsor". A BCP project is only possible if the project team is of high quality (in terms of competency). Who or which departments have to be represented in the project team in order to guarantee a smooth-running project with a swift, successful conclusion? I consider it useful to create two project teams – an inner team and an outer team. Whereas the inner team, i.e. the core team, carries out only the project work, the outer team comes in when specialist knowledge is needed. Thus, the outer team does not work on the project all of the time, but has tasks to perform in the day-to-day business too. So why have two project teams? For the purpose of resource planning, the project manager has to have access to all resources when devising the project plan. This is guaranteed if the members of the outer team are committed to the project work and their line managers can free up capacity in accordance with an estimate of the capacity required to complete the project. Appropriately skilled staff from the

- organizational,
- auditing,
- IT,
- risk management,
- legal and
- accounting

departments should be assigned to the inner team. Depending on the main areas of business, particularly affected departments or sections can or must be added to this list. For example, a bank involved mainly in dealing, say an investment bank, would have to include the dealing section in the team.

There is one point which I have not mentioned so far. The drafting of a BCP for a global group is a considerable economic factor. The investigations of who has to be reachable and able to continue work, when and how quickly, plus the appropriate measures, have a significant impact on costs. However, this point has to be examined by the internal auditing department *before* the actual project work begins. An assessment of the approved budget gives a clear sign, right from the start, of the BCP's real status in the company. On the basis of my own experience, I can only warn everyone against starting work when the budget is hopeless. In such cases, the project manager or, better still, the project team, depending on the corporate culture, has to argue the matter out with the sponsor and explain that the project is doomed to failure.

To summarize the project work of the internal/group auditing departments, all members of the project team are equally committed to reaching the goal. Because of their auditing activity, the internal auditing employees contribute cross-section and/or cross-site knowledge. The internal auditing department's usual reporting procedures should – after consultation with the main manager responsible – be modified so that the audit report is replaced by regular project-status reports, approved unanimously by the project team, for the course of the project. Only in cases where the project team is not unanimous or where the auditor has identified faults which are omitted or not described clearly enough in the status report, does the auditor need to write an audit report in line with the usual internal company specifications. Before being distributed, this report should be discussed with the project manager responsible and then supplied to at least the project manager, the project sponsor and the main manager responsible for auditing.

# 3 Assessment of an Existing BCP by the Internal Auditing Department

Assessment of an existing BCP is very different from involvement in a BCP project. In this type of audit, the auditor is no longer a team member, but is involved in an ex-post audit.

The first audit step, which also lays the foundation for the subsequent steps, is concerned with whether the business continuity (BC) documentation is correct, complete and up to date. The internal auditing department checks the documents to determine whether they comply with the company's internal documentation guidelines, whether they are adequately comprehensible and whether they have been properly distributed. The quality of the BCP implementation will depend on the degree to which the BCP is up to date, complete, known and understood. The original project documentation and the risk analyses (risk-oriented audit plan), with whose assistance the auditing department carries out its work on the project, serve as the basis of the audit. The auditing department also requests the change documentation drawn up at the end of the project and compares it with the company's present status.

It is advisable to obtain the business instructions for the individual sections and sites in order to carry out this comparison. These instructions should illustrate the tasks and types of transaction. A further basis for the audit is provided by information concerning the number and volumes of the individual types of transaction, which can be obtained from the controlling department or from the reports for each audit. This information and the current risk-weighted audit plan can be used to check up to dateness and completeness. Other aids for these audits can be brought in from the organizational section – the areas of organization of structure and operations, to be precise.

Structural changes, process analyses and modifications, altered room plans and/or altered staff numbers in the individual sections are all grounds for the internal auditing department to carry out a comparison with the status in the BCP implementation or for a comparison with the status during the preceding audit. A comparison of the various versions of the organizational manuals helps round off the comparison, as do audit reports on all of the sections and sites affected, and a collection – from the legal section or the auditing department itself – of official regulations and amendments of laws. In addition, test and/or exercise reports contain information of relevance to the internal auditing department.

And here's another tip: the expense accounts and the investment lists have often provided me with useful information for assessing up to dateness. Both minor-value assets and newly acquired or replaced capital assets give indications of processes and procedures which have taken place, are planned or have been changed by individual sections and plants acting independently. Periodic invoices also help create an up to date impression of the situation (e.g. monthly invoices from information suppliers, which are generally not planned by the company and which individual employees, working groups or departments may have requested independently in order to perform certain tasks). If such information is not passed on to the BC team, be it intentionally or unintentionally, no precautions whatsoever can be taken. This creates an unknown weak spot. If this happens whilst specific dealing strategies are being practiced and the dealers can suddenly no longer check certain prices – because precisely the supplier of that information has not been included in the BCP because the BC team was unaware of it – the possible consequences are easy to imagine.

In order to examine, condense and appraise the copious information given by the documents described above, it is a good idea to create a table based on the project documentation (or the documents from the preceding audit). This table should include the types of transaction (divided into sections and sites if necessary), with numbers of units and volumes, the originally agreed resumption time (the period for which a section or site can be cut off from the other sections and/or the IT systems without causing a risk or breakdown for the company), the agreed measures for individual risks and the risk weighting (the possible amount of loss multiplied by the probable loss frequency in one business year, but also the individual loss possible owing to breakdowns). This table is updated using knowledge, gained from the other documentation mentioned, concerning changes in the *entire* company. The internal auditing employees responsible are thus provided with an up to date summary of the existing risks. The table also indicates any shifts in the quality of the individual risks. The employees in charge of auditing the existing BCP must then appraise this table and examine and assess the individual measures. An analysis of variance is used to reveal the quality status of the BCP on the audit date.

Another audit item is the structure of the BC team. Auditors who have carried out the examination just mentioned realize that it is impossible for the BC team to maintain the BCP without information from the business departments, the branch offices, subsidiaries and the group's organizational section. A plan which is not maintained or can only be kept up to date if the BC officers make their own inquiries is bound not to reflect the current situation. The structure of the team and its integration into the company must take this into account. This means that the question of when the BC officer has to be informed of planned changes to processes and strategies is also of particular importance to the internal auditing department. If he or she is not informed properly or at all, a weak spot will develop, not due to one single oversight or one error, but a permanent weak spot which has to be reported as such in the audit.

If the BC team is audited to establish the minimum competencies required by a BC officer, the following questions are relevant:

- What are the minimum competencies which a BC officer must have?
- How does the company handle budgets?
- How are necessary changes which the BC officer identifies implemented?

- Who has to be informed about changes to the approved plan and who has the final say on any changes?
- Who administer the budget required for financing modifications to the plan?

These and other, similar questions are company-specific and must be treated as such by the internal auditing department. The key point is, and this must never be overlooked, that the BC officers have proper authorization to obtain information and have direct access to the company's top management level so that they can immediately resolve cases of doubt and implement requirements which exceed the BC team's authority.

The economic aspects of the audit are largely covered by the examinations already outlined. The statement that "too much BCP" is of economic disadvantage to the company is mentioned here only to ensure that everything is said. Care must be taken to prevent a "storm of regulation" breaking out. Consequently, the measures must be analyzed not only to establish their completeness and effect, as already mentioned, but also their legitimacy in terms of economics. A foreign branch of a bank which carries out only one, combined refinancing action per day in its dealing activities can quite possibly trade successfully for a few days with a maturity tickler for all transactions which includes the processing instructions. A branch of an investment bank in London – and the parent company – will have completely different requirements here. But what happens if legislation influences the BCP? A country with strict laws on banking secrecy will not permit data to be processed in other countries, which could mean that an expensive solution is needed. Another item in the economic analysis is to determine whether these costs have been included in the breakeven analysis for new or relocated business segments. As with other reasons mentioned above, this point endorses the involvement of the BC official from a very early stage in order to ensure that BC costs are included in the calculations in a realistic manner. This interplay between requests and requirements on the part of those affected and involved is a factor which the internal auditing employees must not neglect in their evaluation of economic efficiency.

At this juncture, I should like to say a few more words about auditing economic efficiency. A BCP is not necessarily just a cost factor – even though the costs will predominate in almost all cases. But I believe that the internal auditing department's audit plan must also investigate whether the organizational department, the administrative department or the person responsible in the company has restructured the premium calculation with the company's insurer. The risk covered by various policies (business interruption, commercial fidelity, computer misuse, etc.) can be limited by a BCP; in many cases, insurance companies are willing – especially for large global companies – to reward the limited risk with lower premiums. The sections responsible should carry out such economic analyses for all relevant contractual relations and document them in an easy-to-trace manner. The contracts for additional associations with information suppliers should be formulated in such a way that the full price has to be paid only if use has to be made of those associations (but the original associations which are not used must also be taken into account).

One also has to ask whether the company has checked to see if common and thus more cost-effective, measures are possible. It might be possible to provide the BC environment to other companies under contract and thus recoup some of the costs (as in the case of the emergency IT centers run by various manufacturers). These questions regarding economic efficiency are intended only as examples of the wider range of company-, industry- and environment-specific possibilities. However, they stem from traditional audit plans and are therefore also mentioned here only to ensure that all aspects are covered.

## 4 Testing by the Internal Auditing Department

This is where I let out a heartfelt groan! This is a difficult topic, which causes heated debate in internal auditing circles. As this article shows, a BCP project and day-to-day work with the BCP necessitate foresighted inclusion of *all* of the possible circumstances which can cause business to be interrupted. My question is intentionally provocative: can the individual auditors or the internal auditing department actually manage this?

The executive management expects the audit report to provide information on the BCP's quality. If we take into account also the internal auditing department's information sources outlined in the previous section and its authorization to obtain information, including the information from the minutes of board meetings, of which at least the management of the internal auditing department has to be notified, we can see that there are so many individual factors that only a meaningful test can provide a conclusive evaluation of the plan's quality. A meaningful test is not concerned with quantity.

In order to test a project as complex as a BCP, a large number of individual tests are required. Thus, in addition to the usual IT tests, as developed in the existing emergency scenarios, tests have to be developed to determine whether the activity concerned can be continued in various other situations. Examples here would be an evacuation and the ensuing commencement of activities at other workplaces, breakdown of communication equipment, elimination of information sources, restriction and shifting of authorization and conditions of access to software and data, plus many other, company-specific individual tests.

Rather than serving as a substitute for the audit activities described above, these tests assist the auditor in the appraisal and evaluation of the audit subject. The internal auditing department documents the expected test results in meticulous detail before the individual test or test series starts. By this, I do not mean the qualitative results, but statements on the relevance of the test and the analyses, proposals and measures based on those statements.

Companies are very uneasy about these tests and that's the reason for my heartfelt groan! Their uneasiness stems from the following facts:

- the preparation for such a test and the testing itself are very time-consuming and considerably bind staff in a global company;
- the company requires the support of specialists, either from inside the company or from external sources;
- this kind of test is very cost-intensive;
- even when prepared with the greatest of care and detail, such a test is risky and might result in losses in certain lines of business; and
- many employees and often, unfortunately, managers do not display the necessary motivation when carrying out tests and exercises.

In order to establish the reservations in your company and to arm yourself for discussions, I recommend that you analyze the test and exercise reports from previous emergency tests, the last building evacuation, etc. If you request a test, you will probably be told that such tests are not meaningful or have already been conducted and that you only need to combine the results of those tests to reach a conclusion. Whatever you do, don't get involved with such daring exploits. Although an emergency plan is an important means of preparation for a company, it is only one part – usually *only* the technical part – of a BCP and it is geared to the local environment. To test a BCP, much more preparation and knowledge are necessary including specialist knowledge, which might not necessarily be available in this form in the internal auditing department. For example, all of the technical equipment in the company. Are the auditors familiar with the communication equipment? Are they aware of the risks of routers, bridges, etc. breaking down? Can auditors measure or calculate the throughput of data in backup networks? What happens – or does anything happen at all – if the air-conditioning breaks down in one of the large trading rooms in an investment bank? How long do the persons involved have to react?

It is crucial that this test be carried out. The internal auditing employees who have already worked on this audit subject have realized this. The BCP officer will also be very interested in the result of such a test. So, is a joint test by the BC officer and the internal auditing department possible? From the point of view of economics, a joint test is not only possible, but also the only sensible, feasible path. However, to provide a conclusive answer to this question, we have to return once more to the role of the internal auditing department as an independent and neutral authority in the company.

Does a test prepared together with the BC officer contradict the requirements for independence and neutrality? Of course, one may tend to say so. How can a test be independent if the person tested or the developer of the procedure tested is involved in the testing and developed the test and if the performance assessment depends on the test result? I totally agree with this train of thought, but...

The alternative is that the internal auditing department agrees with the manager responsible for the BCP which employee is responsible for the tests in general or, at least, in a specific period. Of course, after the test, the test results plus, and I go much further here than is normal in some auditing departments, all of the test preparations and processes are discussed intensively with the BC team. I view this as a profound discussion, not a "discussion of the audit report". It should deal in extensive detail with the auditors' ideas regarding the development of the test, and with the monitoring of the test and with the test results. Explaining these steps to the top management level and the BC officer usually eliminates straight away any obstacles to the internal auditing department conducting the test.

Another possibility is for the BC team, the BC project team, the organizational department, IT department and all business departments involved, as well as the internal auditing department, to draw up a basic test plan together. All of the sections/departments involved prepare the steps necessary for the test together. These steps specify the various simulatable failures which can lead to the BCP being used, and document the expected results in advance. These results can be use of backup data lines, use of modems instead of the usual fixed lines, transfer of data from the host to a defined backup computer and many other things. The final documentation can also be agreed in advance.

This is the method I prefer. It enables the internal auditing department to gather an incredible amount of knowledge from all of the parties involved and thus minimizes the risk of overlooking some steps. This basic plan serves as the basis for audit planning.

Once the auditing manager has been presented with a positive decision, the test is incorporated as an audit item in the audit plan and carried out, with the auditing department controlling and monitoring it, without notice. The timing and the reasons for using the BCP are agreed between the internal auditing department and the managing director responsible. The test should then be conducted – as used to be the case in banks – in the form of an unexpected cash audit. At a defined time, the factors causing business interruption are triggered and the reactions of the parties involved are recorded.

Naturally, information arising from and deficiencies detected in these tests are reported in accordance with the company's internal rules. The close cooperation between the departments during the preparation for the test is not such that it calls into question the objectivity of the internal auditing department. Nonetheless, the audit reporting is difficult. If the report is to make clear the auditing department's objectivity, it must assess precisely causes, effects and measures. In all audited areas, this is much easier for the assigned auditors because they are dealing with familiar sections of their company, which they know in detail. The report must highlight and present with the utmost of care the causes which led to the deficiencies detected by the test: not only to ensure objectivity but also so that measures can be derived from these reports to bring about a significant improvement in the quality of the BCP.

# 5 Lines of Authority and Internal Auditing System[1]

In the majority of the risk-oriented audit plans that I have seen and produced, particular significance has been ascribed to the internal auditing system. For banks and other financial service providers, there are rules laid down by the supervisory authorities which highlight this subject, and auditors of annual financial statements devote considerable attention to it. Company-specific authority arrangements are also intensively examined by the internal auditing department. The principle of "four eyes" can serve as a background for the internal auditing system and lines of authority.

No matter how comprehensive and well-developed a BCP is, it will never take into account all of a company's staff in a crisis situation. It is usually more likely that the BCP will specify that individuals, teams or even complete departments should dramatically reduce or stop their activities. If workplaces are inaccessible or if there is a lack of technical equipment, employees are instructed to perform special tasks in other sections and plants or to stay at home until a certain time. That's where my favorite example comes in again: the terminals break down in an investment bank which has a large volume of open commitments, has to conduct maturity transformations, etc. In such an emergency, only a limited number of machines are available. Now who's going to get authorization to use these machines? The dealers, who need to liquidate their positions in order to avoid losses? Or the employees in the back offices, whose tasks include monitoring? These examples can be translated completely to other sections and other industries.

The result is that checks are "neglected", i.e. they are performed by employees who do not have the necessary know-how or they are missed out entirely. And that in a situation in which the nerves and concentration of all employees are strained to the limit. That's an extremely dangerous situation for the company.

In many cases, the company's management is likely to support the front offices (for the understandable reasons outlined above). The BC project team has already been confronted, as the auditor responsible now is, by the task of recognizing and appraising this situation. An internal auditing system for the business continuity situation should have been derived on this basis. It is now up to the internal auditing department to assess whether the specified auditing system is adequate and adjusted to the BCP. Once a crisis situation occurs and the BCP replaces the internal auditing system for day-to-day business, there is no more time for explanations, shifting/adjusting processes, assigning necessary equipment, adapting access authorization, etc.

---

[1] This section refers to the "Internes Kontroll System (IKS)", the German kind of internal auditing system. In German banks there is a strong separation between internal auditing, by retrospective checking of process samples, and regular controlling, which is embedded into normal operation.

Adjusting the lines of authority in crisis situations is as important as adjusting the internal auditing system. To guarantee security, the design of the BCP takes the system of authority into consideration and adapts it to the risks. In my view, it is a good idea to use a modular system, as for the whole BCP. This ensures targeted reaction in emergencies where the BCP has to be used in a working group, a department, a section or a branch office/subsidiary.

Why do the lines of authority need to be adjusted? What are the objectives of such adjustment? A high-priority objective is to return to the "normal" work procedure. Depending on the risk weighting, it is of primary or at least equal importance to avoid economic risks, which could cause the company to go bankrupt. From this perspective, lines of authority have to be examined differently. In day-to-day business operations without any particular interruptions, the lines of authority are such that decisions are made by specified employees and put into practice by other employees (depending on the importance of the decisions). In crisis situations, however, the authority structure alters considerably. This means that the lines of authority for normal day-to-day business also have to change. In most companies, authority in the administrative, organizational and IT sections is increased whilst authority for business deals is significantly reduced. Depending on the sector and the corporate structure, this is desirable. In emergencies, risks have to be minimized. This almost always means reduced business activity, which can best be formulated as "processing open items".

However, the administrative, organizational and IT sections need additional authority, which should be restricted to the crisis period. It is crucial that repairs are carried out, new equipment is procured, new contracts are closed and lots of other, similar things are done. Whereas it is certainly desirable and right to restrict these activities in a manner specific to the company in a "normal situation", in crises the way has to be paved for immediate action. Restriction of authority has to be dealt with extremely carefully for this period. An economically oriented auditor analyzes, appraises and reports on the related subjects of the internal auditing system and lines of authority appropriately. Since, as indicated on several occasions, the circumstances have to be observed largely on a company-specific basis, there are no meaningful, generally binding checklists, etc. for this situation. Such aids have to be prepared by the internal auditing department during the audit preparations.

# 6 Validity of the BCP

In the preceding sections, we have discussed the design, the implementation in the company and the special requirements of the BCP from the point of view of internal auditing. And we have established that a BCP structure which is modular in all its facets (internal auditing system, authority structure, etc.) appears to make most sense for a company operating at the global level. This creates additional items to be investigated by the internal auditing department.

If only one branch office or other segment is affected by a crisis situation, it is not always absolutely necessary – depending on the BCP – to suspend the day-to-day processes throughout the company and change over to the BCP processes. But who decides whether the BCP should be activated? To take this decision, it is necessary to have extremely detailed knowledge of the plan and the interaction described in it in order to provide binding instructions for the appropriate modules. I would say that the BC team is the right partner to ask for advice and to hold responsibility. But if we think about the structure of a global company, it becomes clear very quickly that a branch office or a subsidiary might be confronted with a crisis situation first and might even have to deploy the appropriate module at the same as reporting the crisis to the BC team in order to avoid losses. From the point of view of group auditing, there are two conditions that I consider necessary here.

Firstly, the BCP must specify precise criteria as to what circumstances are to be deemed a crisis situation and what measures (modules) have to be implemented. Since the situations and measures in this description depend so greatly on the company, its activities, its structure, the organization of its operations, the risk potential identified and so on and so forth, I am unfortunately unable to provide any generally applicable rules. I would like to see, on the basis of this description, one auditing employee in each working group which is high-risk and/or affected by the BCP, who identifies these criteria and acts as a link and initial port of call for the BC team. Each deviation from the norm, including deployment of the BCP, is documented adequately in such a way that third-party experts can trace the steps, the working group involved, the date and the time.

Whilst other parties can also trigger the activation of the BCP, returning the company to normal day-to-day business is exclusively the task of the BC team. If all resources (humans and machinery) are functioning and the BC team members have established this fact, the BCP is deactivated. This is done in writing by the BC team; the internal auditing department must be given the ability to assess the individual steps using an audit. The arguments which may be presented against doing so are familiar to auditing departments and have been discussed on several occasions.

If deployment of such a plan causes a major revolution in a company, if the plan restricts or expands authority, if crisis situations can result in big losses or large amounts of lost profits,

- it must be possible to trace who did and/or approved what, how much, when and why, so as to provide evidence and protect the employees affected; and
- it must be possible to identify the weak spots subsequently, so as to maintain and complete the BCP and thus be equipped for the future.

# 7 Summary and Conclusion

I am aware that the suggestions made here shake the very foundations of some internal auditors' conception of their role. Involvement in a project group, assumption of responsibility for designing a plan, etc. are not yet a matter of course in all internal auditing departments. However, the procedures outlined above are based on the realization that it is economically impossible, highly demotivating from the perspective of all involved and extremely risky for the company if the BCP is audited only in the form of an ex-post audit. The mere fact that any subsequent appraisal and assessment and the possible ensuing necessity to reject parts of the BCP, amend or improve contracts or replace hardware and software generate immense, superfluous additional costs forbids such a procedure. There is no need to describe here the risk caused to the company by delaying activation of the BCP – it is self-evident. Of course, the internal auditing department's neutrality has to be maintained – in certain sectors (banking) this is stipulated by the requirements of the supervisory authorities. But even if no supervisory authority supports the position of the internal auditing department within the company by enforcing such requirements, it is crucial that the auditing department is objective if it is to fulfill its role in the company.

However, there is one point that cannot be stressed enough. As with all of the other sections of a company, the internal auditing department's first duty is to its own company. There is no question that this also means adhering to laws and regulations and assessing the sections, departments, processes and tasks audited to ensure that they comply with those requirements. To this extent, the internal auditing department has the same objectives as all other sections of the company. But the picture is slightly different if we look at the internal rules and instructions. The auditing department not only checks whether these specifications are adhered to, it also examines, appraises and assesses them. Such an audit can result in a proposal to abolish, change or create specifications.

Where the objectives are the same, the internal auditing department's consultant role in the company becomes ever clearer – without forgoing its special position in the company as an objective, neutral observer. This means that the internal auditing department's involvement in such extensive projects as a BCP has to change. Internal auditing should already have left behind the role of "box-ticker". Altered requirements such as risk-oriented audit plans, companies' global orientation, process analyses and assessments and system and procedure audits have changed the auditing department's range of tasks and will continue to do so in the years to come. So the internal auditing department will have to have two "tracks", that is to say, one or several teams or departments which perform the traditional tasks, mostly ex-post audits, and teams or departments which perform the tasks described above. Since, in my opinion, the necessity of project-supporting audits will become increasingly evident, the managing directors and the internal auditing department's management would be well advised to provide several employees with the basic skills required for this work.

Since I have often started a heated discussion with those last few sentences – a discussion to which I would be happy to contribute – on the basis of my conviction and experience in various countries and companies, I would like you to send me your opinions and views via mailto:beratung@k-m-r-gmbh.de to discuss them with you.

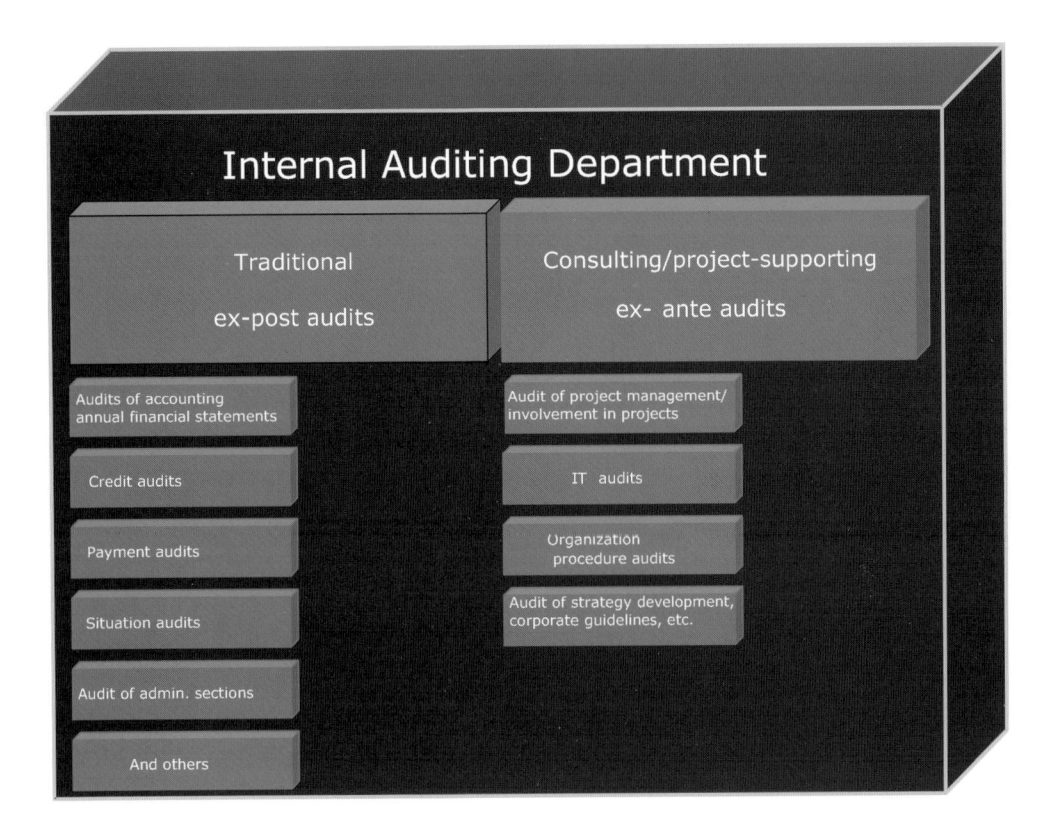

## Internal Auditing Department

**Traditional**
ex-post audits

- Audits of accounting annual financial statements
- Credit audits
- Payment audits
- Situation audits
- Audit of admin. sections
- And others

**Consulting/project-supporting**
ex-ante audits

- Audit of project management/ involvement in projects
- IT audits
- Organization procedure audits
- Audit of strategy development, corporate guidelines, etc.

# Crisis Management for a New Century

Tim Guthrie-Harrison
*Teamworks Continuity*

**Abstract:** Crisis Management has many facets. The pressures it imposes – sometimes almost instantaneously – can change in flavour greatly during an incident. Because of the way in which they interact with one another, these pressures and how to deal with them can confuse crisis managers and participants, not only those in the centre of the problem but also those attempting to plan in advance how to cope with the exceptional issues that arise for most organisations only once in a while, and for many, never.

At the same time, most organisations' ability to handle a crisis has been seriously weakened by the many continuous challenges they experience as part of everyday business life: pressure to perform (to internal targets, to external expectations); reductions in manpower; the constant presence of change; turnover of staff allied with increasing spans of responsibility in ever flatter hierarchies; ever-increasing job focus and channelled activity.

In these environments, the readiness of the individual manager to spend time on "what if" considerations is inevitably and understandably limited, sometimes even to the point of refusal to apply the smallest amounts of quality time to the task.

The need for a straightforward approach to Crisis Management that can be easily grasped and applied whatever the size of the organisation is clear. This chapter seeks to draw out and apply some general lessons to provide a sound structure for Crisis Management that can be adapted to particular circumstances.

**Keywords:** Crisis Management, Business Continuity planning, Contingency planning, Disaster recovery, Mitigation, Preparedness

"We learn geology the morning after an earthquake" (Emerson, *The Conduct of Life*)

"I keep six honest serving men: they teach me all I know – How and What and Why and Where and When and Who" (Rudyard Kipling)

"The most elegant forms of managerial decision involve problems that never have to be solved because they are prevented from occurring.... They are anticipated and sidestepped. The deliberate non-catastrophe is one of the most effective contributions a manager can make." (James Martin)

# 1 Introduction

The references listed at the end of this chapter represent only the tip of the Crisis Management (CM) iceberg: and indeed, the tip of my particular, personal iceberg at that. Take, for example, the journal *Contingencies and Crisis Management*. Every quarter, this learned and lucid publication contains perhaps three to six major articles plus reviews, often based around a specific topic in CM. Over the course of a year, in around 15–25 major dissertations and 50 or so books, it is unusual to find the same subject covered more than once. Let's take a few examples:

- oil spills
- Ebola viruses
- national infrastructure
- monetary crises
- political unrest
- cyberspace crises
- bio-terrorism

… and that's before (a) we get down to anything that is specific in terms of country, industry or operations and (b) we mention the type of CM most commonly associated with the term: media and reputational CM. The subject – and the implied scope of planning – seems inexhaustible. Then along come the events of September 11th 2001, and we all begin to feel that maybe we need to start again from the beginning. How do we know where to start? How do we know if we are getting it right in our particular organisation? Will our plans stand the test? What, indeed, is the test we should plan for?

Can there really be one paradigm in there that could, on the one hand, apply to any organisation preparing for its own particular nightmare and, on the other hand, avoid being so generic as to be instantly useless? I firmly believe that there is.

My proposals for CM contained in this chapter are based on over 35 years of operational experience in both the military and the commercial environments. My premise is that it is possible to have a basic CM philosophy that will span the requirements of any organisation. In outlining its main constituent parts – and in this space that is all that I can do – I shall hopefully make clear and logical to the reader a starting point for real-world CM planning that can be adapted to his or her particular needs.

## 1.1 The Different Types of Crisis Management Plan

From the above title, the reader might expect that a list would follow of all the eventualities that need to be covered by a CM plan. This would of course, in the context of my earlier remarks about the Crisis Management iceberg, be futile – every reader would be able instantly to spot gaps relative to their own needs. We therefore need to take a different approach, that of the extent of integration.

CM plans can be standalone (for particular situations, or even particular aspects of single situations) or they can be integrated into a wider context of:

- corporate policy and standards or
- Corporate Governance or
- Risk Management (RM) or
- Business Continuity (BC).

The single most useful perspective that brings these all together (remember, we are in single-paradigm mode here!) is as follows:

- Corporate Governance makes it necessary to have …
- Risk Management (i.e. recognition and containment of exposures), which drives …
- Business Continuity preparations, which must be complemented by …
- Crisis Management planning, which must cover any conceivable crisis.

If we get this "nesting" right, it is always possible to audit the extent and scope of plans, be they for RM, BC or CM. We can always (and this is an essential feature) *justify and validate* our preparations.

En passant, the best international approach to Risk Management to date is listed in the references: the Australian/New Zealand RM Standard AS/NZS 4360:1999. There is no European equivalent, although early 2002 may see the publication of a United Kingdom standard by AIRMIC (the Association of Insurance and Risk Managers), ALARM (the Association of Local Authority Risk Managers) and IRM (the Institute of Risk Management). However, it is difficult to see how they can improve on AS/NZS 3360, built as it has been on the quite exceptional breadth of expertise and input of Joint Committee OB/7, the participants in which are listed on the Australian Standards web site, from which the document can be downloaded for a very reasonable charge.

Another useful perspective to recognise about crises is that they can be differentiated (and the span of our concept must extend) as follows:

- Internal and/or external.
- Ours and/or someone else's.
- Local and/or remote.
- Contracting or expanding.
- Volatile or stable (i.e. capable of being made much worse or not).
- Either our CM plans should be able to cope with them all or there should be specific exception statements to make clear that the scope of the plans is not infinite.

## 1.2 The Factors affecting Crisis Management Plan Development

Allusion has already been made to the need for CM planning to be understandable and capable of implementation by busy managers who would, frankly, rather be doing almost anything else. In judging the priorities in their working life they are, in my experience and like all of us, driven by:

- meeting short-term targets
- financial and career rewards
- management and peer recognition
- status in the organisation
- security of employment.

Where in this list does CM planning (by definition, planning for the *unexpected*, interpreted by our busy manager as *unlikely and therefore not immediately important*), bring anything to the table that will concentrate a manager's mind?

Even the "big stick" approach (directives from the highest levels of management) rarely works, mainly because it comes from levels well above those where day-to-day management – based on comparison with operational targets – is more locally affected. The managers are already being beaten by so many other big sticks that one more – from a greater distance – has no impact on the individual's agenda and prioritisation. We must therefore be more *clever* about what we encourage or require managers to do. We need to enable them to work *smarter* and achieve what is needed in a more acceptable (*i.e. shorter*) timescale.

Part of making CM smarter is to recognise that, when dealing with a complex subject, the shorter the attention span, the simpler the message needs to be. What we as professionals can and are prepared to discuss, understand and develop may be a world of planning away from what the reluctant manager can even contemplate. Ideally, we need simple CM models and approaches: if not simple, then at least *easy to understand*. We also need to be *relevant* – in terms of the organisational level and the scope of the individual's role in it. Being relevant across the organisation means that we also need a CM concept that is *general* and *flexible*. Above all, we need to be *pragmatic*, but *not defeatist*.

In summary then, our CM approach must:

- Be clever, to enable smart participation.
- Aim to take the minimum time consistent with the need.
- Be:
    - easy to understand (both approach and deliverables)
    - relevant
    - general and flexible.

It's quite a tall order, but not an impossible one!

## 1.3 The Central Nature of Information in a Crisis

To meet these requirements, our CM model needs at its centre a core that is immediately apparent in terms of its relevance and its value. The CM capabilities that this core must support in a crisis are:

- increasing the balance of proactive to reactive actions
- reducing the confusion or doubt surrounding events
- limiting the sources that need to be tapped to gain an understanding of where we are and where we are going (or may, if we are not careful, go).

In the words of Yogi Berra (a 1940s American baseball star with a gift for truisms): "If you don't know where you are going, you could end up somewhere else!"

We now come to the reason for my first two quotations, from Emerson and Rudyard Kipling: our concept for Crisis Management must ensure (a) that the crisis *geology* (i.e. what could happen, why, and how it may react once started) does not have to be learned "on the fly" and (b) that the "*serving men*" (i.e. the basic facts about the crisis and its development) are always available, up to date and assembled as well as possible. We must of course recognise that – to stretch the analogy a little further – our particular seismic event may be bigger and less controllable than anyone expected.

There is one way to achieve our three essential CM capabilities: to recognise the primacy of *information* at the heart of the CM plan and its supporting organisation. It is a principle that is tried and tested in those organisations that "do crisis management" all day every day: the world's armed services. They all recognise that intelligence about what may happen, what has happened and – as a result – what could happen is essential. One could argue – and, at the time of writing, many do – that lack of good intelligence enabled the events of 11 September 2001 and contributed to the early sense of concern about "what do we do in this situation?"

The Crisis Manager must regard good information as a vital resource in the same way that a manager planning for business recovery regards restored systems and reasonably up-to-date applications data as essential: without them, one may eventually cope with the situation but (a) the job will be that much more difficult and (b) the outcome will be a great deal less certain.

Although almost all organisations will need more, it is theoretically possible at the most basic level to define a CM plan purely in terms of the answers to the "Kipling Six", that is (for example):

| Questions | To answer in the CM planning process | That management will ask at the time |
|---|---|---|
| How ... | ... Can we best use our organisation's assets in a crisis? | ... Did it happen? |
| What ... | ... Type of events should we anticipate (and which should we not)? | ... Are we doing to improve the situation? |
| Why ... | ... Must we do this (e.g. regulatory demands, stakeholder confidence)? | ... Are the impacts of this crisis worse now than at another time? |
| Where ... | ... Might a crisis originate? | ... Can we get assistance appropriate to the event that we are experiencing? |
| When ... | ... Would be the worst time for a crisis? | ... Will the situation improve? |
| Who ... | ... Should we involve in our planning (internally and externally)? | ... Is responsible for what? |

To support the flow of information, we need a *Communications Plan*. We can base this around the following "egg" model:

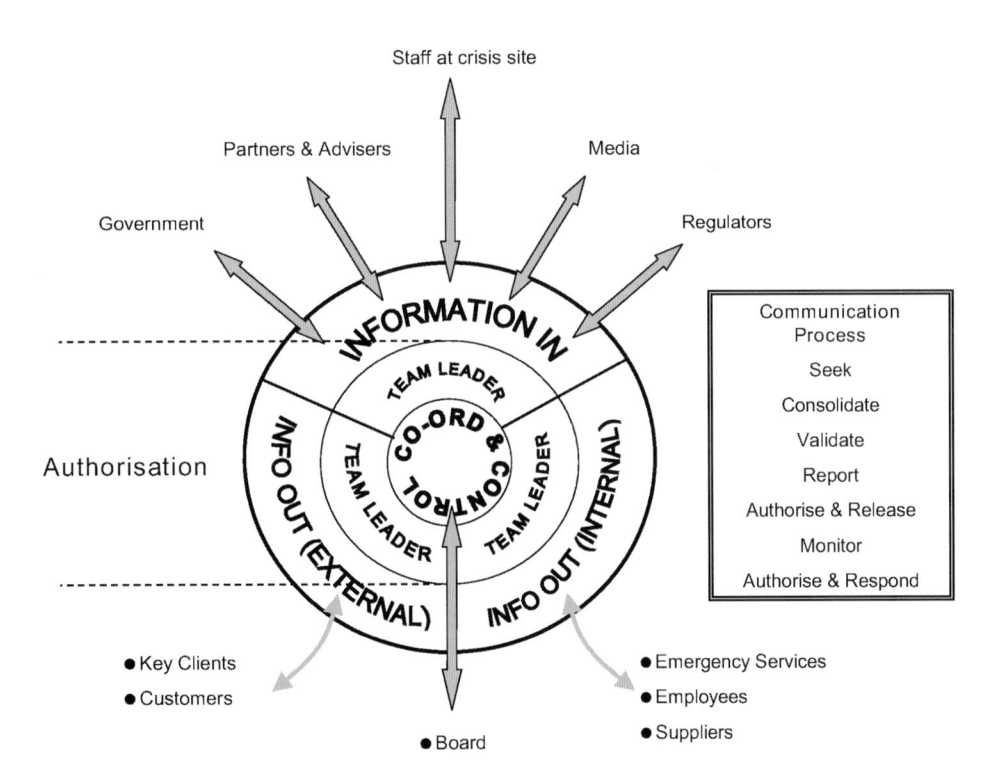

The central information service can be linked to whatever elements we bring into our CM team. It is a model that has been tested during many CM exercises and has proved very effective: there are several major advantages of making this the central hub of the CM effort:

- It presents a "one stop shop" for news – anyone with a question regarding the event or its development knows that this is the single best place to go to for the definitive answer.
- It provides the Corporate Communications (or PR/Media) department with a role and a place in a crisis that best complements its normal role.
- It recognises that many sources of information will have to be tapped to get an overall picture of what has happened and how it is developing.
- It acknowledges that gathering and interpreting information are best separated according to the organisational need – for instance, contrast business impact identification (limited information scope but great detail) with Human Resource (HR) needs (as accurate as possible across a wide board – employees, contractors and visitors – and fast).
- It incorporates all the necessary stages in the communications process, from Seeking through to Response.
- It facilitates the preparation and passage of information to two different audiences, internal and external, and best avoids the possibility of conflicts between the two demands.

In one possible application of the CM concept, we might see the Communications Plan being played out by a Communications Team interacting with other CM elements as follows:

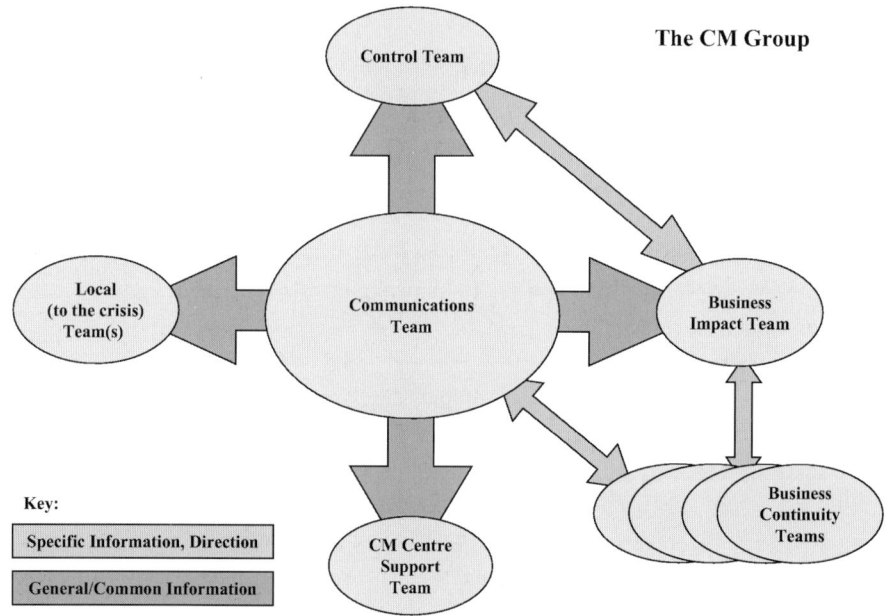

**The CM Group**

[Diagram: Communications Team at center, connected to Control Team (top), Local (to the crisis) Team(s) (left), Business Impact Team (right), CM Centre Support Team (bottom), and Business Continuity Teams. Key: Specific Information, Direction; General/Common Information.]

# 2 The Basis for a General-Purpose Crisis Management Plan (CMP)

Using the above "info-centric" approach to CM organisation and the Communications team, we can relate the teams' roles one to another and provide a general basis for an organisational CM Group (be warned, the terminology is somewhat limited in Business Continuity and Crisis Management planning – one does tend to get teams within teams unless one is prepared to use other terms, such as "cells" or "elements", which can have unfortunate and confusing connotations).

The roles of the teams in the suggested basic CM organisation are:

- *Control (or Command or Direction or Management) Team:* Provides direction to the overall activity; liases "upwards" (to higher organisational levels) and "outwards" (e.g. to regulators); monitors the overall situation, invoking additional resources as and when necessary.
- *Local Team(s):* Stay as close to the physical site of the crisis as possible (typically at a pre-designated Incident Control Point (ICP); feed information to the Communications Team at the CM Centre; liase with the emergency services; provide local representation to the media and others, e.g. relatives and contractors; bridge responsibilities in due course to the Restoration Project Management Team. Note that in, for example, a trans-national crisis, there may be several or many Local Teams providing support to the centre and representation locally. In each situation, the composition of the Local Team should reflect the nature of the incident itself (i.e. more Information Technology (IT) members if the crisis is a systems one, more HR if casualties are significant).
- *Communications Team:* Seeks, consolidates, validates and reports the facts as best they can be established at a point in time; prepares and passes information – authorised as appropriate – internally and externally; provides central briefing resources beyond those available at the site of the crisis; updates all participants in the CM process over time.
- *Business Impact Team:* A "think tank" of key managers reflecting the affected processes and areas of the business; identifies the specific impacts of the event depending upon its timing; defines the business impact timescale and duration; advises the Control Team regarding strategy for mitigation and recovery; members of the team direct the actions of their respective Business Continuity teams.
- *CM Centre Team:* Supports, logistically (including administration, transport and accommodation) all the needs of the CM Teams; implements (opening and closing) the CM Centre regarding communications, systems and office resources; acquires additional administrative support (e.g. secretarial) as necessary.
- *Continuity Teams:* Maintaining or recovering normal levels of activity and/or business in vitally important areas of the business or organisation.

… 88    Tim Guthrie-Harrison

# 3 The Relationship Between Crisis Management and Business Continuity

Although this chapter concerns Crisis Management, it is necessary at this point to define the correct relationship between the CM Group and the Continuity Teams, which latter should be regarded as being made up of two essential constituent parts:

- *Infrastructure Continuity Teams – the "Lifeline Teams" (HR, IT and Facilities):* As well as recovering their own functionality and processes when these have been affected, these teams must provide critically important support to other areas of the organisation, specifically because it is experiencing a crisis. They must therefore, as it were, operate at well above normal levels of performance in a crisis – especially in its early stages.
- *Business Continuity Teams:* From affected areas of the organisation, these seek to restore essential organisational and business services within predefined timescales. They will expect and need predefined levels of service from Lifeline Teams.

Typically, Continuity Teams will continue to report to their own lines of management and it is best not to disrupt this expectation: the last thing anyone needs in a crisis is to have to remember to act differently from normal. Performance will continue to be monitored by higher levels of line management. Taking the overall organisation of the continuity effort up a level or two therefore, we can see it as follows:

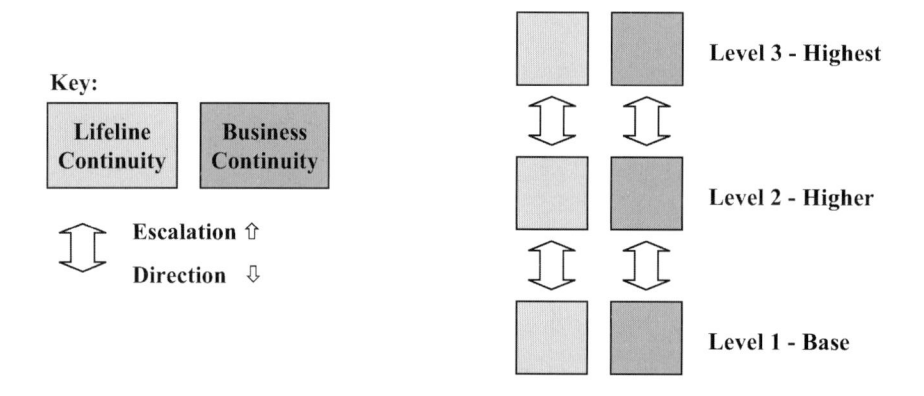

Key:
- Lifeline Continuity
- Business Continuity
- Escalation ⇧
- Direction ⇩

Level 3 - Highest
Level 2 - Higher
Level 1 - Base

Crisis Management will best complement continuity at its various levels, while providing equivalent escalation and direction routes. In this way, line management can stay focused on delivery to customers (i.e. maintaining or recovering *normality*), while CM can focus on managing and dealing with those things that are only happening or upon which there must be special emphasis because there is a crisis (i.e. containing *abnormality*). Thus:

**Key:**

▨ Crisis Management

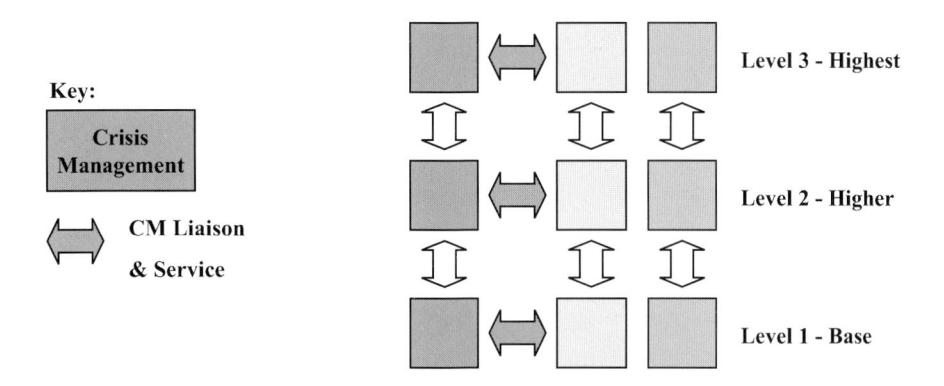

⇔ CM Liaison & Service

Level 3 - Highest

Level 2 - Higher

Level 1 - Base

The above organisation also makes it easier to activate successively higher levels of all three constituent parts (CM, Lifeline and Business Continuity) and reduces the span of any one level of command and control.

# 4 Manning the Crisis Management Group

The complementary style of CM described above will gain much strength if it is manned (i.e. populated) from across the organisation or business. Five key benefits of this approach are:

- There is *no doubt about overall responsibility* for managing the crisis.
- There will be *a greater cross-organisation presence* within the (therefore) generalist CM Group, increasing the ease with which it can be expanded or have greater emphasis applied in a key area if necessary – rapidly – and yet still retain its original coherence and esprit de corps (as colleagues introduce additional colleagues into the Group).
- The *mutual understanding* (within and between the CM and Continuity teams) will be enhanced and increase greatly (a) the quality of comprehension of what has happened, its impacts on the organisation's constituent parts and how particular courses of action might therefore have good or bad outcomes, and (b) the empathy between the CM and Continuity groups.
- *Key area managers can be left in place in a crisis*, rather than diverted into a hierarchical CM organisation that is built on top of every line level of management, and yet those managers can feel that they have a representative at the centre of how the crisis is being managed.
- *No need for specialist CM personnel to be recruited.* Such personnel would have no "peace-time" (i.e. non-crisis) role and the tendency would therefore be to recruit

the absolute minimum and to regard them as specialists with little or no understanding of mainstream activities, priorities or impacts. Conversely, "manning from within" provides (relatively) an almost limitless number of CM Group members, shielding the CM Group somewhat from one of the ever-present challenges, that of employee turnover and retraining. The availability of a "pool" of personnel for the CM Group also raises the probability at any point in time of a high turnout of team members vis-à-vis holidays and other absences.

Regarding the level of staff to be placed in the CM Group, the activity and training for it represent a great opportunity to develop and test those junior managers who are seen as being the lifeblood of the organisation's future. The Control Team can include the necessary maturity and seniority but the other CM teams can have a much more junior membership which – coming from many different parts of the business or organisation – will benefit from the opportunity to understand the priorities, strengths and weaknesses of an organisation in crisis, the way in which the management structures work and interact and the personalities of the current generation of leaders. It is hard to imagine a better training ground for the directors of tomorrow.

## 5 Monitoring the Crisis

Little thought is normally given in CM strategies as to how the progress of the situation can be monitored and it is well worth looking at a possible approach to doing so. As far as I know the idea (a personal one) – Crisis Profiling – is unique but it has proven its value in many CM exercises.

The concept is to break down the crisis into its *aspects*, which can be standardised for any crisis, in any organisation. Then, one takes a series of standard *considerations* within each aspect and writes a "Best Outcome" and a "Worst Outcome" statement for each one, placing these in the left- and right-hand column, respectively, of three columns down the centre of a table. A central column is left between the extremes to allow a middle, or "neither Best nor Worst", evaluation to be made on each line.

The crisis aspects would be:

- scale and timing
- (scope for) escalation
- public relations situation
- (extent of) external impact
- (extent of) external involvement
- site operability.

The evaluation process should be completed by available Control Team members, on the basis of the then best available information, in a matter of minutes rather than as a long-drawn-out exercise. The Control Team quickly work down the aspects and – for each consideration – decide whether (from what they know at the time) the situation is best represented by the "Best" or "Worst" statements, or something in between. A check or tick mark is placed in the appropriate column for each consideration, and a crisis profile rapidly emerges.

Depending on where the predominance of ticks is seen (more towards the left, Best, or more towards the right, Worst, side of the profile), an objective assessment can be made of the appropriate classification for the crisis *at that moment* into one of three categories (in a three column table), say *Emergency* (lowest-level crisis), *Serious Incident* or *Disaster* (the highest classification). Because the profile can be worked up so quickly, it can be refreshed as often as necessary. Ideally, this reclassification would be carried out frequently at the beginning of a crisis, and less often as the situation stabilised.

By completing such a profile initially and at various stages during a crisis, and linking the resultant shape of the profile to a Crisis Classification, the following advantages can be achieved:

- Once the classification is published internally, *everyone in the organisation can describe the event in the same, agreed terms*, avoiding the possibility for confusion and concern of one person calling it "an absolute disaster" while another describes the event as "something of a challenge".
- The *number of possible classifications is reduced* to a minimum.
- The shape of *the profile indicates relative priorities for action*, i.e. where activity in respect of a particular consideration may help to reduce the crisis profile.
- Over time, *a picture of the development of the crisis emerges,* enabling a view to be taken as to whether the action taken is helping and how quickly.
- The profile documents provide *an audit trail for later review*.

A typical profile table might look like this:

The minimum classification, suggested if all ticks are under column (a), is an EMERGENCY. If any ticks appear to the right of column (a), the event should probably be considered a SERIOUS INCIDENT. If any ticks appear to the right of the "Between (a) and (b) column", the event should probably be considered a DISASTER. The CEO is the final arbiter of the classification to be used at any time.
The classification should be renewed on a regular basis for the duration of an interruption.

| (a) BEST situation/outcome | Current expectation: | | | (b) WORST situation/outcome |
|---|---|---|---|---|
| | (a) | Between (a) and (b) | (b) | |
| **SCALE AND TIMING** | | | | |
| Single event | | | | Multiple event |
| CM Group not activated | | | | CM Group activated |
| Management continuing normal duties | | | | Management attention diverted for weeks |
| Injuries minor or non-existent | | | | Serious injuries and/or fatalities |
| Impact will be apparent for a short time only | | | | Impact will be apparent for months |
| Single organisation group can contain/control | | | | Multi-group/cross-site co-operation needed |
| Lack of current business criticalities* now | | | | Important and urgent business criticalities* |
| **ESCALATION** | | | | |
| Situation stable, unlikely to escalate | | | | Escalation or deterioration is probable |
| No legal, regulatory implications | | | | Inevitable legal, regulatory implications |
| **PUBLIC RELATIONS SITUATION** | | | | |
| No media interest in the event/impact | | | | Media interest certain |
| No single-interest group involvement | | | | Single-interest group involvement certain |
| **EXTERNAL IMPACT** | | | | |
| No impact on customers | | | | Many/key customers affected |
| No impact on business operations | | | | Severe impact on business operations |
| No pollution/environmental impact | | | | Severe impact on environment |
| Event not noticed by local community | | | | Severe impact on local community |
| No impact on image/competitiveness | | | | Severe impact on image/competitiveness |
| **EXTERNAL INVOLVEMENT** | | | | |
| Emergency services not called | | | | Emergency services called out |
| No external agencies** involved | | | | External agencies** must be notified |
| Notification beyond the office affected is not necessary | | | | Corporate executives need to be informed immediately |
| **SITE OPERABILITY** | | | | |
| Site access not affected | | | | Access to site denied for a week or more |
| All site operations can continue now | | | | Full off site relocation necessary |
| No effect on next working day's activities | | | | Not resolved fully for many weeks |
| Site services to normalise within 4 hrs | | | | Site services remain disrupted for weeks |
| Systems to normalise within 4 hrs | | | | Systems remain disrupted for weeks |
| External services/utilities will be normalised within 4 hours | | | | External services/utilities will be disrupted for weeks |

\* Criticalities: including product launches, major systems enhancements, site events, meetings and functions.

\*\* External agencies: including insurers, local authorities and regulators (including health and safety and others relative to incident).

# 6 Pointers for CM Documents

Remember the basic requirement for CM planning to be smarter? This applies to the documentation of the plan as well. To achieve the correct design, we need to be entirely pragmatic about the facts of the circumstances in which the material will be used:

- We do not know where the CM Group's participants will be when called out.
- We can make no assumptions about the likelihood that they will have business material of any sort with them.
- We cannot assume that because we think the CM plan is important to have with them at all times, they do too.
- We can be sure that, if called in an emergency, they will want to start doing rather than start reading.

We can deduce from these facts that our ideal CM plan – which will necessarily have to contain a lot of information – should:

- Be easy to understand: lots of bullets, a concise and clear style, no repetition.
- Lead the reader in to where they need to go in an emergency.
- Avoid the necessity to plough through a lot of logic and background information before getting to the (action) point.
- Feature individual and team checklists over time.
- Contain – as far as practicable – everything in one place with minimum references to other documents (or indeed cross-references within the CM plan itself).
- Look good – be well presented and laid out with appropriate use of colour.

Working with the CM Group themselves and giving them the opportunity to participate in the document design themselves during exercises is probably the best way to achieve a thoroughly workable solution. Over the course of many such exercises, I have found the ideal combination to be:

- *An "Aide Memoire" or "Vade Mecum":* a short, ideally credit-card-size reminder of the key CM ideas and resources, with enough action and contact information to support the reader until he or she either arrives at the command centre or gains access to a full version of the plan. It is surprising how much information you can fit on such a folding card – for instance meeting points, team contact numbers, a flowchart showing early stages of activity of the key groups, in- and out-of-hours default procedures plus detailed tasks for the leader of the team activation process, and recovery facility locations!
- *The CM plan itself:* Complementing the Aide Memoire (and therefore not repeating information), and heavily sectionalised with coloured tabs taking the reader direct

to the information they need *now*. The plan should contain separate sections for each CM team (with checklists for leaders and members), notes that apply to all CM group members and supporting information for all teams (such as a CM Centre kit list for the CM Centre Team). The logic and basic facts about the CM concept should also be in there, so that the document can be used for briefing and familiarisation purposes. I have found it useful to "hide" this latter information (which is certainly not required in an emergency) between the cover and the first team divider tab. I also use the cover itself to map out the layout of the plan and carry the reader into their section.

In both the Aide Memoire and the plan, it is advantageous to point the CM participant to the importance of making notes of key requests, actions and timings.

# 7 Looking Ahead: September 2001 and Beyond

Let us look back a short time to 10.00 a.m., 11 September, 2001, New York. America – and the world – are just beginning to see pictures of what later proves to be the single most devastating act of terrorism yet experienced by any nation or group. As the origins of the events at the World Trade Center (WTC) and at the Pentagon in Washington unfold, many interpretations will be put on what has happened, why it happened and what should be done about it. Many viewpoints will be expressed – some of them varying markedly over time. Many pundits will advance their (sure-fire) theories as to who, what, why, when, where and how. Pressures will be applied for action: hard, targeted, *now*. The scale of the losses, of people, of property, of reputations will grow over the next few months.

In considering the lessons of these events for CM concepts and planning, one feels that the sheer scale of the WTC catastrophe must demand something different. However, after a lot of hard reflection, I am not sure that the basic ideas that I have put forward in this chapter have been so rapidly outdated.

What I did was to consider, from the personal experience of colleagues touched by the events of that day and the reports in the media, the CM needs of the management of the following:

- An airline whose aircraft was involved: managing an even worse combination catastrophe than the most imaginative scenario planner would dare to suggest.
- A reinsurance broker that lost all its New York office staff.
- The company whose London personnel were traumatised by the breaking of voice links with colleagues who already had a clear idea of what was going to happen to them.

- The New York Fire Department, which suffered a major loss of personnel whose expertise was badly needed and for whom there was little opportunity to pause to mourn colleagues.
- The small catering company located in the main shopping mall at ground level.
- The many organisations, in many industries located elsewhere, whose business have been affected, in some cases devastated, by the day's events and the follow-on losses of confidence amongst consumers and traders.

In each case, most if not all of the elements of a disaster were present: human, operational, technical, organisational and reputational just for a start. What was and is unique is the scale of the impacts and their geographical spread and the capacity for the reaction by the United States and the coalition against terrorism of itself to be the cause of other political and confidence crises in other places.

Nevertheless, I believe that the features of the basic model I have outlined would still have been useful in any of the above organisations. It is clear that the preparedness of many of those companies and institutions affected by 11th September have stood up well, even if the scale, violence and callousness of what they could have anticipated came nowhere near what actually happened. Perhaps because their management had, knowingly or not, taken on board Franklin D. Roosevelt's words of April 25th, 1936 in that same city: "Nationwide thinking, nationwide planning and nationwide action are the three great essentials to prevent nationwide crises for future generations to struggle through".

Try removing each occurrence of the word "Nationwide" and substituting "our organisation" for "future generations" and I think you will have a sound principle for Crisis Management for the new century.

# Part II

# Business and System Operation

# Business Continuity Planning (BCP) in a Globalised Bank

UWE NAUJOKS
*Business Continuity Coordinator for WestLB Banking Group*

**Abstract:** Business Continuity Planning (BCP), in combination with crisis management, is a wide spread and modern subject. Nearly every company has more or less structured and tested guidelines for emergencies (e.g. fire alarms). However, what comes after this? – Not the cause of an incident but the effects are important. This chapter sets out a possible procedure for developing a worldwide framework for business continuity planning. Of course, every company and even every branch or subsidiary has to adapt individual aspects and has to develop its own plans.

**Keywords:** Operational risks, Business continuity planning, Emergency, Short-term mission-critical activities, Cost/benefit, Business continuity management, Phase model, Continuity plan

## 1 General Considerations

Business Continuity Planning (BCP) is becoming, more and more, a central topic for nearly all companies – this is not only because of the events in New York on 11 September 2001, but those events have forced companies to look at this matter more closely.

In former times, IT recovery and data security were the main subjects of BCP, but this focus has changed completely to continuity planning based on the business processes.

Because of the increase of global business and global dependencies, continuity planning should follow the same strategies by thinking about cross-border solutions and by using global networking, especially in emergencies and for crisis management.

# 2 Definitions of Terms

## 2.1 Operational Risks

Operational risks are classified and described below using examples. This list is by no means exhaustive. All threats are to be analysed locally or at the business unit level, where they are expected and relevant locally.

### 2.1.1 Denial of Access to a Building or Part of a Building (Including Equipment)

The main characteristic of denial of access to a building is that the building, including all equipment within it, cannot be used for a short or medium-term period. That means that the measures and plans to limit the impact are independent from the causes of the denial of access. Concerning preventive measures such as fire protection, however, the causes are of great importance.

**Causes of Short Term Outages**

- Loss of services, e.g. electricity, or water.
- Outage of important equipment (e.g. air conditioning).
- Serious criminal acts such as hostage-taking, sabotage, bomb threat, robbery, or break-in.
- Denial of access to city/town districts.

**Causes of Long-Term Impacts (often Linked with Physical Damage on Buildings)**

- Fire.
- Explosion (bomb, gas, etc.).
- Environmental – natural disasters (e.g. lightning strike, flood, or earthquake).
- Environmental – industry (e.g. chemical industry).

### 2.1.2 Information Technology Failure or Denial of Service, including Telecommunications

This includes IT systems run by a bank and its external suppliers. The following list shows possible types of failure or denial of service but should not be considered complete. Causes of failure or serious dysfunction are not listed, because they can vary.
- Failure of hardware (host, server, or network components).
- Failure of back-end equipment (especially in the trading environment).

- Failure or serious dysfunction of software (system and application software).
- Failure or serious dysfunction of data interfaces to the outside world (e.g. Reuters, or EAF communication).
- Failure or dysfunction of internal nets (LANs).
- Failure or dysfunction of internal wide-area networks (WAN).
- Failure of phones/faxes.

### 2.1.3 Unexpected Unavailability of Personnel

The major impacts resulting from the unavailability of personnel can be compared to those of an outage of buildings in that resources (in this case key personnel (internal and external) or a large proportion of the staff) are not available for some reason.

- Strike.
- Epidemic.
- Demonstration.
- Breakdown of public transport.

## 2.2 Emergency

An emergency is an event that has lasting, serious impact on the mission-critical and/or important tasks of a business area or on the infrastructure required to support them at the location of the business activities.

Not every outage (partial or complete) is to be regarded as an emergency. Outages often end quickly. An emergency arises only when the potential outage exceeds the critical restart time (availability target) and is declared by a person with the responsibility to do so. It is important that, when any kind of trouble arises, the impact is assessed before it is classified as an "emergency". The definition, of what troubles are to be regarded as emergencies, must to be assessed and decided by each individual area.

The definition of an "emergency" is not limited to major events, such as those caused by fire or a bomb explosion. Less serious troubles may cause serious damage but may not jeopardise the whole company.

In practice, any incident has to be treated either as a trouble or as an emergency. The distinction between a trouble and an emergency can be made on the basis of an analysis of possible scenarios and their impact on the bank.

- Troubles will be removed within the normal organisation.
- Emergencies are so severe that they have to be treated within a special emergency organisation.

- Emergencies are characterised by
- predetermined scenarios (impact scenarios) and
- availability targets of defined business tasks or systems.

Experience teaches us that the scenarios of emergencies should be really big ones – such as destruction of whole buildings. It is much easier to derive continuity plans for smaller scenarios from a big one than the other way around (derive continuity plans for a big scenario from many small ones).

In order to avoid situations that become difficult simply because nobody knows whether to treat a situation as a trouble or an emergency, an organisational procedure needs to be set up.

## 2.3 Short-Term Mission-Critical Activities

Short-term mission-critical activities are the focus for business continuity planning because their outage can endanger the existence of the company.

The activities that are regarded as mission-critical and have to be kept functioning are defined below:

- Measures for maintaining health and safety in order to prevent damage to people
- Activities that minimise physical damage
- Activities that minimise direct and indirect financial losses. These can be categorised as below:
- The bank must be able to fulfil or negotiate out of contractual responsibilities: payments (in/out) for deals already complete (e.g. in trading) and payment transfer, including all supporting activities (e.g. liquidity control).
- The bank must be able to close and secure trading positions (maintaining a minimum level of trading – to be able to respond to market changes), including the necessary settlements and controls.
- Activities that maintain compliance with legislation and regulations (e.g. external regulatory reporting, and MaH).

To give further guidance, the activities listed below are not regarded as mission-critical:

- Broad service availability for clients.
- Signing of new business.
- Long-term strategic business operations.
- Non-operational activities.
- Project work.

There is not a single definition of "short-term" in this context. The definition depends mainly on the difference between the time, for which a task is allowed to fail and the time within which the task must be recovered without special measures, being prepared in advance.

# 3 Objectives

The main objective of BCP is to ensure, that short-term important and mission-critical tasks continue and that operational risks (especially those that could have a long-term impact) are countered by the implementation of:

- reactive measures to be used in an emergency including the necessary preparations
- preventive measures to avoid threats, to reduce their probability and to reduce their impact.

The scope of the operational risks is:

- failures of facilities or denial of service by them,
- failures of information technology systems (hardware, software and networks), including telecommunications, or denial of service by them
- unexpected unavailability of personnel.

This includes the bank's own risks, as well as those of outsourced services which support mission-critical or important business tasks.

Preventive measures, for example duplicate hardware systems, are a permanent task of all business units, but they must be considered again in the context of business continuity planning in order to achieve an adequate relationship between preventive measures and the measures and preparations for an emergency.

Focusing on long-term failures (e.g. loss of premises due to fire) can be justified as follows:

- their impact is much higher
- the preparations for a long-term failure can often be used for short-term failures also, although they may not provide an exact match to the requirements.

Identical tasks and identical redundant systems at different locations can provide a cost-effective solution. In this way, in an emergency, the business activities are very quickly available to other business units or the affected unit can move to another site, not always at the same capacity level but with minimal disruption to business tasks (loss of capacity instead of functionality).

In principle, this sort of high availability should be preferred to measures designed for an emergency because it provides a high degree of resilience and a low cost level for business continuity planning. The design of such systems must include the ability to test.

Contrary regulations must be taken into account where such regulations apply.

Overall measures for the safety of information systems (such as assigning responsibilities for the use of IT, data back-up and access controls) are assumed, and the continuity framework is based on this assumption.

For detailed description of *operational risks* see the explanation later in this chapter.

Emergencies at a bank caused by business problems of clients or business partners (e.g. credit or settlement risks), and liquidity problems are outside the scope of this framework.

Risks from external suppliers that might affect important or mission-critical tasks at a bank, have to be managed by appropriate agreements and contracts and in accordance with the requirements described in this chapter, and have to be controlled.

# 4 Overall Requirements

*Business continuity management has to be 'lived' (part of the culture).*
For each business continuity plan, a senior responsible person must be named, who is responsible for regular, frequent maintenance and testing.

The task of maintenance, testing, education and training has to be audited. Only by regular and frequent checks can accurate plans be maintained.

An early involvement of the Business Continuity Coordinators in projects which influence the business continuity planning is absolutely necessary.

*Business continuity plans have to be easy to follow.*
- Continuity plans for dealing with a disaster have to fulfil the following criteria/attributes:
- practical, and user-friendly
- up to date
- testable
- easy to maintain
- independent of people (neutral)
- readable.

"Practical" means that (if possible) activities can be carried out according to checklists in which they are described in a short but precise way.

"Easy to maintain" means that the plans are (as far as necessary and possible) independent of organisational structures. In some cases it is unavoidable to take the organisation into account.

*An important basic rule is: Speedy responses are vital with regard to emergency response activities. Since these activities often differ greatly from day-to-day business, it is important that they be defined precisely – the greater the difference from normal activities and the faster one wants to see results, the greater the amount of precision that is required when defining the action plan.*

# 5 Minimum Standards

The following minimum standards apply:

- In the case of denial of access to a building, the technical and organisational prerequisites to sustain the important and mission-critical tasks including the necessary support activities, within an acceptable minimum capacity, must be met.
- Preventive measures must be taken (mainly through redundant hardware), to deal with loss of mission-critical tasks through hardware failure.
- There must be business continuity plans for the loss of mission-critical tasks through software failure.
- Connections to global systems, as far as they are needed for sustaining the important and mission-critical tasks, must be especially safeguarded. Hence, business continuity plans and/or preventive measures are required.
- Connections to real-time settlement systems, stock exchanges and market data suppliers, as far as they are needed for sustaining the important and mission-critical tasks, must be especially safeguarded. Measures and procedures for an emergency offered by the supplier should be used.
- Every task – regardless of its short-term urgency - must be recoverable or phased out within an appropriate time frame.
- For each branch and subsidiary, there must exist plans for crisis management.

More than one point in this list can possibly be covered by the same plan, e.g. hardware failures and denial of access to a building. But, often, redundant hardware cannot counter software failure.

The requirement to recover or phase out every task must be covered mainly through infrastructure-related measures such as data back-up and redundancy of vital records; business continuity plans are not explicitly required. A lot of the activities needed should be usual already.

Regarding the unforeseen unavailability of personnel, no independent minimum requirements exist.

## 5.1 Cost/Benefit Ratio of BCP

The main focus of the expenditure should be on the important business elements. The expenditure for all other tasks should be the minimum required to ensure post emergency recovery but on a timescale appropriate to the business priority.

An important factor in deciding expenditure is the impact of potential damage and the likelihood of its occurrence. Probabilities cannot always be accurately defined. However, there must be measures for the protection of people and, for the prevention of damage that could risk the bank's existence.

According to a proposal of the BIZ, Basel, operational risks should be covered by the bank's own capital. With respect to efficient use of resources (the bank's own capital), operational risks should be reduced as far as possible and economically acceptable through adequate business continuity planning (optimisation of the cost of security and the benefit from increased operational security).

# 6 Procedure for Business Continuity Management (Phase Model)

The first time a continuity plan is put together a project team should be formed to implement the first four phases described below. If there is already an existing business continuity plan, then the existing parts can be used as far as possible and, by further additions, the standard of the framework described here can be reached. The fifth phase "Maintenance and Development", is then normally handled as a line responsibility.

The processing methods will depend on whether the continuity plan is being written from scratch or an existing continuity plan is being revised. For example, the following entities can be the object of a BCP study:

- a branch
- a business unit
- a centralised infrastructure component such as Lotus Notes
- an individual information technology system
- a single building

Business continuity planning is an iterative activity. For optimisation of the plan the activity has to be repeated from time to time. This may happen to the whole plan or to part of it for example because of test results or specific changes. The next figure illustrates this procedure.

## Life Cycle of the Phase Model

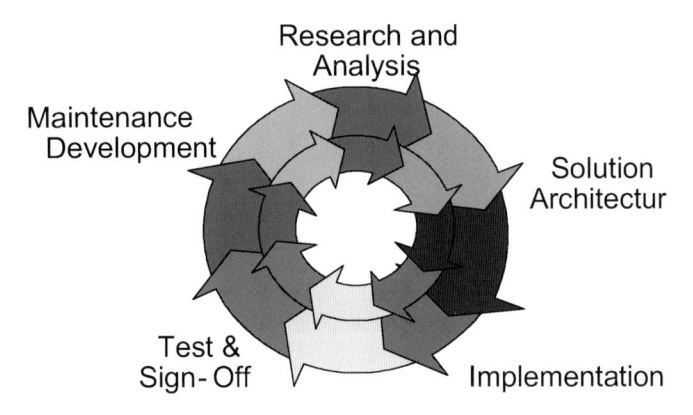

- Research and Analysis
- Solution Architectur
- Implementation
- Test & Sign-Off
- Maintenance Development

The above-mentioned phases are illustrated in the following diagram and in the subsequent sections.

## Phase Model

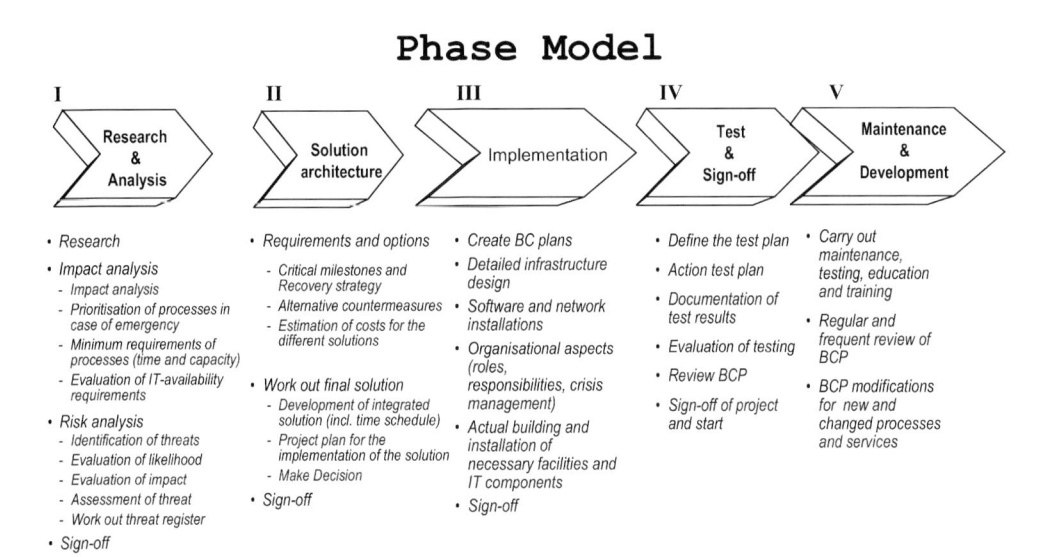

**I — Research & Analysis**
- Research
- Impact analysis
  - Impact analysis
  - Prioritisation of processes in case of emergency
  - Minimum requirements of processes (time and capacity)
  - Evaluation of IT-availability requirements
- Risk analysis
  - Identification of threats
  - Evaluation of likelihood
  - Evaluation of impact
  - Assessment of threat
  - Work out threat register
- Sign-off

**II — Solution architecture**
- Requirements and options
  - Critical milestones and Recovery strategy
  - Alternative countermeasures
  - Estimation of costs for the different solutions
- Work out final solution
  - Development of integrated solution (incl. time schedule)
  - Project plan for the implementation of the solution
  - Make Decision
- Sign-off

**III — Implementation**
- Create BC plans
- Detailed infrastructure design
- Software and network installations
- Organisational aspects (roles, responsibilities, crisis management)
- Actual building and installation of necessary facilities and IT components
- Sign-off

**IV — Test & Sign-off**
- Define the test plan
- Action test plan
- Documentation of test results
- Evaluation of testing
- Review BCP
- Sign-off of project and start

**V — Maintenance & Development**
- Carry out maintenance, testing, education and training
- Regular and frequent review of BCP
- BCP modifications for new and changed processes and services

# 7 Phase 1: Research and Analysis

The first phase is one of the major parts of the project and should be treated very intensively and carefully. This phase is devided into two subparts, the Business Impact Analysis (BIA) and the Risk Analysis.

When starting the BIA it is very useful to set priorities by classifying the various tasks analysed by estimating the possible damage in the case of a task failure.

## 7.1 Damage Estimate

Before the damage which could be caused by a task failure can be estimated the criteria according to which the estimate is made must be defined. The following criteria for damage estimates have been chosen. The order of the criteria in the list indicates their importance for a banking institute and can be amended if necessary.

- Financial.
- Image and reputation.
- Legislation and supervisory regulations.
- Loss of control over business (e.g. the missing transparency of the current profit/loss ratio of a business unit)

The progress of impact analysis should be documented using the "Damage Estimate" form shown below. The damages after 4 and 8 hours should be filled in only if relevant damages arise in this timeframe.

### Damage Estimate

| BU: xxxxx | | | | | | | |
|---|---|---|---|---|---|---|---|
| Task name: | | | | | | | |
| Timeframe | After 4 Hours | After 8 Hours | After 24 Hours | After 48 Hours | After 1 Week | After 4 Weeks | Remarks |
| Criteria | | | | | | | |
| | | | | | | | |
| Financial | | | | | | | |
| Image and reputation | | | | | | | |
| Legislation and supervisory regulations | | | | | | | |
| Loss of control over business | | | | | | | |
| | | | | | | | |

### 7.1.1 Financial Impact

The financial damage should be described in millions of euros per task. In addition to the amount, in the _"Image and reputation" row of the form a point rating should be filled in.

In the trading departments, there are three major parameters which should be added together to determine the financial damage:

- Value-at-risk limit
- (In the case of value at risk, the likelihood of an outage is calculated according to the standard of the institute, e.g. a 95.0% confidence interval with a one-day trading stop of the portfolio).

- Settlement risk.
- Foregone income.

The financial impact from the loss of a task may depend on the market conditions on the day. Therefore, for assessment purposes, an average trading day should be assumed. Where there are expected to be large fluctuations in the risk profile from this average (i.e. volatile or illiquid markets), such factors should be recorded in the "Remarks" column.

### 7.1.2 Image and Reputation

The image risk will depend largely on the role played by the bank in the market (e.g. as a market maker) and on the client group affected. If warranted, a multiplier effect should be included in this calculation.

### 7.1.3 Legislation and Supervisory Regulations

The impact with regard to legislation and supervisory regulations depends on whether the bank has a statutory or supervisory obligation to maintain the affected task at all times or only at certain points in time. This should be indicated under timeframe as critical times and deadlines.

### 7.1.4 Loss of Control over Business

This criterion records the impact of losing access to information which is required to control the bank's business, e.g. profit/loss ratio of a trading department.

## 7.2 Determining the Recovery Profile

During the impact analysis, the maximum admissible outages must also be defined, as well as the minimum capacities at which the tasks must be maintained at all costs. The sum of these data results in the recovery profile. These profiles are used in Phase II as a basis for determining the requirements for the solutions which are to be defined.

The following diagram provides a schematic illustration of the recovery profiles of three different tasks. The diagram describes the following facts:

- Process 1 must not be interrupted and has to be permanently available with a minimum capacity of 50%. After one week, the process must be fully recovered.

- Process 2 is allowed to be unavailable for two days as a maximum. Subsequently, there must be a minimum capacity of 30%, and after one week the process must be fully recovered.
- Process 3 is allowed to be unavailable for two weeks as a maximum. After that, it has to have a minimum capacity of 120%. The additional 20% is necessary to recover from the backlog.

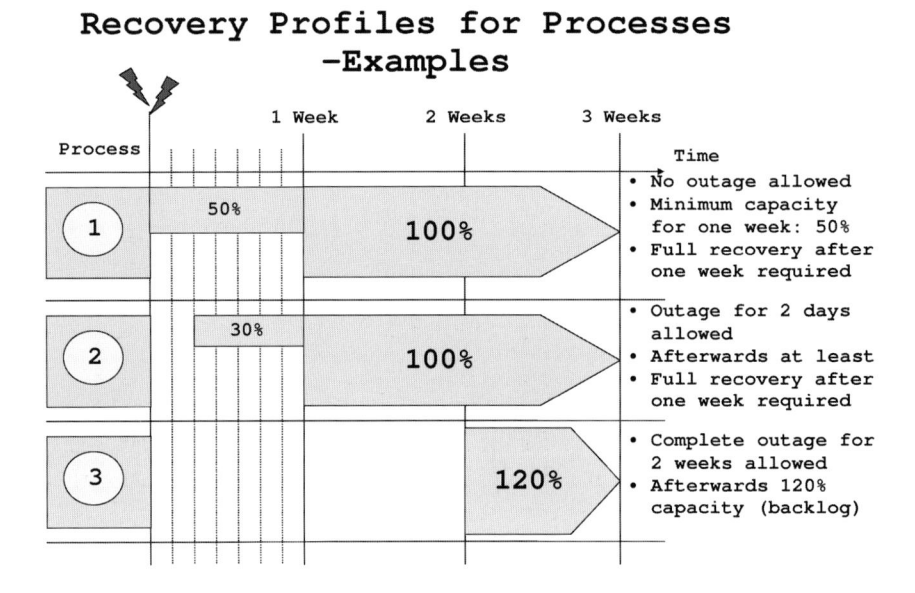

```
Recovery Profiles for Processes
           -Examples
```

                1 Week      2 Weeks     3 Weeks
Process                                          Time
                                                 • No outage allowed
    1       50%        100%                      • Minimum capacity
                                                   for one week: 50%
                                                 • Full recovery after
                                                   one week required

                                                 • Outage for 2 days
                                                   allowed
    2           30%      100%                    • Afterwards at least
                                                 • Full recovery after
                                                   one week required

                                                 • Complete outage for
                                                   2 weeks allowed
    3                          120%              • Afterwards 120%
                                                   capacity (backlog)

The recovery profiles for all tasks and applications of each business unit should be recorded by means of the following tables.

## Tasks

| BU: xxxxx | | | | | | | | | | Recovery profile | | | |
|---|---|---|---|---|---|---|---|---|---|---|---|---|---|
| Task name | Org-No | Description | Remarks | Location | Classifi-cation | No of desks | Gets data from BU BU | Gives data to of data (in h) | Accep-table loss | Time 1 (in h) desks 1 | No of alternate | Time 2 (in h) desks 2 | No of alternate |
| | | | | | | | | | | | | | |
| task 1 | org-no 1 | | | | | | | | | | | | |
| task 2 | org-no 2 | | | | | | | | | | | | |
| task 3 | org-no 3 | | | | | | | | | | | | |
| task 4 | org-no 4 | | | | | | | | | | | | |
| task 5 | org-no 5 | | | | | | | | | | | | |
| | | | | | | | | | | | | | |
| | Sum | | | | | 0 | | | | | 0 | | 0 |

## IT Recovery Profile

| BU: xxxxx | | | | | | |
|---|---|---|---|---|---|---|
| | | \multicolumn{4}{c|}{Recovery profile} | |
| Application | Acceptable loss of data (in h) | Time 1 (in h) | Capacity 1 (in %) | Time 2 (in h) | Capacity 2 (in %) | Remarks |
| application 1 | | | | | | |
| application 2 | | | | | | |
| application 3 | | | | | | |
| application 4 | | | | | | |
| application 5 | | | | | | |

## 7.3 Determining the IT Availability Requirements

Once the maximum admissible outage for each task has been defined, it is possible to determine the availability requirements for the IT applications. If one IT application supports several tasks, then the figure should be calculated using the task with the shortest admissible outage.

A direct transfer from the recovery profile of the tasks is not adequate every time. For example, it is possible that in an emergency one system may substitute for another so that the required recovery time can be shifted backwards.

## 7.4 Generated Information

After the impact analysis has been completed, the following information will have been gathered:

- assessed impact on the business of task failure
- classification of tasks into "mission-critical", "important" and "not relevant"
- recovery profile of each task
- IT availability requirements.

## 7.5 Determining the Likelihood of Occurrence

The threat checklist contains as far as possible information about the likelihood of different threats. These probabilities have to be checked taking account of the unique conditions at a given office.
A standardised, five-point scale is used:

- very low (= less than once in a hundred years)
- low (= more than once in 100 years but less than one in 25 years)
- medium (= more than once in 25 years)
- probable (= more than once in 5 years)
- very probable (= more than once a year).

These values refer to the likelihood of an event (e.g. a fire) occurring, not the likelihood that the event will have a certain impact (e.g. complete denial of access to a building).

## 7.6 Impact Scenarios

The definition of an impact scenario is, in a broader sense, the result of a threat analysis. An impact scenario is one containing the biggest possible impact that any threat can have. An impact scenario causes a wide outage of tasks that drop out simultaneously because of their topological vicinity. These may be for example all tasks performed within one building.

Causes are no longer of interest at this point, only impacts. This is the reason for the term "impact scenario". Since scenarios of this kind provoke severe damage to the bank, they must be treated within a special emergency organisation. This is the reason for also using the term "emergency scenario" or just "emergency".

Each impact scenario implies, that all tasks and IT applications affected in that scenario fail simultaneously. The business continuity planning process must take this into account. In cases of doubt, bigger and more comprehensive scenarios should be selected. Continuity plans drawn up for big emergency scenarios can also handle smaller ones - but not vice versa.

Impact scenarios that are sufficiently far apart from each other – that is, more than 2 km – never happen simultaneously, because the likelihood of occurrence for each individual scenario is already quite low.

### 7.6.1 Typical Impact Scenarios

The following impact scenarios should normally be considered:

- If the data centre and the business unit reside in the same building: loss of the building that houses the business unit and loss of the primary IT equipment (not the back-up equipment).
- If the data centre and the business unit do not reside in the same building:
- loss of the building of the business unit
- loss of the primary IT-equipment (not the back-up equipment).

These assumptions may be changed or refined as a result of the analysis phase, e.g.

- Loss of nearby buildings at the same time
- For each group of rooms (e.g. the whole data centre or nearby decentralised server rooms), where primary IT equipment for productive applications (not network servers or other active components) resides, a separate impact scenario is required
- specific scenarios (e.g. a strike)

If flexible solutions are found for those impact scenarios, in most cases smaller emergencies and even failures should also be covered.

## 7.7 Deliverables/Results

Once the first phase has been completed, the following information will have been gathered:

- impact with regard to statutory requirements, financial damage and loss of image and control over business
- categorising of tasks
- recovery profile
- potential threats
- likelihood of the threats occurring
- impact of threats
- list of known weaknesses and of single-point-of-failures
- Impact scenarios

At the end of Phase I, a decision must be taken on the basis of the information gathered as to how large the scope should be, i.e. which impact scenarios, tasks and threats are to be considered relevant for the future business continuity plan. This decision must be taken by management.

# 8 Phase 2: Solution Architecture

## 8.1 Stages of Recovery

The procedures for managing an emergency can be divided into stages. This aids communication, prioritisation of response activities and resource planning, both in the preparation of the recovery solution and in its use following an emergency.

There are three stages of recovery, preceded by an pre-recovery escalation phase.

### 8.1.1 Escalation

The escalation is triggered by a notification. The management, once notified, assesses the situation to decide if the continuity plan or parts of it should be invoked. If needed, the business continuity solution is activated.

### 8.1.2 Recovery Stages

**Initial Response**

This stage concentrates on gaining and maintaining control of the emergency. The primary activities relate to the welfare and safety of employees, public relations, security of the site, assembly of business continuity teams, and communications (staff, customers, and agencies).

The Initial Response may cover a period of four to eight hours, or sometimes longer, depending upon the business continuity solution.

**Initial Recovery**

The focus of this stage is to restore the operation of predetermined business tasks (core tasks) within the time frame and to the level required. This, however, must be done under an overall management of the emergency that continues to address the issues of staff welfare, public relations and communications (staff, customers, and agencies). The aim of this stage is to establish temporary normality.

During this stage, the assessment of the emergency continues to determine what actions will be required to re-establish normal business operations. Where there has been physical damage, matters such as salvage and insurance must be considered. When the physical damage extends to the total loss of a building, there are considerations of business strategy to be decided as part of the return to normal operations.

Some elements of the Initial Recovery stage will overlap with the Initial Response stage. Typically, these elements relate to the recovery of technology that supports critical business processes.

**Long-term Recovery**

In some cases the Initial Recovery solution provides a business operation environment for a limited period. If normal operations cannot be established within this timescale then a second phase of recovery may be required. The business continuity solution should include long-term recovery requirements. The decision about the long-term recovery requirements is based on the business priorities, the time provided by the initial recovery solution, the resources available, the amount of preparation that would be needed and the costs involved.

### 8.1.3 Normal Business Operations

The recovery process is terminated, and normal business operations are re-established.

Returning from a recovery location to normal operations will typically cause some disruption to service.

## 8.2 Work Out Final Solution

### 8.2.1 Steps

- Prepare a draft of a fine-tuned solution proposal (including a timeline).
- Plan a project for implementation of the draft solution.
- Effect a decision (remember to include all relevant departments).

### 8.2.2 Procedure

The combination of different solution options will result in a fine-tuned solution proposal which the relevant bodies will then have to decide on.

The proposed solution must describe the preventive measures and/or those which are to be implemented in an emergency.

A project plan must be drafted to handle the implementation of the measures.

### 8.2.3 Generated Information

The above considerations wrap up Phase II, "Solution Architecture". The following information will have been generated in this phase:

- preventive measures
- emergency measures
- a project plan for implementation of these measures.

# 9 Phase 3: Implementation

The primary activities are:

- Write up continuity plans and staff information.
- Draw up detailed infrastructure design.
- Determine all required software and network installations.
- Define procedural organisation and organisational structure to be used in an emergency situation (activities, responsibility, and crisis management).
- Carry out construction work and have IT components installed.
- Sign-off.

## 9.1 Procedure

The business continuity plans are written and documented in this phase. All measures implemented in the project should be recorded at this point and subjected to a consistency check.

The measures in a business continuity plan can be preventive or reactive. The preparations made with regard to the business continuity plan constitute the core of any reactive measures. Systems or infrastructure required in an emergency should be installed, procedures should be defined and it should be clear who is responsible for what.

In the planning process, it is recommended to proceed in the order of priority assigned to the processes and the likelihoods of occurrence determined in the threat and impact analyses.

# 10 Phase 4: Testing and Sign-Off

When the efficacy of the business continuity plan is being tested, the focus should be on the emergency measures. The preventive measures are possibly already being used in day-to-day operations, which provides the best situation in which to test their efficiency.

In addition, the information technology department can apply its usual testing procedures for the use of new or modified systems (test system, developer test, user test, etc.).

The primary activities are

- Work out a test schedule.
- Test preparation (e.g. test scripts of what will be tested).
- Perform tests.
- Document tests.
- Evaluate tests.
- Revise business continuity planning.
- Approve and implement business continuity planning.

More details concerning the test activities can be found in this book in the chapter entitled "Verification/Testing and Monitoring of Business Continuity Plans".

## 11 Phase 5: Maintenance and Monitoring/Reporting of the BCP

The primary activities in this phase are:

- Maintenance, testing, education, training.
- Further development when new processes are added or existing processes are modified (including the support for the processes).

More details concerning the test activities can again be found in this book in the chapter entitled "Verification/Testing and Monitoring of Business Continuity Plans".

## 12 Conclusion

In conclusion, we can say that BCP can be written down with "only three characters" but has much more content. This article can give only an example of a possible approach to handling this important topic. Every company has to find its own individual BCP strategy. The author wishes everybody good luck with these activities and hopes, that their BCP plans will never have to be used in a real crisis.

# Verification/Testing and Monitoring of Business Continuity Plans

UWE NAUJOKS
*Business Continuity Coordinator for WestLB Banking Group*

**Abstract:** An old German proverb says, "nothing is older than a newspaper of yesterday". Transferred to BCP, this means, "having no plan could be better than using an old plan". Quality assurance of the BCP activities is therefore absolutely necessary and has to be repeated on a regular basis. Test schedules, test scripts (e.g. performing tests) and document tests are basic assumptions. Testing should include the IT part as well as the process part. Monitoring the whole BCP life cycle is an important part of the overall risk management. This chapter gives an overview of the main test activities, including a suggestion of an annually based test schedule and a possible methodology for a monitoring procedure based on a self-assessment.

**Keywords:** Business continuity Plan, Test scenario, Test plan, Test schedule, Testing procedure, Awareness, Desktop test, Scenario test, Technical Test, User exercise, Training, Maintenance, Monitoring, Reporting

## 1 General Considerations

As described in the chapter entitled "business Continuity Planning (BCP) in a Globalised Bank", BCP activities are integrated into a cycle from "analysis" through "solution architecture" to "implementation", followed by test activities, which will normally lead to review of the analysis. For the basic project work, the final sign-off is performed after all tests have been completed successfully. After that signoff, the line function "Business Continuity Planning" should be set in place and should be maintained and monitored on a regular basis. The test scenarios set out below, do not describe the various types of "software testing", but are mostly focused on tests relevant to BCP. Specific details of software testing can be found in [WiMe01].

## 2 Testing and Sign-Off

When the efficacy of the business continuity plan is being tested, the focus should be on the emergency measures. The preventive measures are possibly already being used in day-to-day operations, which provides the best situation in which to assess their efficiency.

In addition, the information technology department can apply its usual testing procedures for the use of new or modified systems (test system, developer test, user test, etc.).

The primary activities are

- Work out a test schedule.
- Test preparation (e.g. test scripts of what will be tested).
- Perform tests.
- Document tests.
- Evaluate tests.
- Revise business continuity planning.
- Approve and implement business continuity planning.

## 2.1 Test Plan

Various options are available when it comes to performing the tests and exercises. They differ sharply in the degree of penetration attained (see section 2.2 for more details).

The following figure illustrates a sample test schedule.

**Sample Test Schedule**
for Business continuity plan sign-off

| Draft Plan | Awareness<br>• Training<br>• Education | Walk Through<br>• Plan validation<br>• Logic<br>• interfaces | Scenario<br>• Management<br>• Integration | Test<br>• Functionality | Execise<br>• Management<br>• Integration<br>• Logistics |
|---|---|---|---|---|---|
| Crisis Management Team | ● | ● | | | |
| Press and Media | ● | ● | | | |
| Human Resources | ● | ● | | | |
| Business Team 1 | ● | ● | | | |
| Business Team 2 | ● | ● | | | |
| Business Team 3 | ● | ● | | | |
| IT-Team | ● | ● | | ● | |
| Facilities Team | ● | ● | | ● | |

Plan Sign-off

## 2.2 Testing Procedure

The following types of tests and exercises are available.

### 2.2.1 Awareness

Awareness sessions have to do with the basic introduction and preparation of the employees in the context of BCP.

Objectives:

- Appreciate need for BCP.
- Education and training.
- Understand and test the interfaces to and requirements of other teams/departments.
- Verify validity of the organisational rules and manual tasks.

### 2.2.2 Desktop Test

This is a written test which simulates an emergency and is based on the various business continuity plans of each business unit. This test should be done before starting the real tests to find major mistakes or differences without spending a lot of money on technical equipment and additional resources during a live test.

Objectives:

- Train the employees to understand the structure and logic of the business continuity plan.
- Test the interfaces with the other teams.

### 2.2.3 Scenario Test

In a scenario test, the employees act out their roles in a contingency plan against the background of a simulated emergency, which should be made as real as possible. The scenario unites the contingency plans of the various units.

A simulation team works out the scenario and provides the employees with additional information if necessary. The goal is to make the simulation as authentic as possible.

It is important that as many elements as possible of a real emergency are built into the simulation (e.g. camera teams performing on-the-spot interviews, which are recorded and can be evaluated at a later point).

A scenario test can sometimes last for more than one day. The employees are made aware of the time frame beforehand, but do not know how deeply they will become involved in the events. This will crystallise during the course of the simulation, which can develop a momentum of its own. It is important that the simulation team is able to react interactively to the actions of the persons involved in the test during the simulation.

Objective:

- Exercise contingency plans in a safe environment.
- Rehearse and understand the way communications affect disaster responses.
- Understand the reporting structure in a disaster situation.
- Identify gaps in logic or practical obstacles that would stop or affect a recovery to normal service levels.
- Comprehensive interaction of the contingency plans across all units (CMT, banking operations, IT and facilities) in order to find gaps.

### 2.2.4 Technical Test

The main objective of this test is to determine the limits of the technical skills of the employees with regard to the starting of (redundant) machines and setting up of installations in order to determine whether or not the times planned for this work are realistic. Such tests should be applied only to single cases. The results must be recorded and an action list with the improvements required has to be set up.

It is mainly employees from the IT section or internal services (e.g. in the case of a test of back-up power supplies) who are involved.

Objectives:

- Test the functionality of technical and IT equipment.
- Assess the skills and confidence of the employees in an emergency.
- Determine the time required for recovery of installations from a technical point of view.

### 2.2.5 User Exercise ("Dress Rehearsal")

An exercise significantly exceeds an IT test. The exercise is carried out in the same environment as that used in an emergency and is even more authentic. The results must be recorded and an action list with the improvements required has to be set up.

A lot of people, at a minimum the business and infrastructure teams are involved.

Objectives:

- Simulation of running the business under the conditions of an emergency.
- Assess the skills and confidence of the employees in an emergency.
- Determine the time required for recovery, including the organisational aspects.
- Prove that regulatory obligations can be met.

# 3 Maintenance and Development

The primary activities in this phase are:

- Maintenance, testing, education and training.
- Further development when new processes are added or existing processes are modified (including the support for the processes).

## 3.1 Maintenance, Test, Education, Training

Ongoing BCP development comprises:

- Adapting the plan to meet modified situations.
- Testing to establish whether the contingency plan is still up to date and effective.
- Educating staff to refresh their knowledge of business continuity planning and their awareness of the topic. This includes inducting new employees into business continuity planning and "retraining" when employees move from position to another, thus taking on new responsibilities under the plan. At the same time, this enforces quality assurance since employees can point out inconsistencies and impracticable procedures in the plan.
- Training exercises to run through the practical procedures that are to be used in an emergency.

It is necessary to regularly review business procedures at a bank and to audit the contingency plans. This is done through testing. Which tests need to be performed and how frequently will depend on the specific circumstances at each location. The minimum requirements are set out in the following section.

## 3.2 Development of BCP for New or Changed Processes and Services

When processes, or the systems and services supporting them, undergo major changes, adjustments will have to be made to the contingency plan. Time and effort will be saved if the persons responsible for business continuity planning are involved in the planning of the modifications at an early stage. This is the best way to fully exploit all opportunities and, at the same time, to ward off the creation or aggravation of potential threats.

Should in-depth modifications occur, component tests will have to be performed to determine whether gaps have opened up in the logic of the plan.

Because of the ongoing modifications and improvements being made to processes, the contingency plan will only ever be as up to date as the last review.

## 3.3 Minimum Requirements for Maintenance and Testing

The maintenance and testing activities have to be controlled very seriously. Therefore a structured plan is one of the best ways to support these activities. The following diagram can be used as an example, but has to be adapted to individual needs.

### 3.3.1 Annual Maintenance Plan

Each BCC who is responsible for maintaining a contingency plan must put together an annual maintenance plan. This plan must comprise the following components:

- Which tests, exercises and maintenance activities are be to performed, and when.
- Factors expected to have an influence on BCP (e.g. removals, new buildings, IT projects and reorganisation), with expected dates.
- Check of Service level agreements.

## Example Annual Schedule

Annual Maintenance and Testing

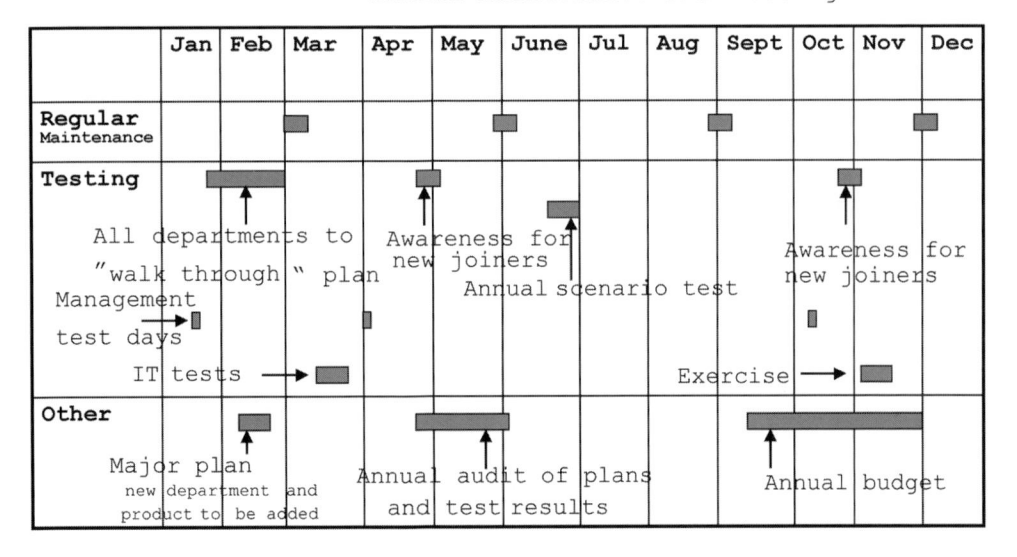

| | Jan | Feb | Mar | Apr | May | June | Jul | Aug | Sept | Oct | Nov | Dec |
|---|---|---|---|---|---|---|---|---|---|---|---|---|
| **Regular Maintenance** | | | ▇ | | ▇ | | | ▇ | | | ▇ | |
| **Testing** | | ▇ | | | ▇ | | | | | ▇ | | |
| | All departments to "walk through" plan | | | Awareness for new joiners | | | | | | Awareness for new joiners | | |
| | Management test days | | | | | Annual scenario test | | | | | | |
| | | IT tests → ▇ | | | | | | | Exercise → ▇ | | | |
| **Other** | | ▇ | | | ▬▬▬▬ | | | | | ▬▬▬▬ | | |
| | | Major plan new department new product to be added | | | Annual audit of plans and test results | | | | | Annual budget | | |

## 3.3.2 Regular Intervals

The effectiveness of the contingency plans must be tested with tests and exercises at regular intervals. The following intervals are minimum requirements. In special circumstances, the tests and exercises may need to be performed more frequently. Since these tests and exercises can disrupt regular business operations, the frequency of the tests and exercises should reflect the risk level of the threat, however, the emergency tests and exercises should be performed at least once a year.

| Activity | Testing interval (minimum requirements) | Remarks |
|---|---|---|
| Check that employee lists are up to date | At minimum semi-annual, for larger locations monthly | |
| Revise threat register and IT availability requirements | Annual | |
| Review and maintain plans | Annual | If warranted, more frequently |
| "Employee awareness sessions" | Annual | |
| Test of the IT production with back-up machines | Semi-annual | More frequently for important machines or complex environments |
| Exercise at alternativ location | Annual | If warranted, more frequently |
| Test uninterruptible power supply | Annual | |
| Test working order of back-up power | Annual | |
| Building safety inspection | Annual | |
| Evacuation drill | Biannual | Only for large or complex buildings or parts of them |
| Test notification plan | Annual | |
| Test call tree | Annual | If a call tree is planned |
| Test back-up procedures (manual or partly manual procedures) | Annual | |

# 4 Monitoring and Reporting

After completion of the BCP project work, it is extremely important to maintain a permanent overview of the BCP activities and occurrences. The more branches a company has, the more difficult it is to prepare the annual BCP report.

The purpose of real business continuity planning is to keep the process linking BCP-live (the active protection against dangers that is being applied) and BCP (the production planning for BC-live) functioning permanently, as shown in the following figure:

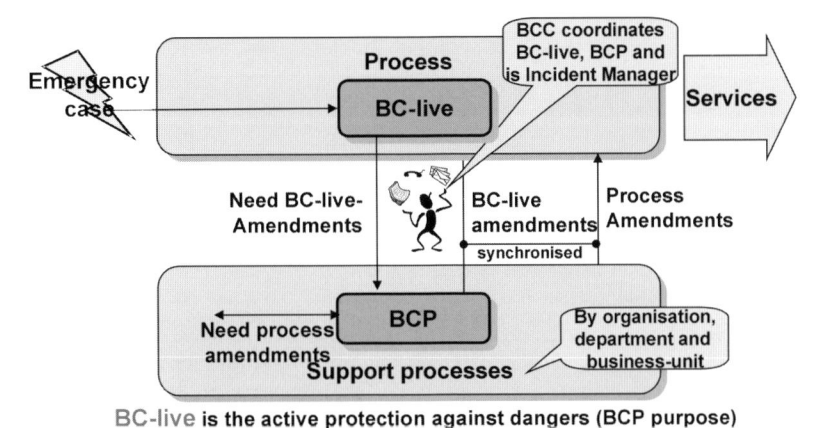

BC-live is the active protection against dangers (BCP purpose)

BCP is the production planning for BC-live.

Normally, the management would like to have both a comparison between the different branches (e.g. sorted by executive board departments) and a year comparison. This report should be short, highly informative and comprehensible.

One possible solution for obtaining such a report is a structured self-assessment with a huge number of pre-defined questions, which is to be sent to each business continuity co-ordinator to be filled in an annual basis. These questions can be answered by scoring and – if necessary – by adding comments or by referring to specific plans, so duplication of work is impossible.

With this methodology you will get not only answers but also feedback to improve the company guidelines and rules. The structured way is as easy for every business continuity co-ordinator to use as it is for the central co-ordinator to evaluate.

As the final result, you will get code numbers that can be used in each "section" of the BCP and as a summary for each branch. These code numbers can be classified into "operational business activities" and "future prospects". The following figure explains the "step by step" philosophy aimed at reaching the highest certification, "ideal". The whole assessment is an ongoing process with a constantly changing environment.

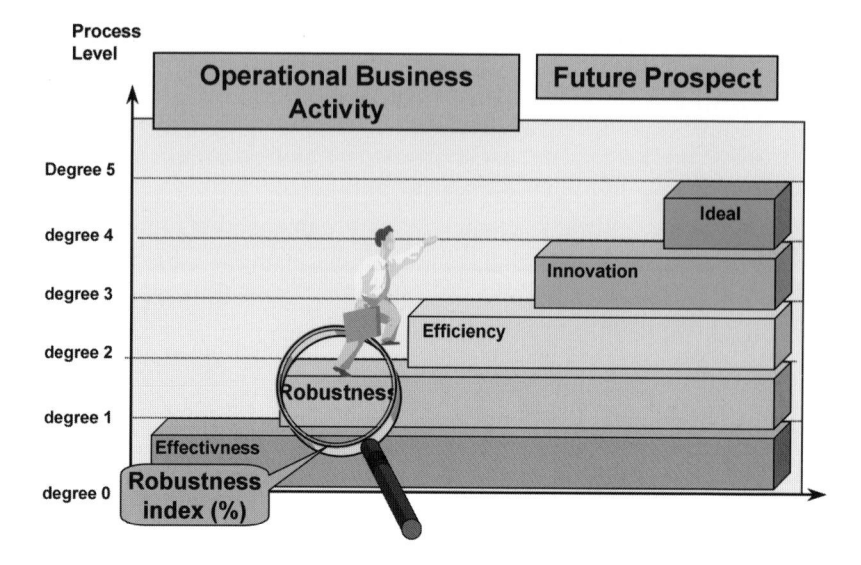

Only those companies with well structured "BCP standards" – including a well prepared monitoring system – will get a "best practice certificate" from their internal and external auditors.

The author wishes everybody good luck in solving outstanding problems and in preparing BCP standards. Keep always in mind:

"Business continuity planning may be cost intensive until something happens, but will save a lot of money or even the whole company in the case of a real disaster."

ripped # The Benefits of BCP Tools, with Special Reference to CAPT® and CM®

Lothar Goecke
*Heine & Partner GmbH (Germany)*

**Abstract:** Maintaining business continuity and the recovery of the mission-critical business functions after a disaster are some of the most important tasks of a company management. A growing number of companies regard BCP as a main factor for success in business. Contingency planning is a precondition and requires documentation in contingency manuals for different departments, the crisis management team and the company's management. A suitable BCP documentation tool supports this task.

In this chapter the benefits of using one of two specific tools, either CAPT® or CM®, are described.

In a separate section it is discussed for which purposes you should use a BCP documentation tool and for which purposes you should not.

**Keywords:** Business continuity tools, Disaster recovery planning tools, Documentation, CAPT®, CM®

## 1 Why do we Need Another Tool for BCP?

Imagine you have your BCP documentation in "flat files", one file for every team, maintained with a text-processing tool such as MS Word or something similar. It contains your team members in PowerPoint sheets and their addresses and phone numbers in EXCEL sheets. Both of these sets of data are included in the Word files.

Then the following usually happens: somebody has left the company, others have joined, and many of those who are still in the company have taken up an offer of a new, better provider for their mobile phone, which means they have new telephone numbers.

You, as the person responsible for BCP documentation, have to go through all the Word files, make the changes, go through all PowerPoint slides and Excel sheets in every Word document and make the same changes to all of them. This is definitely a boring job and not the best way to keep your documentation in a good state. A tool should help you not only to make these changes only once but also to keep data consistent!

You need a tool that provides BCP data without redundancies and with a high level of data integrity to keep the effort of maintenance as low as possible:

- All BCP data must be stored in *one* database although you need several manuals for certain teams and several types of manuals (see below in Section 3). If, for example, a supporting company is listed in several manuals, you want to change its telephone number only once; the company's new data should then appear in all manuals. You change the data only once, and after that no additional work needs to be done.
- If you are faced with the task of changing specific data, you must know where these data items are used. Only a full-text search in every manual or in the whole database will give you sufficient support. Furthermore, it may be helpful to figure out where a specific data item is used (in which plans) and to whom you have to deliver a new version or an update of the corresponding BCP manual.
- Usually more than one employee is responsible for the maintenance of BCP data. There is always one person responsible and at least one deputy. In this situation it is worthwhile to know who has made what changes and at what time. Your auditors may want to know who has changed, inserted or even deleted any data in a certain period of time. Only a complete logging of all changes to the database will give you this information and will your BCP documentation into a revisable status.
- Storing BCP data with a tool on your server is one thing, in an emergency you need to have access to this machine or any backup server, so don't forget that you need to have access to it. Additionally we recommend you to have a printed version of your BCP manual available at any place you might need it. Then you can look at the manual on line and look at a printed version as well.
- Nowhere else is it so important to have a consistent terminology for your BCP documentation. No tool will avert the input of inappropriate data but a good tool can help to produce a consistent terminology for the emergency guides.
- Because BCP documentation cannot be the leading data in your company (see below in Section 6), you need to have import and export features to connect it to other databases in your company.
- As an overview, a graphical presentation always gives more information than any written documentation. Therefore the activity planning should be presentable as a PERT diagram (or something similar). But, on the other hand, this diagram must correspond to the written documentation.
- Those who know what to do in an emergency won't look at the written documentation, but they may like another form: a checklist generated out of the written documentation. This means control over the sufficiency and validity check of your documentation.
- If the features mentioned above are regarded as more than "nice to have", it is clear that you need a tool to fulfil all these requirements. A BCP documentation tool helps you to organise your activities when responding to an emergency.

## 2 Quality of BCP Documentation

### 2.1 Aspects of Documentation

It is strongly recommended that you establish quality requirements for the BCP documentation in your own company. They may be grouped as follows.

#### 2.1.1 BCP Documentation Needs a Comprehensive Scheme

The restart after an emergency has to be described exactly. That means that anybody who has a certain standard of knowledge can act properly with the help of the emergency guide.

Therefore the factual information must be comprehensive. No person from another discipline will be able to do a job he/she has never done before, but, for instance, a system administrator of a Unix system should be able to rebuild any Unix system with the help of the documentation, if the factual information is comprehensive.

All resources that you need in an emergency are described to a certain level of completeness. There is no general advice as to what level you have to do this to, but everybody in the process must be able to rely on the written documentation.

No team nor any person will act unless they are alarmed according to a proper alarming procedure. For every team a "contact list" is required. The more information that the list contains about every person in it, the more team members you can inform, and they will help to cope with the emergency.

We recommend the following table of contents on the chapter level to be used in your documentation:

1. *Distribution list:* file of all recipients of the manual and where they store their copies
2. *Contingency scenarios:* each specific manual applies only to specific scenarios
3. *Availability targets and recovery strategies:* the recovery strategies meet the requirements of the availability targets, which refer to your business impact analysis.
4. *Alarming procedures:* how is the alarming procedure performed?
5. *Emergency teams:* who are the members of the crisis management team, the operational teams and the emergency teams, who are leader, deputy and secretary, who is the press-spokesperson, etc.
6. *Emergency procedures (activity plans):* what has to be done to recover a location, a computing centre or business premises?
7. *Checklists:* any emergency plan in form of a checklist.
8. *Supplements:* company contact lists, glossary, inventory, and predefined messages.

### 2.1.2 BCP Documentation Needs to be Clear and Understandable

During recovery processes you cannot afford any discussions about the actions to be done; therefore the description of each action is clear and precise; it is formulated in a business-like manner.

The functions and roles of all team members are clearly defined and described. This enables anybody who has basic knowledge to act according to a specific instruction sheet in the emergency guidelines.

If you can generate checklists from your action plans, they will help those who know what to do to ensure that they don't forget anything.

If there is a glossary in your BCP documentation that describes your company-specific usage of all important terms, everybody will use the same terms.

Every plan is set up in such a way that it meets the requirements of the team performing it.

### 2.1.3 BCP Documentation Needs to Have a Good Layout in a Standard Format

To describe what a good layout is either takes many pages or is self-explanatory. But one thing should be mentioned: if there is a workflow representation available in a graphical style, it is regarded as an advantage.

But nevertheless: only if your BCP documentation meets the formal requirements of your company will it be accepted.

### 2.1.4 BCP Documentation Should Be Regarded as a Binding Agreement

The organisation of processes an emergency is different from normal. For example, the replacement of EDP equipment will be done by an emergency team and not by your central buying department. This fact needs to be agreed prior to the emergency to avoid trouble. This also applies to the alarming procedure and to the functions and responsibilities of the crisis management team.

Therefore the BCP documentation is a binding agreement for the whole company. Formally, this can be achieved with a signature of a CIO on a release document in the documentation.

### 2.1.5 BCP Documentation Should Always Provide the Latest Information

The documentation always images the current state of your production environment; the resources you need in the recovery process are also described in a way that corresponds to the current state. You have to decide how sophisticatedly you describe the environment (for further information see Section 6).

As already mentioned, you need all available information from every person involved in the recovery process, in the latest state – otherwise they will not help you. As an optimum there are the phone numbers of each persons office and home, any mobile numbers and, last but not least, the persons private addresses. Even pager numbers, private mail addresses or fax numbers will help.

### 2.1.6 Access to BCP documentation Should Be Obtainable at All Times and Wherever it is Needed

Make the storage of your BCP documentation (stored electronically and physically) safe and secure. Only authorised persons need access. In your BCP documentation there is a lot of information that no unauthorised person – or company – needs to know; it may even cause serious trouble if it falls into the possession of the wrong people.

But everybody involved should know the storage location of the BCP documentation. You may also regard it as necessary to give certain people a home-stored version of their manual. This way, they can start acting from home.

Finally, the BCP coordinator needs access to the electronic version of your documentation, as well as to the commonly accessible printed versions (e.g. at meeting points or in the crisis management meeting room).

## 2.2 Aspects of Tools

When you have finished reading this chapter you may want to buy a BCP documentation tool. In addition to the reasons mentioned above, you should then consider the following questions:

- Does the provider do anything else in the BCP business besides selling the tool? You may need some help from the provider to understand how the tool is intended to be used. Therefore the provider needs some knowledge of Business Continuity and Business Recovery.
- Can the software be run on an operating system that is in common use or does it have exotic software and hardware requirements?
- Does the tool support network use?
- Is it a multi-user piece of software?
- Can you give sophisticated access rights to any user of the tool?
- Does the tool enable you to keep several versions of different emergency manuals at the same time?

- Does the tool provide an English version besides the native language of the company that produces it?
- Is the tool distributed, sold and supported outside its home country?
- Is the product a currently maintained piece of software or has the provider released the last update quite some time ago?
- Does the tool have a reasonable purchase price to buy and an acceptable maintenance fee?
- Is there an adequate pricing model for stand-alone, network and enterprise-wide version?

# 3 Types of Manuals

As mentioned above, a company needs different types of manuals. Every manual contains at least one emergency plan. We divide them into the following:

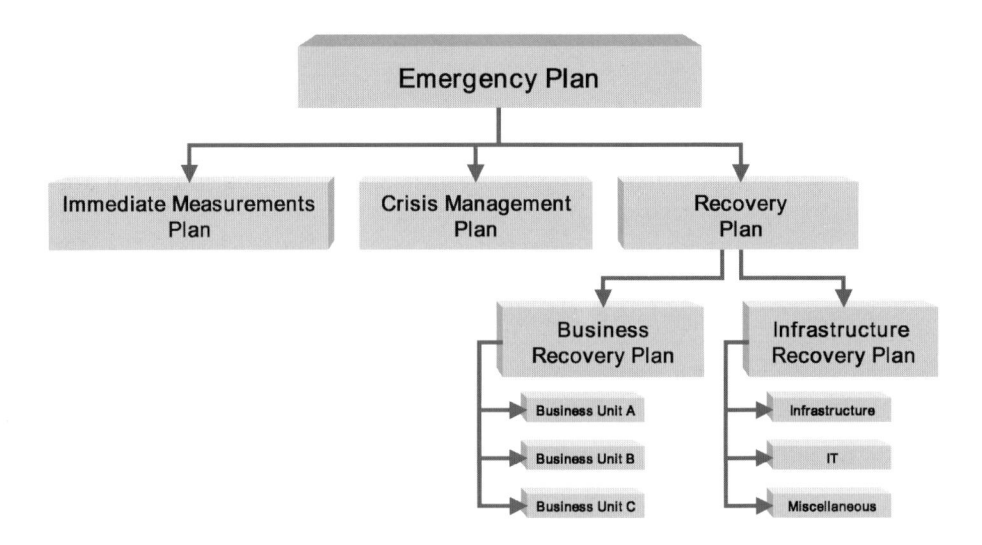

```
                          Emergency Plan
                                │
        ┌───────────────────────┼───────────────────────┐
        ▼                       ▼                       ▼
Immediate Measurements   Crisis Management         Recovery
       Plan                    Plan                  Plan
                                                      │
                                            ┌─────────┴─────────┐
                                            ▼                   ▼
                                        Business           Infrastructure
                                      Recovery Plan        Recovery Plan
                                            │                   │
                                      → Business Unit A    → Infrastructure
                                      → Business Unit B    → IT
                                      → Business Unit C    → Miscellaneous
```

- *Crisis Management Plan:* contains everything required to steer any recovery actions by a central coordination unit.
- *Immediate Measurements Plan:* contains all actions such as save and rescue which take place on the spot.
- *Recovery Plan.*
- *Business Recovery Plan:* contains all actions required to get one business unit to emergency business after a disaster.
- *Infrastructure Recovery Plans:* establish the back-up solution for premises, etc.

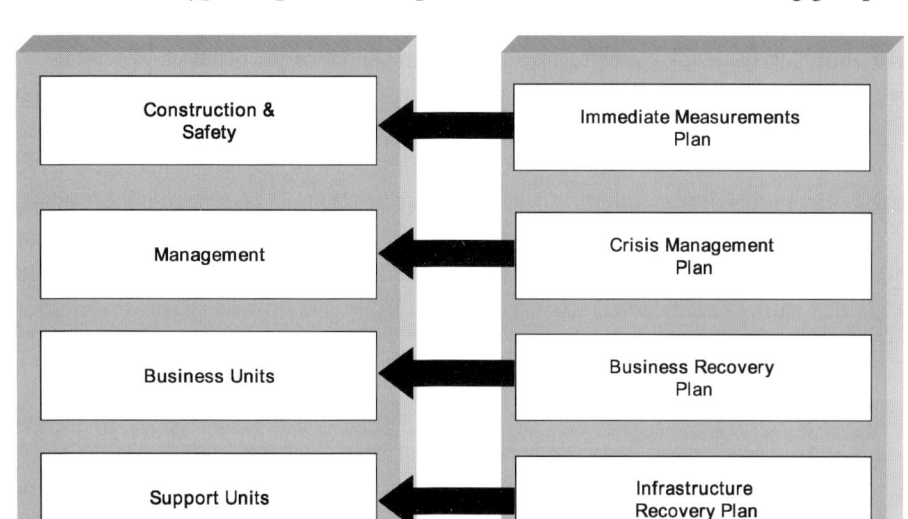

The various types of plans are of particular interest to the following groups:

*Construction & Safety* ← *Immediate Measurements Plan*

*Management* ← *Crisis Management Plan*

*Business Units* ← *Business Recovery Plan*

*Support Units* ← *Infrastructure Recovery Plan*

## 4  CAPT® (Continuity Action Planning Tool)

CAPT® is an MS-Access-based application and runs on Windows NT or 2000; it does not require a workstation with a special configuration.

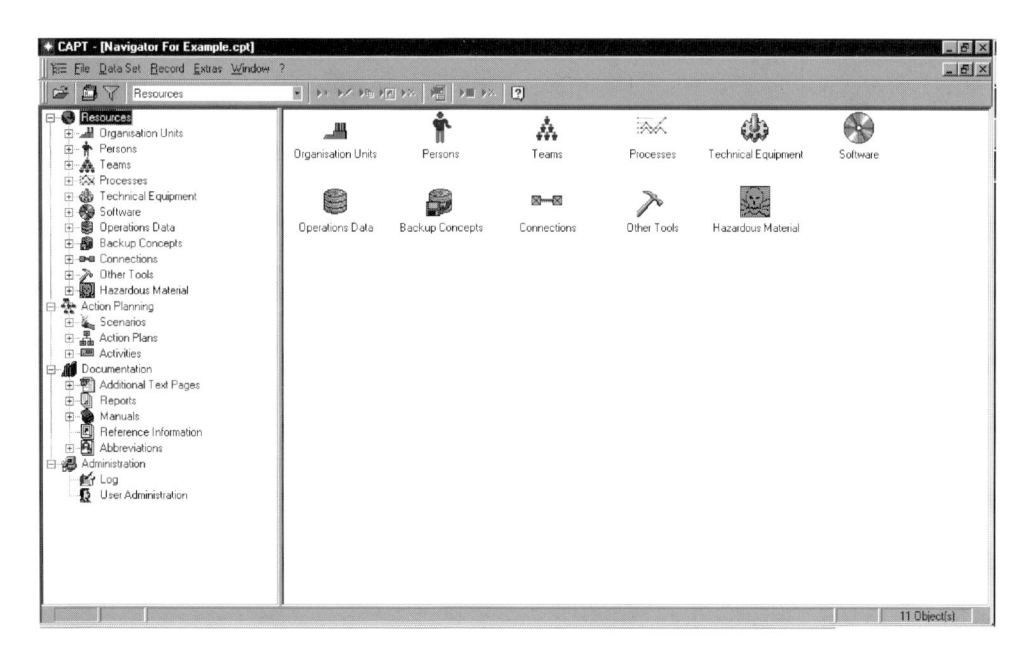

All data is stored with encryption using a specially designed algorithm. CAPT® requires MS-Word for editing, storing and printing manuals.

The data model has a lot of predefined links between several data sets. Hardware, software and infrastructure are linked to one another and to activities in action plans. In many data sets, it is possible to categorise.

Organisations, teams, business processes and activities in plans can be arranged hierarchically to an arbitrary depth.

Import and export are possible for the most important data sets.

The output is either an MS Word file or an HTML version readable with browsers such as Netscape or MS Internet Explorer. All internal links in the data are realised as HTML links. For instance, you click from a team to member to his/her address, etc.

The user interface is simple to use. In many views, user-defined sorting and filtering with conditions are possible.

Plans can have sub-plans and activities are grouped into plans. The representation of activities in plans is performed graphically, as shown in the picture below.

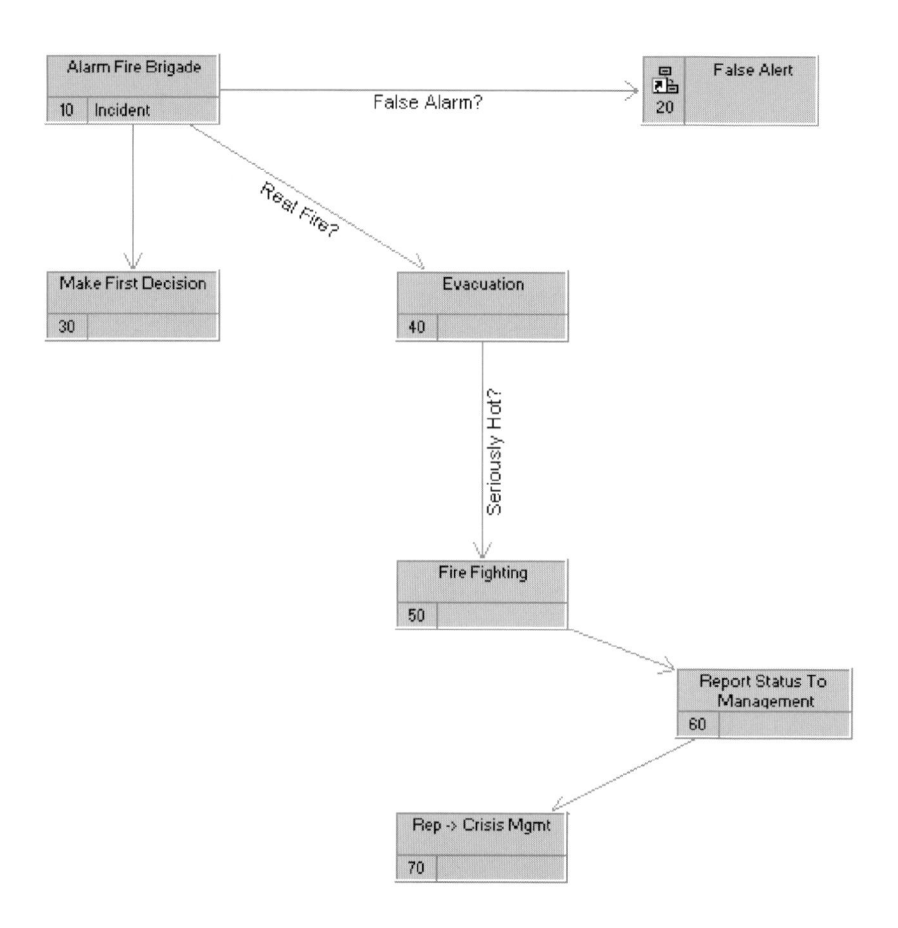

There is an extensive report generator for producing lists of any entries. For every report, the contents and layout are predefined and changeable by the user.

Access rights are simple to define for each individual user. Logging can be switched on or off for all important actions in the database.

CAPT® is an easy-to-use, mature tool which is recommended for any size of company or any of its units that has a Microsoft environment. It is produced and sold by Heine & Partner GmbH.

## 5 CM® (Continuity Manager)

CM® is a Lotus Notes based application and runs on Windows NT or 2000, it requires a workstation with Notes Version 5.x on the PC, but no other special configuration.

All relevant data is stored in one Notes database, the Notes encryption feature can be used.

Manuals are generated from this database into the *generated manuals database*, here no changes are possible, and manuals can be read or printed. A full-text search is possible in both databases. The generated manuals database can be configured, with access by an Internet browser.

Besides these two databases, there are databases for protocol and help functions. Furthermore, CM® has a concept where a global database allows a central view of the decentralised documentation, this is useful for companies where branches have, on the one hand, their own BCP solution and, on the other hand, connections to each other.

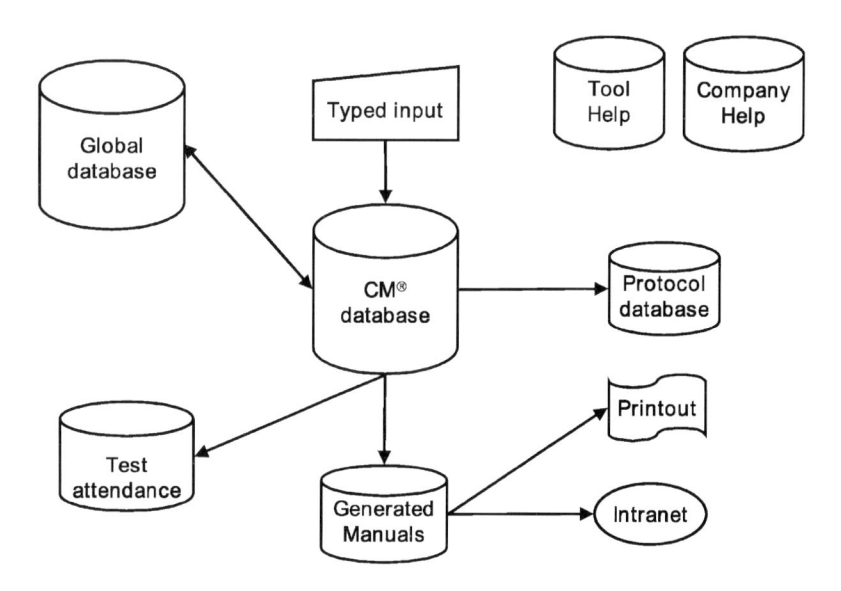

No additional editor is needed, Notes provides a wide range of layout features. Files of other types (MS Word, Excel, PowerPoint and Visio) can be embedded and stored in the NOTES database or linked and stored outside the Notes database. The content of the embedded or linked files can also be printed.

In CM®, the most important data sets are predefined. For extended usefulness you can arbitrarily define input forms for data and data connections as *free objects*. This feature is mostly used to define an inventory to the depth that is needed. As an example, we have defined desks for workplace recovery, with extensive descriptions of the equipment required. A further usage was to store the results of a business impact analysis.

Activity planning is grouped into a four-level hierarchy. If the duration of the activities is maintained, the critical path of the activities is calculated. For a graphical representation of activities, an export to MS Project is possible.

Access rights are granted via user groups of Notes. In addition these access rights can be specified down to record level.

To co-ordinate simultaneous maintenance, it is possible to check out and in documents. While being altered by one person the document cannot be changed by anybody else.

The quality state of a document can be marked as being one of six levels: in development, for release, for correction, read, released, or generated.

In CM®, every document has an ID (a structured sequence of ten digits and letters). Some like it – others don't. You can ignore the ID if you wish. You can use it for pre-structuring if you want to.

CM® is a good tool for large companies and uses Lotus Notes as a well-known basis for its applications. It is produced and sold by Heine & Partner GmbH.

## 6 Do's and Don'ts

With a tool, you always can do many things, even things the tool was not designed for. BCP documentation tools are specialised, and thus we recommend the following split:

Do:
- *Contingency Plans.* These tools were programmed for producing recovery guides or recovery plans.
- *Alarming procedures.* There is no recovery without an alarming procedure being performed. BCP documentation tool are designed to keep the data and information about such procedures.
- *Immediate measurements.* Usually you have your immediate measurements recorded in flat files. After you have decided to use a BCP documentation tool, you should integrate them there.
- *IT-Processes.* The processes in a computing centre look much like recovery procedures and use the same inventory. Therefore it is possible to put down the documentation of the work in your computing centre in a BCP documentation tool.

Don't:
- *Inventory management.* Although you need a lot of inventory information in a BCP, the documentation tool should not be the leading system. There is only one exception: if your company is small and you don't have your inventory listed somewhere else then you can use it, because it is the first time ever that you have recorded this information. But for your HR data, you usually have a personal administration system, this is the leading system and feeds your BCP data set.
- *Project planning.* Don't use a BCP documentation tool for project planning. For this task, there are other tools (better ones).
- *Don't think that you buy a tool and the work is done.*
  It needs an effort to introduce any tool to your company. It needs even more effort to keep plans maintained. A tool doesn't help at all if you don't have any BCP solution. It doesn't do the planning for you, but it helps you to stay on track.

- *Use a book of samples.* There is no template for all emergency manuals for your company; they are all different for every company, and only the structures for the various types of manuals may look alike.
- *Connection to technical software.* There is no general connection or compatibility with safety engineering department software or security force software. Don't get the recovery started by an automatic alarming procedure, there must always be a clear decision by the crisis management team before you start your recovery.

# Creating the Complete Environment for the Survival of a Bank

ULRICH VELDENZ, FRANZ-JOSEF WEIL
*Banking Services Luxembourg S.A*

**Abstract:** In Luxembourg, a cooperation of banks founded a company to share the costs and benefits of a disaster recovery center. The business model based on the recovery requirements of financial institutions, and the organizational and technical architectures implemented are described. The necessary documentation of business continuity plans is described by means of an example.

**Keywords:** Alert, BCP business model, Breakdown scenarios, Business continuity plan, Business impact analysis, Business recovery plan, Disaster management, Disaster recovery manual, Disaster scenario, Emergency plan, Emergency planning tools, Emergency teams, IT logistic team, Network computer concept, Period of tolerance, Recovery capacity, Recovery management team, Recovery organization, Recovery plan, Recovery strategy, Recovery teams, Recovery tests, Recovery time, Restart plan, Restart procedures, Restart strategy, Risk evaluation study, Risk scenarios, Structure of a DRM, Technical team, Workplace recovery site

## 1 The Business Recovery Business Alliance

### 1.1 The BCP Business Model

Every bank must keep its essential functions operational at all times, even in a *disaster* (Instructions of CSSF[1], MAH, Basel II).

In the case of an interruption of business operation due to an external or internal incident, the business operation of a bank needs to be recovered as soon as possible. This can be guaranteed – without a major impact for the customer – by including all bank activities in a *business continuity plan (BCP)* (abbreviations used in this chapter are defined in Section 5) so that the bank is able to immediately recover business operation after any interruption. This requires the implementation of backup infrastructure and the definition of recovery processes. Setting up the entire technical installation for a bank frequently means purchasing or renting a new building as well as IT investments. Using an operating company means that the costs of business recovery can be reduced, but if this is done the confidentiality of bank data should be carefully analyzed.

---

[1] The Luxembourg bank supervisory body.

Several banks in Luxembourg have now equipped themselves with a complete emergency plan, the necessary premises and a backup data-processing infrastructure. This is provided by Banking Services Luxembourg S.A (BSL), working together with other Luxembourg banks. In comparison with other providers of *workplace recovery sites*, BSL differentiates itself by the following two particularities:

- BSL does not offer the basic IT backup for the computer center of a bank. The assumption behind this is that most of the banks in the Luxembourg banking center already have IT backup facilities located in a different building which they use regularly outside emergencies for system tests, software upgrades or load balancing. Owing to the strict banking secrecy in Luxembourg, an IT backup operation by outside staff is hardly possible.
- BSL offers a workplace recovery site developed in a bank in Luxembourg to other banks. BSL was created as an preventive measure by two banks; by including further banks and using the workplace recovery site, these two banks managed to reduce the high costs of such measures. The priority is cost sharing rather than maximizing profit.

The reliable operation of the recovery center and recovery management are the main responsibilities of BSL. A restart after a disaster can only function perfectly if emergency processes for the bank are clearly established and are written down in an emergency manual. Thus, as a rule, the following steps precede contract conclusion with the recovery provider:

- Setting up the business impact analysis and restart strategy.
- Setting up the business recovery plan and disaster recovery handbook.

## 1.2 The Recovery Site

As a result of its *Network Computer* concept, BSL is able to guarantee a restart of business operation within one hour. In order for a bank to be able to comply with its obligations towards its customers, BSL has taken the following measures:

- *Operation in parallel.* First, the available office space has been subdivided in such a way as to allow two banks to use the BSL facilities simultaneously and independently from one another. This, basically, is equivalent to the creation of two workplace recovery sites.
- *Site location analysis.* Second, the Luxembourg banking region was divided into a grid of 100 m squares. BSL accepts a maximum of one customer per square. This prevents congestion.

- *Limitation of the number of participating banks.* Third, BSL has limited its customer base to six banks. Such a limitation offers the highest safety to users, as even in the case of a major catastrophe, the customers can count on using the DRS.

The site location analysis, together with the limitation of the number of participating banks, gives the customer more safety in the case of a disaster. The chance of finding the workplace recovery site usable is higher.

### 1.2.1 The Office Space Backup Server Infrastructure

In addition to the server room and the technical infrastructure services (see section 2.1), BSL offers emergency office space.

The Recovery Site comprises:

- 24 NC-based workplaces with telephones seven of which have two telephone devices
- all workplaces and server connections have UPS
- two Reuters terminals[2]
- one Bloomberg terminal
- photocopy machine, fax machine and shredder
- standard office supplies
- reception with HICOM switchboard
- fully equipped kitchenette
- two sanitary rooms.

### 1.2.2 Server room

This room has:

- limited access
- a closed shop[3]
- a UPS connected, which is supervised and is accessible at any time to authorized persons of the bank
- fire protection, inclusive of immediate power shutdown in case of fire
- Aragonite fire-extinguishing system.

---

[2] The information from the terminals and the Bloomberg terminal will be available on the *NC*. We expect however that a bank using such services will have the relevant gateways and servers even in an emergency.

[3] Access to the server room is restricted to a small number of specialists

### 1.2.3 Telecommunication Connection

This is a 2 Mbit ISDN primary connection or standing line connection in accordance with what the customer has installed.

# 2 Recovery Requirements for Financial Institutions (Banks)

## 2.1 Situation of Banks in Luxembourg

All relevant business processes in a bank are dependent on the operation of front- and back-office systems, as well as that of external communication lines if a central host application is located in the headquarters. If one or several of these systems break down, it is in principle possible to continue business operation for a limited period of time without data-processing support. Frequently, however, there are no instructions or work procedures to ensure continuity of business operation when data-processing equipment is not available. Furthermore, hardly any bank employee is still able to settle transactions without data-processing support.

Despite all safety measures taken in the IT center of a bank, the possibility of a total breakdown of the entire electronic data-processing system should not be excluded. Such a breakdown could cause the interruption of processing at several points and thus shut down bank operation. Table 1 summarizes the typical risk scenarios which should be discussed at the beginning of a *risk evaluation study* for a bank.

Table 1: General risk factors (examples)

| Risk | Reason for inclusion in emergency planning |
| --- | --- |
| • Catastrophe (e.g. flooding, major fire, storm, failure of power supply over a large area) | The Grand Duchy of Luxembourg is significantly smaller than the surrounding countries and, in a natural catastrophe, will suffer greater damage, as the entire country will be affected. |
| • Lightning | Lightning has already hit buildings used by banks. |
| • Risk from the sky | The city of Luxembourg is located in the approach corridor of Luxembourg airport and thus regular air traffic has to be considered. |
| • Risks on the ground (for instance vehicles) | All buildings of the banks in Luxembourg are located beside roads carrying heavy traffic, without restrictions on trucks and goods vehicles. |
| • Industrial hazards (gas, chemicals, etc.) | Owing to the presence of industrial sites in the region, a negative impact on a bank from an industrial hazard cannot be excluded. |

## 2.2 Specific Risks in the Grand Duchy of Luxembourg

This section contains a summary of the risks related to the geographical, political and economic framework of Luxembourg. We describe here the economic area of Luxembourg, with its specific characteristics.

The Luxembourg international financial center hosts more than 200 banks, with premises mainly located in the city of Luxembourg. The premises of at least eight other important banks can be found in the immediate neighborhood of one BSL partner bank. In the case of a major incident in the city, it is very likely that more than one bank would be confronted with the consequences thereof. The high density of banks in the area under review, furthermore, leads us to conclude that minor incidents could also have an impact on more than one institution.

Most of the banks and financial service providers use external services to support the core business (for instance IT, safety services and financial information services). As an interruption of such secondary services would have an impact on the operation of the relevant bank, agreements have been set up which determine reaction and problem-solving times in various cases. Further, a high demand for such contractual services can be expected if several banks have to deal with a business interruption, at the same time.

Given the density of banks already described and the known cooperation between banks in the Luxembourg market, there is a danger that secondary-service providers and appliance providers might not be able to satisfy simultaneous requests for service or delivery. In an emergency, therefore, the agreements described above may not necessarily be put into practise. It is even imaginable that appliances such as PCs or mobile telephones will no longer be easily available.

Table 2 shows typical local risk factors.

Table 2: Specific risks of the Luxembourg banking center

| Risk | Reason for inclusion in BCP |
|---|---|
| • Supply (electricity, gas, water, etc.) | Overall risk, as supply pipes are located close to the building. |
| • Fire | Overall risk, as flammable materials are stored in a bank. |
| • Weaknesses in PC safety (hacking) | High amount of confidential data in the IT systems of a bank. |
| • Robbery | A bank keeps important tangible assets in ints buildings. |
| • Vandalism | The buildings of a bank are accessible to the public and thus are liable to vandalism in areas with public access. |
| • Spying | Confidential information within a bank. |
| • Terrorism | Even if it is difficult to foresee this threat, a fundamental risk exists for all organizations. |

Table 2: Continued

| Risk | Reason for inclusion in BCP |
|---|---|
| • IT | Banks are highly dependent on the availability of IT. IT is a necessary condition for business continuity of a bank. The IT environment is complex and thus needs special attention. |
| • Trustworthiness and public image | The primary customer base of a bank is in the private banking domain. For the individual customer, trusting a bank is paramount. Any loss of trustworthiness could lead to important customers leaving a bank and thus have a negative impact on the bank's results. |

## 2.3 Availability Goals

The priorities for restoring business processes (Table 2) can be derived from a process of data collection, to be carried out in the various departments of a bank. Assessment of the maximum tolerable interruption times is frequently based on statements by managers and employees, taking special account of possible financial damage and consequences.

Table 3: Priorities for restoring business processes (example)

| Priority | Time frame | Business process |
|---|---|---|
| 1 | < 1 hour | • Trading<br>• Private banking<br>• Cash counter<br>• Secretariat & reception |
| 2 | 1–6 hours | • Securities transactions<br>• Private banking department<br>• MM/FX settlement<br>• Mailbox |
| 3 | 6 hours to 4 business days | • Securities management<br>• Risk control<br>• Accounting<br>• Credit business<br>• Account administration |
| 4 | > 4 business days | • Audit department<br>• Legal<br>• Human resources<br>• Steering/organization<br>• Internal operation |

## 3 The Architecture of a Standby Work Area

In 1999, when WestLB International S.A. planned its standby work area, it was obvious that a business recovery time of one hour was a big challenge for the project team. The recovery window of the most important business processes required a powerful new technology to keep the downtime as short as possible. In the case of a disaster the bank would not work with a PC environment but would switch from the PC to a system based on an NC, Windows NT terminal server and Citrix Metaframe.

Even at planning stage, the main consideration was to find a solution which not only would fit WestLB's needs in a disaster but also could be rapidly adapted for other financial service providers. The requirement study stated that the infrastructure to be implemented should be flexibly adaptable to the needs of different financial service providers. In addition to hardware and software installations, the concept was also required to comprise all necessary *restart procedures*. The most essential part of the specification study was, however, the requirement for a short *recovery time*. Seven workplaces should be recovered within one hour and an additional 15 workplaces after four hours.

### 3.1 Technical Concepts

The technical concept is based on a flexible infrastructure, based on a network of NCs used as clients and a server, running the Windows NT[4] terminal server operating system and Citrix Metaframe. By using a Windows NT terminal server together with Citrix Metaframe, time-consuming installations after the declaration of a disaster were made unnecessary. The terminal server concept provides an out-of-the-box solution for the *recovery*. The *restart* is very fast, as the server boots within 15 minutes and the 22 workstations need only two minutes.

The terminal server solution offers an optimal platform for the administration of the entire infrastructure and user support from a central station. New installations, updates and changes need to be made only once, on the terminal server system. The terminal server supports all applications on each client and is thus the ideal platform for workplace recovery sites serving customers with different requirements.

The ICA[5] protocol is optimized for connections with low bandwidth. The "persistent object caching" function reduces transmission traffic. Memory management is optimized for multiple users. Data and applications are located on the terminal server system. There is no download to the clients. All users access the same centrally stored

---

[4] Trademark of Microsoft.
[5] Citrix Metaframe protocol for communication between an NC and an application server.

data. Data traffic between the server and clients is encrypted to comply with the increased safety requirements of financial service providers. The terminal server supports Windows NT safety parameters completely.

## 3.2 Telecommunications

The opening of a connection to a customer, as shown in Figure 1, is, for security reasons, always initiated by the customer. This allows the system to guarantee the highest possible safety with regard to the IT center of the customer. The customer starts the connection between its (backup) IT center and the workplace recovery site, after starting the server in the standby work area in the appropriate configuration. The transmission speed between the customer and the recovery site is 2 Mb/s on a PRI ISDN dial-up line. This generates low connection costs. Safety of transmission was another important element to be implemented. There is a PAP/CHAP handshake at the time the connection is opened. The data transmission is secured by a triple DES. Additional encryptors operate between the routers.

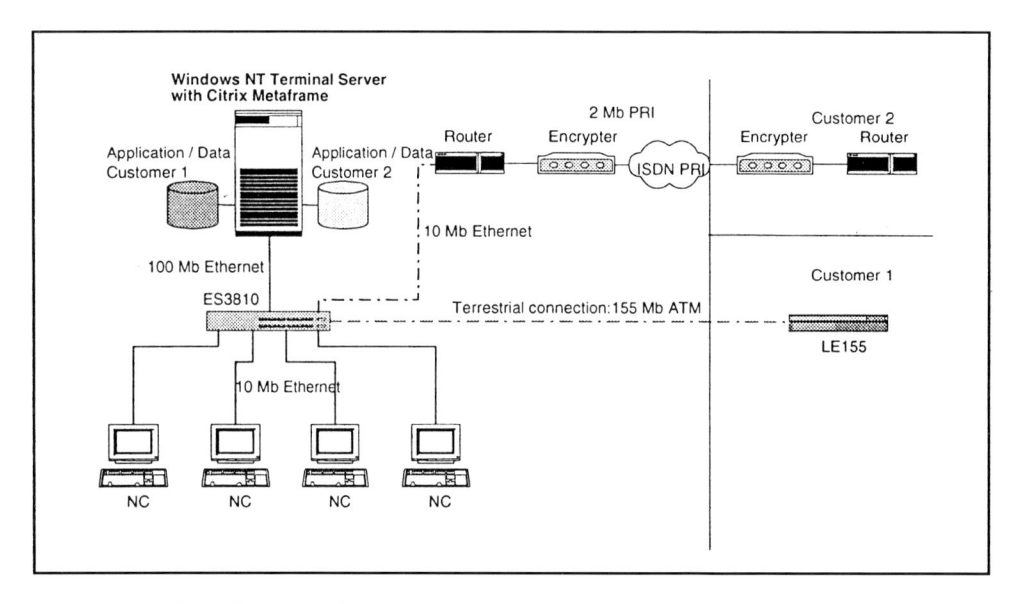

Figure 1: Overview of systemarchitecture

### 3.3 Recovery Procedure

The most important condition for recovery is to implement a business continuity plan. Only such a project will provide the *pre-positional resource* required in the workplace recovery site. This is the basis for a *recovery plan*.

If the recovery plan is available, the corresponding measures for the installation of the important applications on the terminal server system have to be taken. The terminal server system acts as an application server and is configured to connect the logon and data servers in the IT backup site of the customer.

If the applications are adequately installed and tested, only minor work is necessary in a disaster. The customer informs the operations manager of its *declaration of disaster* according to the alert agreement.

The operations manager will immediately prepare the workplace recovery site to be used by the customer, by charging security personnel to open and guard the entrance door and making NT and network specialists available for the support of the customer on site.

In parallel to this, the customer informs its telecom provider that its telephone numbers should be switched to the telephone number of the workplace recovery site and gets the disks for the terminal server from their storage location. At the recovery site, the customer inserts its disks into the terminal server system and boots the system. After this is done, the workstations available can be started.

Generally, it docs not take more than one hour from reception of the alarm to booting the terminal server system and connecting the NC clients. The telecom providers in Luxembourg also guarantee telephone transfer implementation times of one hour at maximum. Thus, it is possible to make the business operational again one hour after the declaration of a disaster.

## 4 The Disaster Recovery Manual

An example of a DRM is described in this section. In addition to organizational and technical measures, and documentation of the *business continuity plan*, the d*isaster recovery manual*, is the third but not the least important part of business continuity.

First, the DRM is a *service-level agreement* for the services to be provided and, second, it is a checklist for *mobilization*. All organizational and technical changes in the production environment have to be immediately described in the DRM with respect to their impact on business continuity. Only an up-to-date DRM may be used as a guidance for restoring business operation in a disaster. Use of the DRM guarantees that all activities and measures are carried out in the right order, at the right time, by the right team or the right person and with the right resources.

We recommend the use of a database tool for the DRM documentation. The emergency planning tools available on the market support a process-oriented representation of restoration. Furthermore, such tools allow one to produce various types of manual for various groups of recipients. As each recipient receives only relevant information, the motivation to read the DRM will be significantly increased. This will necessarily lead to a better knowledge of the information. The structure of a DRM generated with the ICM[6] tool will be described below.

A manual generated in this way comprises the following chapters:

- Organizational Framework
- Strategies
- Activity Plans
- Team Composition
- Appendixes.

## 4.1 Organizational Framework

### 4.1.1 Structure of the Manual

The first chapter of the DRM describes the structure and maintenance of the manual, the alarm plans, the recovery organization charts, the alarm procedure, the team structure and the documentation needed to carry out a recovery exercise.

The ICM approach is based on a three-layer structure:

- First layer: plans, each comprising at least one block.
- Second layer: blocks, each comprising at least one activity.
- Third layer: activities, which are the lowest level of continuity planning.

Every team is linked to a *restart plan*. The actions of a team are described in at least one block. The activities describe the individual actions of managers and teams. A further subject of the chapter is the description of the database structure of ICM. In addition, the introduction provides a description of the *period of tolerance*. In the alarm plan, the requirement for a *declaration of disaster* is stated. This is absolutely necessary, as the hectic activity generated by minor production interruptions should not lead to disaster measures.

---

[6] Supplied by: Info AG, Hamburg, Germany.

### 4.1.2 Disaster Organization

A further part of this chapter is the description of *breakdown scenarios*. In this context, major catastrophes that are not considered to be disasters even if the operation of the company may be interrupted should also be covered; an example might be an incident at a nuclear power plant. Owing to the spatial extent of the disaster in such a case, it should be assumed that both the production site and the workplace recovery site would be equally hit. In this case nobody is going to proceed to apply disaster measures; instead, everybody should try to get to a safe place if possible.

In addition to the disaster scenario, there are disaster situations which require immediate action before the alarm is given and the disaster organization is established. Such scenarios should be listed in this part of the manual together with a description of the particular measures.

A very important part of the introduction describes the status that business continuity planning has in the company. The most important statements should read:

- *Emergency planning* has to be "lived".
- *Emergency plans* have to be "livable".
- Emergency plans have to be, as far as appropriate and required, linked to one another.

The following principles must always be complied with, in this order of priority:

- Protect persons before protecting objects.
- Limit the extent of the disaster and fight causes.
- Guarantee the primary vital business processes.
- Avoid losses before avoiding income interruptions.
- Manage consequences (press, customers, counterparties, supervisory body, etc.).
- *As a general rule: Short decision lines, clear established competencies.*

To avoid any time-consuming discussions as to responsibilities in the case of a disaster and the consequences thereof, another part of the introduction describes, as shown in Figure 2, the recovery organization chart. It shows the organizational structure applicable in the case of a disaster. The organization is adapted to the needs of the situation and is thus very lean. It also differs from the standard organization chart from the point of view of personnel. There are only four bodies here; the business continuity coordinator(s) and the emergency management team together form the disaster management team and the IT logistic and technical team.

## Recovery organization chart

### Disaster management team

**Emergency management team**

Responsibility for:
* declaration of disaster and start of restoration
* survival of the enterprise
* image of the enterprise

Main tasks:
* definition of the actual tasks of the crisis management team
* Public relations

**Business continuity coordinator(s)**

Responsibility for:
* overall responsibility for coordination of the recovery process

Main tasks:
* advise and support the emergency management team
* manage the IT logistic team and the technical team
* control the results of ongoing restoration process

**IT logistic team**

Main tasks:
* implementation of the infrastructure
* help desk and hotline
* support the technical team recording the damages

**Technical team**

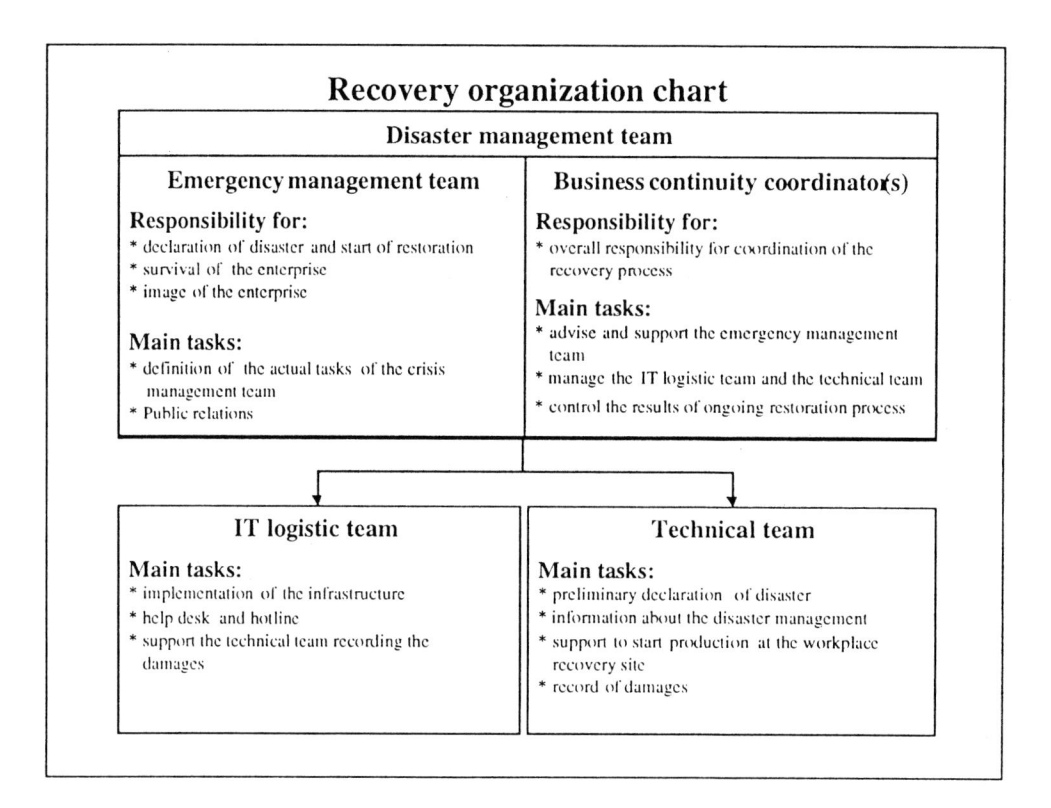

Main tasks:
* preliminary declaration of disaster
* information about the disaster management
* support to start production at the workplace recovery site
* record of damages

Figure 2: Recovery organization chart

The organization chart describes the responsibilities and tasks that the various persons have in an emergency.

The alarm plan (see Figure 3) describes the various types of alerts, for example fire, robbery, flooding or disaster, and the alarm chains to the fire brigade, the police and the security company.

A further subject is the subsequent handling of an alert after it has been recorded by the security company up to the assessment of a disaster in the sense of the emergency management plan and the subsequent informing of the relevant recovery teams.

### 4.1.3 Testing

Another main item of business continuity planning is testing. All components which are part of the Business recovery have to be tested in order to guarantee their functionality at least once a year. For this purpose, an annual plan for recovery exercises should be established with the relevant teams.

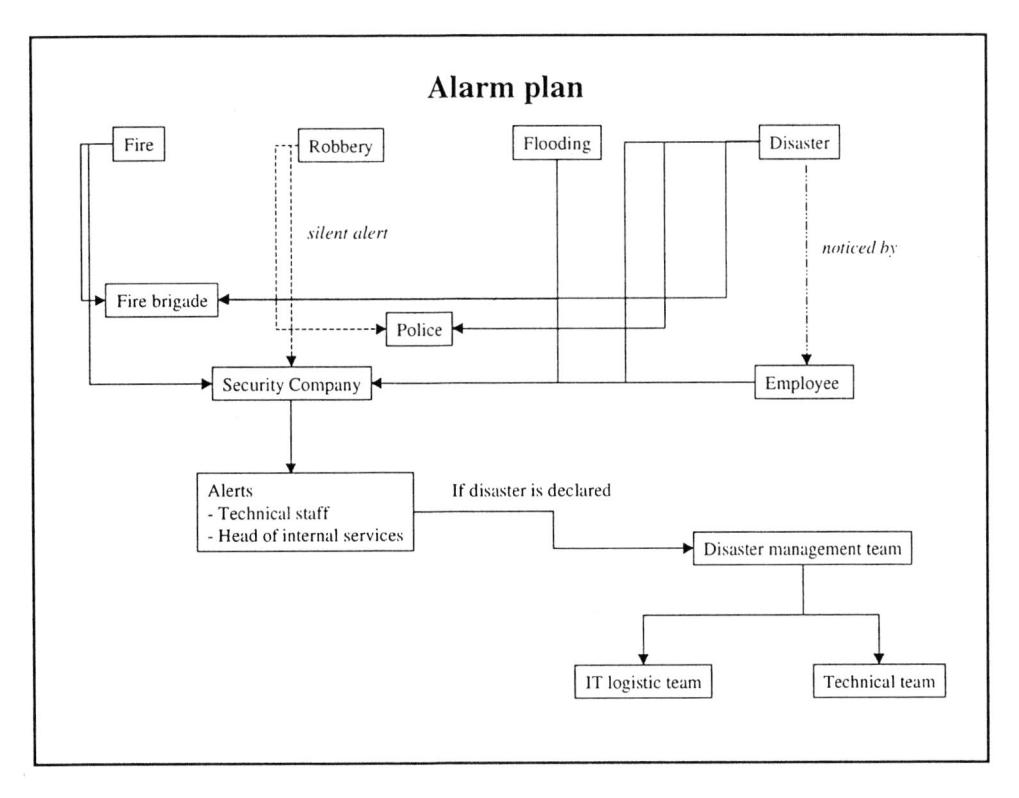

Figure 3: Alarm plan

Preparation of recovery tests should start very early. It is useful to fix the dates of the tests for a given year at the end of the previous year or, at the latest, at the beginning of the test year. Building on this framework, the content of the tests can be discussed in general terms with all participants and users.

The various possible ways of structuring recovery tests can be classified. We have defined four classes of recovery tests, which individually produce meaningful results and together whole cover all requirements. These tests are:

- basic tests
- functional tests
- application tests
- overall tests.

Even though the test classes reflect different statuses of the tests with respect to the ability to achieve recovery, it is our experience that each test has its own -entitlement to exist and that all test forms should be used again and again. The mixture of large and small tests is decisive. In the case of substantial changes in procedures, this mixture is of particular importance and special tests could be necessary.

Tests of the alarm procedure can be carried out within the framework of the application and overall tests or independently of the recovery tests.

The class of basic tests is the lowest level of the test classes. Tests of this class are a precondition for all other tests. A basic test will cover the fundamental functions of one or several production systems. Later on, that basic test will form part of other tests. When preparing a basic test, one should check that all documents that have been stored for the system team are available. The normal procedure after a disaster as described in the DRM should be followed. This procedure can be interrupted rather quickly, as the aim is only to cover a small part of the recovery capacity. Only few persons are necessary to carry out a basic test. There is no alarm, and thus alarm procedures are not tested. The test is previously agreed on with the participants. After any change in our NC /terminal server –environment, we run a basic test in the workplace recovery environment.

Functional tests guarantees that all systems are available and operational on site. Functional tests should always be carried out when individual components of the configuration have undergone major changes. A functional test comprises all components of a basic test and, in addition, a check of the functional capacity of the system. Spot checks on applications allow one to verify the access protection measures, as well as the existence and coexistence of the data which are accessed. It is assumed, for a functional test, that all lines required in an emergency will be available. All backup lines can be checked independently from recovery tests; for instance, one can test their ability to transfer the individual data streams of the kind that generally occur in the case of a line breakdown. Functional tests are carried out mostly without the intervention of outside IT staff. After successful completion of the functional tests, the probability is high that the applications are functioning as they should. Only after completion of these tests should the departments be involved in further measures. We run a functional test after each installation of a patch or of new software. Thanks to the NC /terminal server concept, the expenditure is less than it would otherwise have been.

Application tests should be the class that is most frequently used. These tests show the recovery capacity of individually selected applications but, generally, also provide insight into the other domains. An application test will contain all components of a functional test and thus also of a basic test. This covers not only the formal possibility of working with the application under test but also the adequacy of the results. For this reason, participation of the relevant departments is absolutely necessary. Application tests require the same preparation as functional tests. In addition, precise dates should be fixed for the tests with the users and, especially, the times of test runs should be agreed with the departments. The activities necessary for building the environment are the same as for the functional tests; all of these activities should, of course, be carried out strictly in accordance with the DRM. The procedures should, however, be run completely at least once beforehand.

Overall tests are the highest level of tests. These tests cover all components of business recovery and are therefore rather extensive. The factor most important to the organization, however, is the risk linked to overall tests and their impact. The aim of an overall test is to assess absolute recovery capacity. This assessment is, of course, valid only at one specific moment and must be questioned continuously as changes are made to the system. The basis of an overall test is the recovery capacity of all applications. All participants have to work together. Planning has to be done months before with the relevant users and must cover:

- the expected workload on test days, taking into account work at the end of the month or end of the year and holiday periods
- the support that users will receive in the case of problems, together with problem management during the test
- key points where accuracy must be checked, as it is impossible to reproduce the entire operation (this is covered by application tests)
- the procedure for checking the results.

It is our experience that an overall test should be carried out only after all other test classes have been completed. All applications should have been tested at least once before in the application tests. If significant problems have been experienced in previous tests, no overall test should be carried out. Users, where their participation is not simulated, should work as in normal business operation. Together with management and the test teams, they should comply strictly with the procedures in the DRM.

Preparation of a test includes preliminary discussions, which are written down as minutes. These minutes show which preparation tasks should be carried out by whom, together with the relevant deadlines. The progress of the tests is documented by the business continuity coordinator in charge, on the basis of a checklist. Minutes should be taken regarding the tests. It is important to evaluate the recovery capacity in these minutes. Experience has shown that it makes sense to carry out this evaluation on the basis of a previously agreed scheme.

## 4.2 Strategies

This chapter of the DRM describes the disaster scenarios, the decision point, the tolerance threshold and the recovery strategy. Further, it describes the extent and requirements of continuity planning, as well as the strategies for handling emergencies. The extent of the continuity planning and the corresponding preventive measures are determined by the range of disaster scenarios which have to be taken into account; the requirements of recovery planning should be given in the form of restart objectives. Handling a disaster presupposes that within the framework of a recovery strategy, the availability of the broken-down components of the IT infrastructure has been determined. The personal responsibilities of those carrying out restorations plans in the form of emergency teams are set out. For every system, a backup strategy (hot, warm or manual) and the process for restoring system availability should be described. The availability objective should be described for each business domain. This description also covers the definition of tolerable interruption time, loss time and the number of persons necessary for continuity operation.

## 4.3 Activity Plans

At the center of gravity of the activity plans are the *recovery* plans and activities, checklists and documentation for handling an *emergency*, and a detailed description of *restoration*.

The first of the activity plans describes the creation of a disaster management and the associated teams. In addition to detailed planning, the DRM includes a presentation of the processes in the form of checklists. The first plan mainly serves as a decision support for the disaster management, whereas the checklists are tools to be used by the teams in the case of a disaster. The following four plans have to be complied with:

- Creation of disaster management and teams.
- Production responsibility to be taken by disaster management.
- Restoration of production in the backup center and the workplace recovery site.
- Restoration of production in the production environment after the disaster is resolved.

Every plan is described, together with its blocks (see section 4.1.2). Every block is subdivided into activities, which are the smallest units. Activities and their relation to one another are described, as well as the corresponding responsibilities and the duration of these activities.

## 4.4 Team Composition

This chapter of the DRM is dedicated to the disaster management team, the IT logistic team, the technical team and the organizational units. A list provides the names and addresses of the persons involved, as well as their office and private fax, mobile-telephone and fixed-telephone numbers.

## 4.5 Appendixes

The appendixes of the DRM comprise the addresses of all providers, administrations, doctors and other institutions that need to be contacted in an emergency. In addition to these addresses, the appendixes contain prepared press releases and damage reports for insurance companies. These letters are readily drafted and need only to be completed with the relevant date and signature.

# 5 Abbreviations

The following table lists the abbreviations used in this chapter.

| Abbreviation | Full form |
|---|---|
| BCP | Business continuity plan |
| BSL | Banking Services Luxembourg S.A. |
| CHAP | Challenge handshake authentication protocol |
| DES | Data encryption system |
| DRM | Disaster recovery manual |
| DRS | Disaster recovery site |
| FX | Foreign exchange |
| HICOM | High Communication (Computerized automatic branch exchange (Siemens)) |
| ICA | Independent Computing Architecture (Citrix) |
| ICM | Integrated Continuity Manager |
| IT | Information technology |
| MAH | Minimalanforderungen für die Abwicklung von Handelsgesellschaften (Minimum requirement for treasury) |
| MM | Money market |
| NC | Network computer |
| NT | New Technology (Operating system manufactured by Microsoft) |
| PAP | Password authentication protocol |
| PC | Personal computer |
| PRI ISDN | Primary integrated services data network |
| S.A. | Société anonyme (joint stock company) |
| UPS | Uninterruptible power supply |
| WestLB | WestLB International S.A., Luxembourg |

# Robustness Provided by Internet Monitoring Systems

Barry Dellar
*SIM Group Limited*

**Abstract:** Internet applications such as Wealth Management Banking Programs require a very high degree of robustness. To attain this continuous testing – that is monitoring the systems over a period of time – is suggested. The preparation of an appropriate site-monitoring process during application development and for use during operation is described.

Transition states are used to link program operation to business workflow. They are associated with releases, especially to save the workload on the "continuous monitoring suite" in an incremental way for reuse of tested test assets.

The "generic" requirements of an Internet offering are considered from a testing viewpoint. They can always be met by the continuous testing/monitoring of the application in the development, soft launch and live environments.

**Keywords:** Internet, Monitoring ystems, Robustness, Continuous testing, Test environment, Site monitoring, Transitional state, Internet offering, Testing recommendation, Soft launch, Requirements

## 1 The Monitoring Suite

One of the great fears of an Operational Project Manager in the run-up to the live operational date of any Internet-related offering is "will this application be robust enough for my customers – or will we be flooded with calls of dissatisfaction on day one?" This is a fair question to ask of a Test Manager or Test Project Manager – from a genuinely worried person – as the Operational Project Manager is under extreme pressures in what is a genuine race to meet the market demands upon Internet offerings such as Wealth Management Banking Programs today.

Historically, general wealth management has meant either exclusive private banking for ultra-high-net-worth individuals or retail relationship banking for those with more complex needs than the average high street customer. These worlds are rapidly converging, with both the retail and the private banking sectors discovering that their customers are demanding a different approach to the management of their wealth. This is leading to a succession of new offers being launched into the market place.

All of these developments are finely tuned into development programs – incremental application builds requiring specific test approaches – and none more so than continuous testing to provide operational robustness.

So – how does the Test Manager ease his/her fears, mitigate the risks and add confidence to the operational teams' expectations *prior* to the live date and *during* the live period?

There is no doubt that the 10_000 or so functional and technical tests that have to be run against the software time and time again now have next to zero failure rates. But that s*till* is not enough to completely satisfy the committed professional Business Managers – or the operational stakeholders!

The answer to this of course is *continuous testing* – or attaining the required application robustness by monitoring the systems over a period of time. Large coverage of compatibility tests – all hardware and software combinations within the marketplace can support this.

Test automation and market research obviously play a big part in this solution – the most key and integral business events are automated as test scripts and looped together in one test suite.

This suite can then be used and developed alongside the live development path as shown below.

The Central Test Environment, or *main* test environment would be the starting point for the build of the monitoring suite. It is here that all of the connections and interfaces are complete and ready for full system testing prior to launch. From this point, companies are now more comfortable in moving into a *soft launch phase*. This is where the launch of the offering does not actually get released to all clients or to the World Wide Web; it is a case of building up the application and running through a "live trial" period.

As the diagram below indicates, the site-monitoring process is built and developed through the development stage and into the live stage. It is vital that the test suite is developed early in the project lifecycle – the first main target is to run alongside the application in the "soft launch" stage in order to refine the processes and reporting and to develop the method.

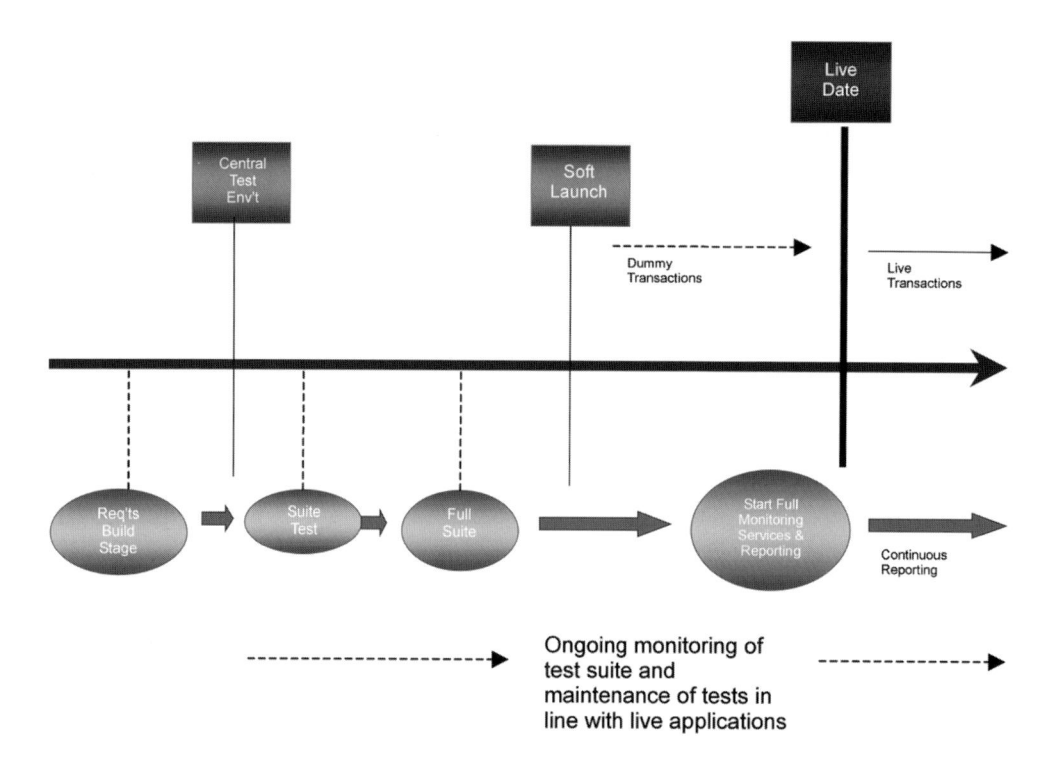

[Diagram: timeline showing Req'ts Build Stage → Suite Test → Full Suite → Start Full Monitoring Services & Reporting → Continuous Reporting, with milestones Central Test Env't, Soft Launch, and Live Date above the timeline. Dummy Transactions run before Live Date; Live Transactions after. Ongoing monitoring of test suite and maintenance of tests in line with live applications spans across.]

The main highlights of the test suite are:

- Early identification of test requirements:
- Early build of test suite inline with the above:
- Early suite test versus test system.
- Run against "pre-production" or "soft launch" environment prior to live date.
- Continuous monitoring of site once live.

Internet programs, by their nature, demand co-ordination of activity across several areas of IT and with the business partners. They also require the management of conflicts between programmes that are driven by differing business strategies, i.e. revenue growth versus cost efficiency. This requires cross-programme control and control over significant risks to the delivery of the set of IT systems that meet business requirements and integrate end-to-end with the business model.

## 2 The Transition State

Internet programmes go through the stages of idea initiation then design/build and then implementation. They have identifiable transition states that link into business plans. A transition state represents a major change to the way the business carries out its business and is represented at high level by the diagram below. In IT terms, a transition state is often associated with a major release – this is where the workload for the "continuous monitoring suite" can be saved increment upon increment.

Therefore, the transition state represents an island of benefit, where the test team can rebuild upon the test asset for future increments, while at the same time securing tried and tested test assets for separate releases.

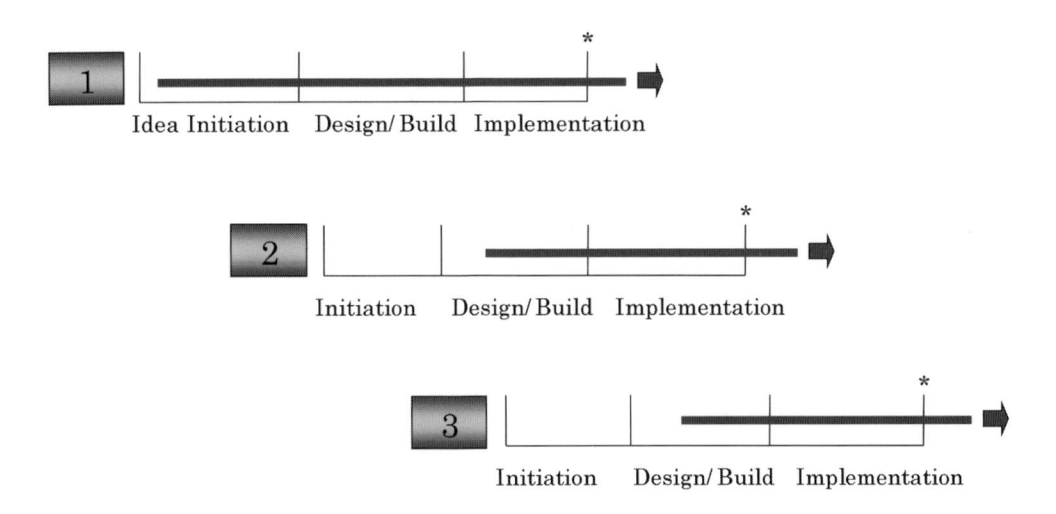

*[Diagram showing three iterations, each with phases: Idea Initiation / Initiation, Design/Build, Implementation]*

The thick lines in the diagram above represent when the "live site" monitoring suite overlaps the overall programme design and implementation schedule.

1. The first increment of the Internet market offering is normally a straightforward home page with a few links. However, this is the project where *most* of the hard work is done – as there is no suite to actually build upon, nothing to copy, update or script from. That is why the generation, maintenance and refinement of the suite stretch for more or less the entire project length.
2. The second iteration of the program, however does have a base of functionality to build from in the form of the original suite. Therefore, the time taken within the project is shorter – as is the start-up time – and hence a later start-up.
3. Iteration 3 has the latest start-up point owing to 1 and 2 above – whereby the previous increments have created a greater amount of material to build upon – therefore increasing and securing the overall test asset.

The following diagram symbolises how different types of projects relate to a transitional state and/or benefit within the scope of programme management.

The line indicating the pathway of the site-monitoring tool also goes through transition states – where the code, site and usability of the offering are under change – and, by design, so does the monitoring suite, enabling a fully integrated test asset that can be operated in varying environments, i.e. pre-production, test and live, consistently producing accurate reporting for the business to measure responses, sometimes against market competitors.

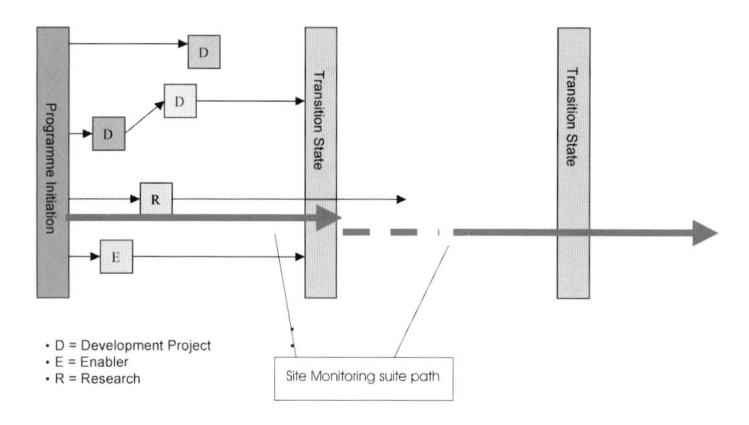

- D = Development Project
- E = Enabler
- R = Research

Site Monitoring suite path

## 3 Considerations Related to the Requirements

The table below shows the "generic" requirements of an Internet offering, and the related considerations from a testing viewpoint. These considerations can always be met by the continuous testing/monitoring of the application in the development, soft launch and live environments.

| Requirement | Considerations |
| --- | --- |
| Reliability | The service will need to be reliable; users will need confidence that it will be able to constantly and continually service their needs. It needs to be available and perform consistently.<br>**Testing Recommendation:**<br>Tests will need to be planned, prepared and executed to ensure that the service is reliable and resilient. These tests should also be integrated into a continuous testing pack. |

| Requirement | Considerations |
|---|---|
| Usability | The service needs to be easy to use. The level of IT or Web literacy among users will vary significantly. It needs to be easy enough to use for the less Web-aware clients.<br>The service needs to be usable by remote users using a variety of browsers and operating systems.<br>**Testing Recommendation:**<br>Usability tests will need to be planned prepared and executed to ensure the usability of the application. The profile of the anticipated user community will need to be determined to help ensure that the tests are defined within the profile's level of experience. |
| Security | Each individual's details and portfolios must be secure. While the legal and regulatory requirements will have been laid down by various bodies, the users will still need to be able to perceive a high level of security within the application. Any erosion in levels of confidence will soon see the service no longer being used.<br>**Testing Recommendation:**<br>Tests will need to be planned, prepared and executed that deliberately attempt to "hack" into the application. Site monitoring before and after going live will also secure live operation faults. |
| Speed of customer service | Customer services will need to be sympathetic and responsive to customer queries – as much information as possible on the quality of the service once in the soft launch or live state will be invaluable. |
| Comprehensiveness of offering in both functionality and quality terms | How will the comprehensiveness of quality be defined, and who will do this? How will a user's perspective on this be defined?<br>**Testing Recommendation:**<br>Plan, prepare and execute a series of user acceptance tests with the users to ensure and agree that qualitative goals have been achieved. |
| "Real time" market information and analytics | How will this be achieved – links to other sites or regular data refreshes from information providers?<br>**Testing Recommendation:**<br>Once the information provider is contracted, planning, preparation and execution of a series of continuous tests to assess the frequency of updating of the analytical information offered by the service. |

Of these, I believe the following are the four most critical to a successful launch:

- reliability
- security
- quality of offering
- robustness of the application.

As an absolute minimum, testing activities must cover these four areas – and they all fall into the categories of design, build and the ongoing test targets of the continuous-testing suite – thereby proving the robustness of the systems to the business by Internet monitoring.

This test asset, when used and configuration-managed correctly, should at least prove to be one sure way of easing the programme and project managers' anxiety a little – and indicates to everyone how test processes can positively change the overall outcome of Internet service.

# Part III

# System and Software Supply

# Risk Management for IT and Software Projects

Dr. E. Wallmüller
*Qualität und Informatik, Zürich*

**Abstract:** Risk management can be defined as a systematic process for identifying, analyzing and controlling risks in projects or organizations. Definitions and illustrations of risks are given; in particular, a list of ten risk factors which occur most frequently in IT and software projects is given. For complex, high-risk projects it is very useful to implement a formal risk-management process, supported by effective methods in the individual process steps. As variants, risk-management processes proposed by Barry Boehm, Ernest Wallmüller and Jyrki Kontio are presented. The importance of a sound operational preparation for each step of the risk-management process is emphasized and illustrated by examples.

**Keywords:** Risk management process, Riskit, Risk management, Quality management, Identification of risks, Analysis of risks, Control of risks, Monitoring of risks, Project risks, Risk scenario, Risk definition

## 1 Motivation

In order to increase the likelihood of a project reaching a successful conclusion, the risks or potential problems of a project need to be identified at an early stage and appropriate countermeasures developed. Tom Gilb put it in a nutshell with the following words: "If you don't actively attack the risks, the risks will actively attack you." Experience shows [Boeh89] that handling risks proactively, as is the case when risk management is used, is less expensive than correcting problems in the aftermath.

## 2 Background

Risk management has been around for some time. The word "risk" is derived from the Italian verb *risicare*. The science of risk management was developed back in the sixteenth century during the Renaissance, a period of discovery. The theory of probability, which is the core of risk management, was developed to help estimate people's chances in games better.

What is a risk? This question can be best answered using an example from everyday life. All cigarette packs are marked with warnings such as "Smoking is dangerous to your health" or "Smoking causes cancer". If one analyzes these statements, one sees that they describe a cause (smoking) of a problematic situation (cancer occurs) and its impacts (shortening of life).

There are many definitions of the term "risk" but no generally accepted one. All definitions implicitly include two characteristics: uncertainty (an event may or may not occur) and loss (an event has undesired effects). This is demonstrated by the following examples:

- used as a noun, the word "risk" indicates that somebody or something is subject to a danger or dangers;
- risk is the potential for the occurrence of undesired, negative consequences of an event [Rowe88];
- risk is the possibility of suffering losses, damage, disadvantages or destruction [Webs81].

On the basis of Webster's description of "risk", we shall use the following definition: risk is the possibility of suffering losses as a result of an event that will quite probably occur.

According to [Kont97], a risk can be illustrated using "risk scenarios" containing the following elements:

- a risk factor is something that influences the probability of a negative event occurring;
- a risk event is the occurrence of a negative incident or the discovery of information revealing negative circumstances;
- a risk reaction is an action which can be carried out when a risk event occurs; and
- a risk effect is the impact of a risk event on a project.

A risk scenario is a chain consisting of a risk factor, a risk event, a risk reaction and risk effects. The example given in Figure 1 includes the following risk scenario: "The database release is still in the beta-test phase. Problems could occur with the database integration. If so, a database expert might have to be called in. This would cause additional project costs totaling DM 20,000."

As opposed to purely textual descriptions of risks, risk scenarios offer the advantage that the risks can be divided into individual elements, making it possible to define targeted measures. On the one hand, attempts can be made to eliminate the risk factor or reduce the probability of a risk event occurring. This type of measure is referred to as a "preventive measure". On the other hand, additional, more effective risk reactions can be defined or the risk effects reduced. These measures are known as "precautionary measures".

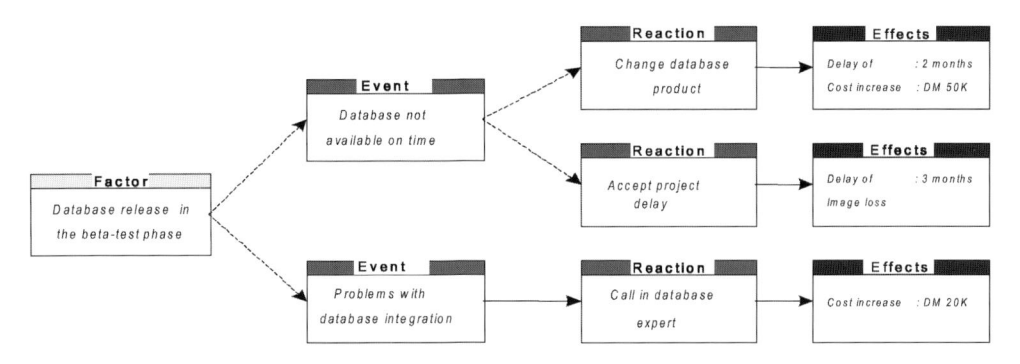

Figure 1: Example of a risk scenario

So risk management can be defined as follows: risk management is a systematic process for identifying, analyzing and controlling risks in projects or organizations.

## 3 Examples of Risks

The literature on this subject describes a plethora of risks which can occur in software development. Many sources suggest measures for decreasing the probability of these risks occurring. According to [Boeh98], there are ten risk factors which occur most frequently (Figure 2).

## 4 The Risk-Management Process

Risk management has always been a part of software development. Project managers and other project staff can usually identify risks intuitively and deal with them. However, as the risks described in Figure 2 show, that is not always enough. A formal risk-management process, supported by effective methods in the individual process steps, needs to be implemented for complex, high-risk projects. The following three examples of risk-management processes will be described in the sections below:

- the first formal risk-management process used in software development, described by Barry Boehm in 1989 [Boeh89];
- a risk-management process, defined in [Wall99], that is applied as an integrated part of project management; and
- a risk-management process which places great emphasis on the project's goals and stakeholders when analyzing risks and their effects. This process was described by Jyrki Kontio in 1997 [Kont97].

| Risk factor | Preventive measures |
|---|---|
| 1. Human error on part of staff | Employ the best people; rewards; team formation; training; peer reviews; adapt process to available know-how |
| 2. Unrealistic schedule and budget | Business-case analysis; incremental development; reuse of software; modification of schedule and budget |
| 3. Standard software and external components (inexperience, incompatibility, etc.) | Benchmarking; prototyping; review of reference installations; compatibility analysis; review of suppliers |
| 4. Requirements and developed functions do not match | Win–win agreements between parties concerned; business-case analysis; prototyping; application description in early phases |
| 5. User interfaces do not fit needs | Prototyping; development of scenarios; description of users |
| 6. Inadequate architecture, performance or quality | Simulation; benchmarking; modeling; prototyping; tuning |
| 7. Constant alteration of requirements | Increased threshold for changes; hiding of information; incremental development; change-management process; change control board |
| 8. Problems with legacy systems | Design recovery; restructuring |
| 9. Problems with tasks performed externally | Audits; parallel design or prototyping by several suppliers; team formation |
| 10. Overestimation of own IT capabilities | Technical analysis; cost/benefit analysis; prototyping |

Figure 2: Boehm's ten risk factors

Apart from [Boeh89], there are numerous other standard works on risk management, for example [Char89], [Doro96] and [Jone94].

## 4.1 Boehm's Risk-Management Process

Risk management was introduced into software development as an explicit process in the 1980s. The father of software risk management is considered to be Barry Boehm, who defined the risk-driven spiral model [Boeh88] – a software-development lifecycle model – and then described the first risk-management process [Boeh89]. Most of the processes defined since then are based on his basic process. His risk-management process consists of two sub-processes, "risk assessment" and "risk control" (see Figure 3).

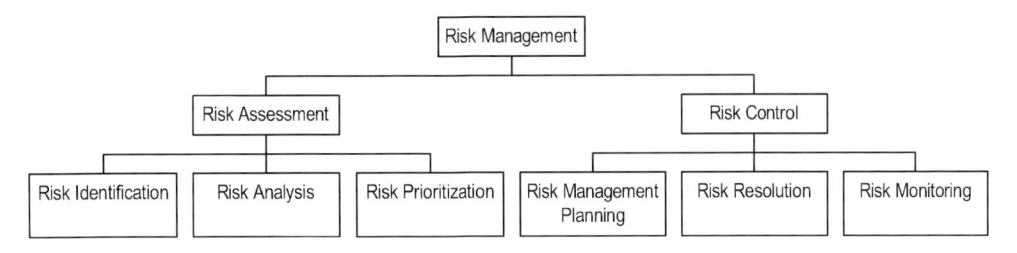

Figure 3: Boehm's risk-management process

The risk-identification process entails listing all conceivable risks to the project. Creative methods, e.g. brainstorming, and analytical methods, e.g. a risk checklist, can be used here. The risk analysis evaluates the risks. This involves determining the probability of occurrence and the possible negative effects for each risk. The risk-prioritization stage is used to specify the sequence in which the risks are to be dealt with. To this end, the losses caused when risk events occur are evaluated.

The process of risk-management planning involves specifying measures intended to reduce the probability of risk events occurring or to diminish the negative impacts following the occurrence of a risk event. Risk resolution is the step of the process where the measures defined in the preceding step are carried out. Risk monitoring keeps track of the efficiency of the measures implemented. In order to do this effectively, risk-monitoring metrics should be specified in the stage of risk-management planning and the appropriate data should be captured during the risk-resolution process.

## 4.2 Wallmüller's Risk-Management Process

[Wall99] describes a process whereby the risk-management activities are conducted by the project team at the same as the activities of cost, time, quality and requirement management.

Unlike Boehm's process, this is a sequential process (see Figure 4). It consists of a risk-planning part (steps 1–8) and a risk-control part (steps 9–11). The risk-planning part starts in the preparation and planning phase of the project before the actual project kick-off. The process runs full circle at least once during a project phase. This is also referred to as continuous risk management.

Many activities are the same as in Boehm's process. A significant new component is the assignment of various risk-management roles. The project manager determines the general risk-management strategy, including the appointment of the risk manager and assignment of risk-management responsibilities. The project manager works with the risk manager and the project team (clients, suppliers and subcontractors) in order to identify risks and define probabilities and impacts. He or she plans and approves

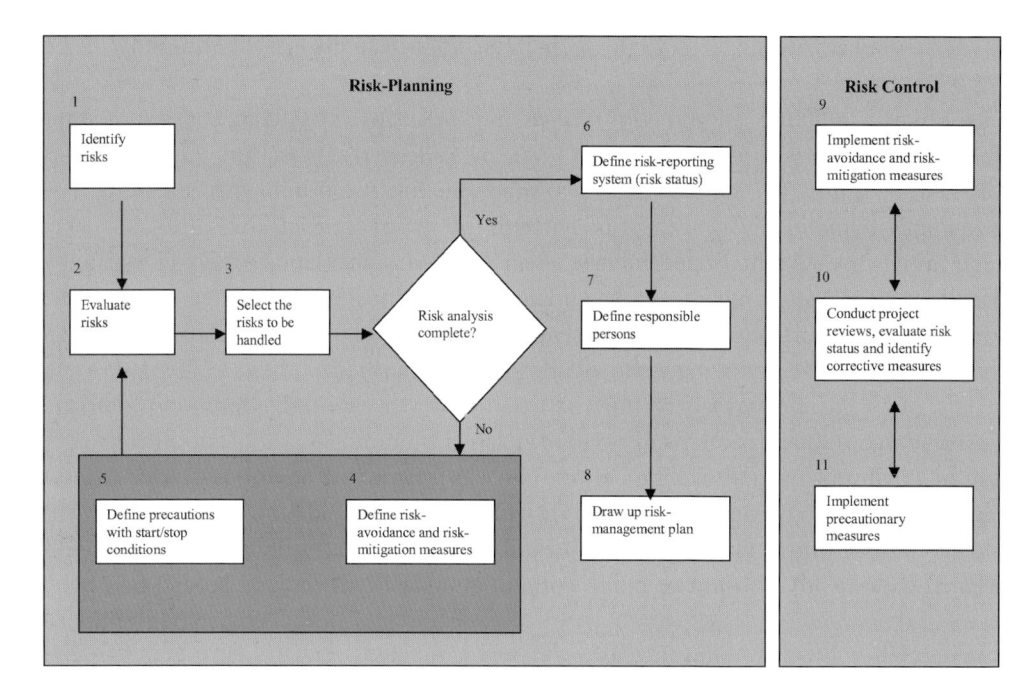

Figure 4: Wallmüller's risk-management process

the implementation of financial, time-related and technical preventive and precautionary measures; he or she also monitors the process and establishes reporting procedures.

The project team identifies risks within its area of responsibility, appraises probabilities and impacts, prioritizes risks, identifies preventive and precautionary measures, reports on the status of risks, evaluates the efficiency of the preventive and precautionary measures, and implements, if necessary, the precautionary measures.

The risk manager supports the project team in the risk-planning and risk-control processes, implements the risk-management plan, organizes and administers risk-status reports, evaluates new risks, and checks the effectiveness of current risk plans and of the implementation of precautionary measures.

## 4.3 Kontio's Risk-Management Process (Riskit)

Riskit is a goal-oriented and stakeholder-oriented style of risk management [Kont97]. Riskit distinguishes between two phases: the initialization phase and the risk-analysis cycle. The latter has many parallels with Boehm's basic process and Wallmüller's risk-management process. This phase will thus not be described in detail here. The foundations upon which the risk-management process is performed are laid in the initialization process.

The aim of the first process step, "Risk-management mandate definition", is to establish a risk-management procedure for the project in consultation with all parties involved (e.g. the project manager, risk manager and project team) (Figure 5). The risk-management process must be adjusted to the complexity and riskiness of the project. In the case of a small project, where no major risks are to be expected, it usually suffices to discuss risks at the project-management meetings from time to time. In complex, high-risk projects (e.g. when new development methods are used), a formal risk-management process, supported by well-developed methods, is required. The results of this first process step are:

- risk-management targets, methods and tools;
- a defined time frame for the analysis cycles (e.g. once a month);
- a definition of risk categories which are not to be considered (e.g. marketing risks);

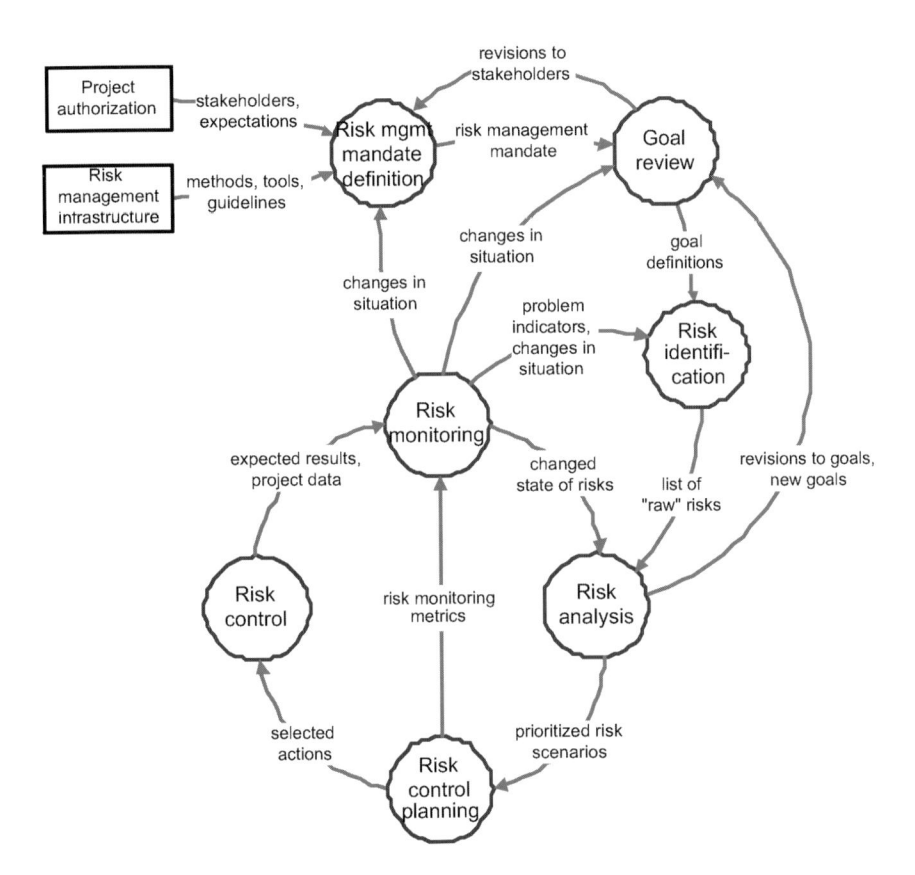

Figure 5: Kontio's risk-management process (Riskit)

- risk-management roles and tasks;
- communication mechanisms and reports; and
- project stakeholders and their expectations vis-à-vis the project results.

In particular, it is the consideration given to stakeholders that distinguishes Riskit from other risk-management methods. The concept is based on the idea that different stakeholders have different goals and different expectations of the project. Consequently, the second process step, "Goal review", examines the project targets and formulates them in as measurable a form as possible. It also analyzes which goals are important for which stakeholder and how important they are.

Goals and stakeholders play a crucial role in the "Risk analysis" step. Each risk is analyzed to determine its impacts on the project goals. These impacts are described in as measurable a form as possible (e.g. project delayed by three months = budget exceeded by $50,000). Since the "Goal review" step defines in advance which goal is important for which stakeholder, it is then possible to estimate who will incur the largest loss if a risk event occurs. These analyses are also of benefit when specifying measures.

# 5 Risk-Management Methods

In order to conduct a risk-management process in a systematic manner, it is important to have well-developed methods for each process step. To list all of the methods described in the literature would be beyond the scope of this chapter, so only a few examples will be given. An extensive assortment of risk-management methods can be found in [Doro96].

## 5.1 Risk-Identification Methods

As a rule, two types of methods are used for identifying risks. Firstly, brainstorming methods, which activate the project staff's creativity. And secondly, there are a variety of risk checklists comprising typical project risks. These checklists can be used in group or one-to-one discussions to identify risks. One very well-known checklist is the "Taxonomy-Based Questionnaire" [Carr93], containing 194 questions, which are divided into various categories, namely:

- Product Engineering (requirements, design, code and unit test, integration and test and engineering specialties).

- Development Environment (development process, development system, management process, management methods and work environment).
- Program Constraints (resources, contract and program interfaces).

Figure 6 shows an extract from a checklist which this author uses.

| Schedule/Location | Subcontractors | Resources |
|---|---|---|
| - Time Frame<br>- Geography<br>- Location<br>- Real Schedule vs. Bid Schedule | - Statement of Work<br>- Price<br>- Terms & Conditions<br>- Resources/Experience<br>- Subcontractor Management<br>- Quality Control<br>- Invoicing<br>- Alternate Sources | - Bid/Proposal Resources<br>- Skills/Qualifications/Capabilities<br>- Implementation Resources<br>- Facilities (e.g. Space, Equipment)<br>- Logistics |
| **Technical** | | |
| - Requirements<br>- Prototypes<br>- Tools<br>- Functionality<br>- Technical Performance<br>- Available and Future Technologies<br>- Architectures<br>- Integration<br>- Support Service (Training, Rollout, Installation)<br>- Baseline Management<br>- Unproven Hardware | **Contract**<br>- Change Control Process<br>- Terms & Conditions/Payment Plan<br>- Acceptance Criteria<br>- Statement of Work /Deliverables | **Innovation Projects**<br>- Market Knowledge<br>- Transformation of Client Needs<br>- Speed Idea => Product<br>- Changes of Requirements<br>- Team<br>- Management Support /Commitment<br>- Number of Projects in Parallel |

Figure 6: Risk checklist

## 5.2 Risk-Analysis Methods

One of the first steps in a risk analysis is to describe the risk in detail. An example of a form used for this purpose can be found in [Doro96]. According to that form, a risk description contains the following information, some of which is not gathered until the control measures or the monitoring phase is planned:

- unique risk title;
- identification date;

- formal description of the risk using risk factor, risk event and risk effect;
- context description containing additional information in text form;
- person who identified the risk;
- priority;
- probability of a risk event occurring;
- degree of impact (risk effect);
- time at which the risk event is likely to occur or at which measures have to be taken;
- classification;
- responsible person;
- strategy aimed at reducing the probability of the risk event occurring or at avoiding the risk;
- action plan to be applied should the risk event occur;
- status and date when the status was last recorded;
- person who accepted the risk, e.g. project manager;
- conclusion date; and
- reason for conclusion.

The risks can be prioritized on the basis of qualitative criteria with the help of a risk portfolio. By this method, the probability of the risk event occurring and the degree of impact are each rated as "low", "medium" or "high". Thus, three categories of priority can be defined:

- high-priority risks (A quadrant) are those which are rated as "high" for one of the two parameters and at least "medium" for the other (see Figure 7);
- low-priority risks (C quadrant) are those rated as "low" for one parameter and at the most "medium" for the other; and
- the other risks are assigned medium priority (B quadrant).

Presenting the risks in the form of a portfolio chart (Figure 7) provides a good overview of the priorities which are important in risk resolution.

A good means of evaluating risks quantitatively and prioritizing them is the risk-exposure method [Boeh89]. In this method, the probability of a risk event occurring is given as a value between 0 and 1 and the impact of the risk is given as a measurable value. The risk exposure is calculated as follows:

Risk exposure = Probability * Impact.

Thus, an impact in the form of a $100,000 loss with a 20% probability of occurrence results in the following risk exposure:

Risk exposure = 0.2 * $100,000 = $20,000.

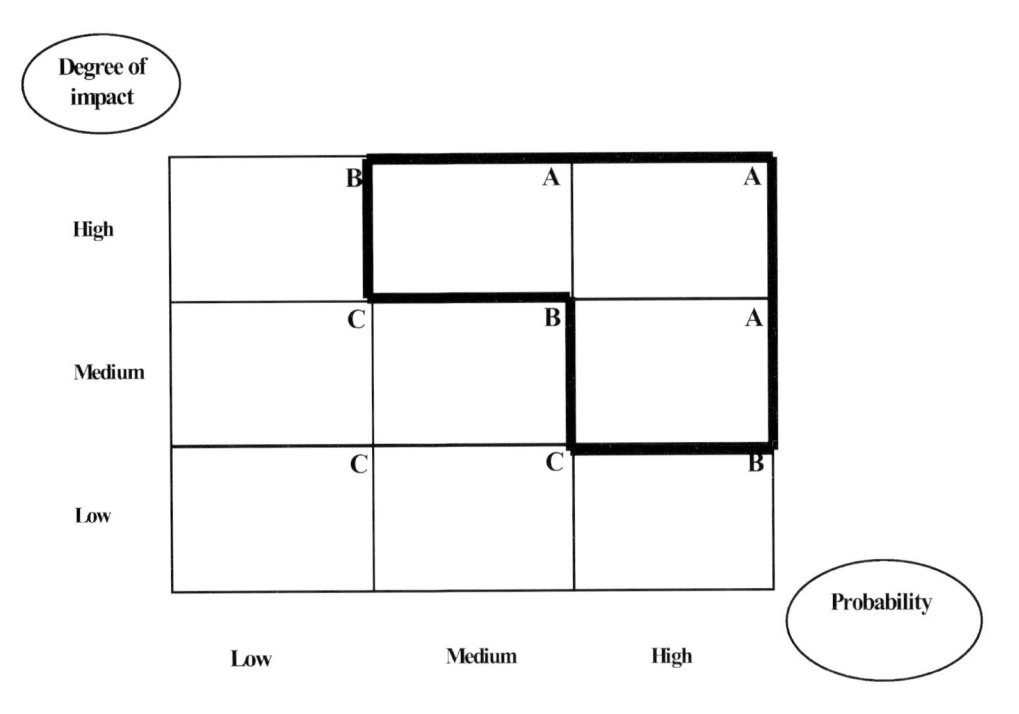

Figure 7: Risk portfolio

## 5.3 Methods for Planning Control Measures

Once a risk has been analyzed, one or several strategies should be defined for how the project members should handle the risk. [Hall98] cites the following fundamental risk strategies:

- Risk acceptance: no action is taken to counter the risk; the impacts are accepted. This strategy can be opted for if the impacts are minor or if the effort required to implement the measures necessary exceeds the impact of the risk events.
- Risk prevention: attempts are made to prevent the risk event from occurring at all. This strategy is chosen when the impact is serious.
- Anti-risk measures: targeted redundancies (e.g. duplicate processors and disks in tandem systems).
- Risk mitigation: this strategy reduces the probability of the risk event occurring or the degree of the impact.
- Risk research: additional information is obtained. This strategy is opted for if the individual risk elements are not sufficiently transparent.
- Risk reserves: reserves are included in the project budget or time frame. This strategy is chosen when there is great uncertainty in the project.

- Risk transfer: the risk is passed on to other persons, groups or organizations. This strategy is used when others control the risk and the measures to be taken.

Once the risk strategy has been selected, a risk-management plan can be devised. This plan is used to add information to the risk description, e.g. the person who accepted the risk, the person responsible, preventive measures and precautionary measures. [Jone94] contains an extensive assortment of possible risk measures.

## 5.4 Risk-Monitoring Methods

In order to monitor the current status of the risks and the measures defined, metrics can be specified for the risks. These metrics can be quantitative, such as the probability of occurrence or the effort and cost of control measures. But they can also be qualitative, e.g. an appraisal of project staff's motivation.

Another monitoring method is to use triggers, which are threshold values for metrics which trigger measures when reached.

Whereas metrics and triggers are used only in well-developed risk-management processes, risk reports are almost always used as a means of monitoring. The literature refers to many different types of report, e.g. the risk description, which is updated when risk measures are completed, or the risk table (see Figure 8).

# 6 The Importance of Risk Management for Quality Management

In many software projects, key business processes are optimized and the supporting software-system environment is redesigned. These projects are complex in that they have a complex structure and generate complex software systems. Migration of different legacy systems and integration of systems into an extensive IT system environment also raise the complexity of such projects.

Project planning and quality planning, as well as problem and risk management, can be used to define and prioritize quality management measures. Risk management, in particular, is an ideal process for focusing the quality management measures on the critical aspects of the project.

### Example I
| | |
|---|---|
| Project: | Major Systems Integration |
| Status Date: | September 1, 1993 |
| Origination Date: | March 20, 1993 |
| Risk Number: | 1 |
| Risk Title: | System Interface Definition |
| Functional Area: | Systems Engineering |
| Responsible Person: | John Systems |
| Critical Milestone: | System Requirements Review (SRR) |
| Risk State: | Active Risk |
| Risk Probability: | 40 |
| Cost Impact: | $1,500,000 |
| Schedule Impact: | unknown |
| Performance Impact: | non-compliance |
| Spec/WBS Ref: | Sys Spec-3.3.1.1/AA200 |

**Risk Definition:**

The client's system specification is incomplete, specifically in the area of system interfaces.

### Example II
**Risk Avoidance/Mitigation Status:**

Three primary risk avoidance/mitigation efforts are underway and include active client participation in the requirements validation effort, the establishment of an interface control working group, and the creation of interface specifications and interface control documents for each interface. Current status is as follows:
1. Requirements validation is in process. The client is actively participating and supporting this endeavor. Systems engineering is assigned to track this effort.
2. An interface control working group has been established with members from all client user groups and end customers. All major interface requirements have been identified.
3. Six of the eight interfaces have a requirements specification documented. The requirements for the remaining interfaces will be defined prior to SRR.

**Risk Contingency Plans Status:**

The contingency plans include utilizing a phased implementation and designing in flexibility in the overall system design for easy accommodation of phase II requirements. Also optionally obtaining schedule and/or milestone payment relief from the client.
An acceptable alternative phased implementation schedule has been created and approved by the client. The implementation of phase II applications will be delayed approximately three months. A separate phase II SRR will be held. This delay will add approximately $100K to our cost. Neither contingency plan is currently implemented. Implementation will be initiated if the remaining interfaces are not firmly established and defined at the System Requirements Review (SRR).

Figure 8: Examples of risk reports

# 7 Conclusion

Risk management is a practice that includes processes, methods and tools for managing risks in a project. It provides a disciplined environment for proactive decision-making to

- assess continuously what could go wrong (risks);
- determine which risks are important to deal with; and
- implement strategies to deal with those risks.

If risk management is applied, there will be a cultural shift from "fire fighting" and "crisis management" to proactive decision-making that avoids problems before they arise. Anticipating what might go wrong will become a part of everyday business, and the management of risks will be integral to the program.

# The Control of IT Risk by Means of Risk-Based Testing

Gary Sutherland
*SIM Group Limited*

**Abstract:** This chapter looks at using risk and risk analysis as a method of defining and implementing a testing strategy. It looks at how testing has matured over the years and how risk and risk management plays a major role in determining the strategies of organisations that strive to maximise their return on investments. As part of this chapter we also examine how the role of testing teams has grown and look at some new ideas to help you understand how testing teams can be resourced.

While the chapter concentrates on e-commerce applications and refers to an actual programme that is under way, many of the principals expressed are applicable to all IT projects and programmes.

**Keywords:** Internet, Delivery channels, Business risk, Project risk, Risk mitigation, Testing strategies

## 1 Background

Many large organisations delayed using the Internet as a significant delivery channel at the end of the 1990s. There were two major reasons for this; firstly, it relied on relatively new and unexploited technologies, and secondly, a large percentage of the IT budget at that time was directed towards addressing the Year 2000 problem.

Once Year 2000 was out of the way, budgets were made available to direct towards major initiatives that had been put on hold. Also, at around the same time, smaller, start-up organisations had made early strides in addressing the Internet as a delivery channel and had exposed some of the major challenges to be faced in that field. Organisations had made what was believed to be significant sums of money available to step into and exploit the Internet marketplace. In many cases, tackling the problems with resources was the approach that was taken; now many of these organisations are realising the cost of this approach and are looking for more pragmatic solutions based on more detailed cost benefits, and added value.

Other organisations were aware that the Internet was a step into the unknown, were keen to appreciate the risks that they were going to be faced with, and wanted to have strategies that were geared to mitigating those risks; this was to be applied to all phases of the programme's lifecycle, including testing.

## 2  What is Risk-Based Testing?

Risk-based testing is basically what the name suggests, the scope of testing is established on the basis of risks (to both the organisation and the project itself) that are applicable to the project or programme being undertaken. The scope and sequence of testing that are defined in the testing strategy are geared primarily to addressing the risks that are considered likely to confront the project or programme.

Boris Beizer's model of a tester's mental development describes five stages of evolution. In brief, these phases are:

1. That there is no difference between testing and debugging.
2. That testing is carried out to prove that the software works.
3. That testing is carried out to prove that the software doesn't work
4. That testing is not a means of either proving or disproving anything, but is carried out to reduce the perceived risk of not working to an acceptable level.
5. That testing is not an act; it is a mental discipline that results in low-risk software without much testing effort.

Risk-based testing is the core technique that is used to move an organisation from stage 3 of this model to the next level of maturity.

The current economic conditions are demanding that organisations seek greater returns from their investments in IT. It is generally accepted that organisations invest grudgingly in testing and that, for testing plans and budgets, they have to show a maximum return for a minimum investment. Such returns would be extremely difficult to achieve at the earlier stages of the testing maturity model. Risk-based testing aims to make testing a more cost effective process by:

- Testing what needs to be tested in a priority order where possible.
- Testing as early as possible in the lifecycle.
- Carrying out specific tests that target identified risks.

Risk-based testing can alternatively be described as "testing what if…" Risk Management looks at problems or potential problems and attempts to grade them from two perspectives, Seriousness and Probability. The risks can then be plotted onto a quadrant:

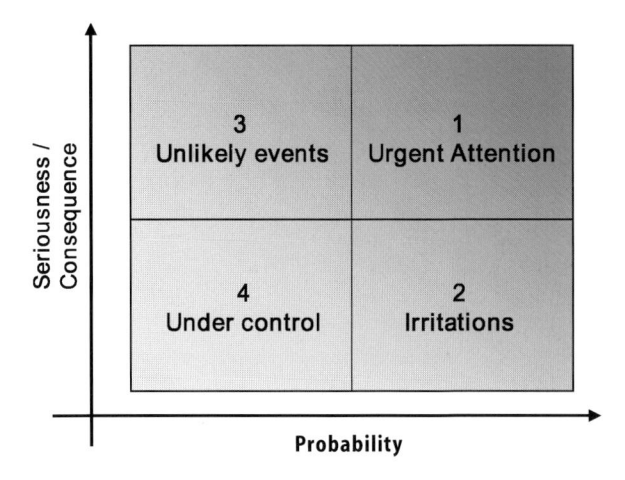

|   |   |
|---|---|
| 3 Unlikely events | 1 Urgent Attention |
| 4 Under control | 2 Irritations |

(Y-axis: Seriousness / Consequence; X-axis: Probability)

Elements deemed as being High Risk and High Probability will need to be addressed during the lifecycle of the project. If testing can help in any way in managing the impact of the risk then these should be included in the strategy. We then need to work our way down the various grades of risk and probability to include the relevant mitigation factors in the testing strategy.

Using the above measures gives an indication as to the relative priorities that must be given to the testing activities.

Some techniques as to how we use testing as a means by which these risks are addressed are investigated later in this chapter.

Another way of assessing the risk of a project, or the burden problems will place on an organisation is to look at the levels of support that will be deployed to service the product or application once it is made live.

Again we can see some interesting trends emerging. In the early days of IT the vast majority of applications were used to support the internal processes that kept the business running: accounting packages, payroll systems, etc. Users were relatively tolerant of errors that occurred when using the systems and often accepted them. Generally, internal applications required two levels of support, an area where the errors could be reported, and an area that was charged with resolving the problem. As client/server solutions emerged, applications moved away from back offices and near to the real customer base, ordering systems, etc. This user community were less tolerant of problems than their predecessors, but still accepted a level of problems when using the applications. Another level of support was introduced: we still had the problem recorders and fixers, but another layer between these, problem management, appeared. Now we are in the Internet age, the users *are* the customers: they are intolerant of problems and will quite happily look elsewhere if you cannot deliver what they want or expect. This on its own adds another tier to the overall support function – customer support.

A fifth layer has also been introduced as a means of supporting a service where there multiple providers of the service – problem determination, a function that attempts to identify the most likely cause of the problem and assign the corrective work accordingly.

Again a Risk based approach to testing uses this information to help define the scope and resources that could be used.

# 3 Identifying Risks

In this section we shall consider what the risks of failure are likely to be to an organisation if the project fails, and what can be done in the testing phases of the project to help reduce the potential impact of those risks.

There is no universally accepted definition of what constitutes a "failure" in IT project terms, so quantifiable research into how many projects fail and, importantly, what that failure means in real terms has been performed. Failure figures vary from, at the lower end of the scale 15% from research carried out by DeMarco in 1982, to the 85% that Cresenzi reported in 1988. In the same time period (1982) Lyytinen's research concluded that 75% of IT projects fail. Despite the vast differences in the numbers, it is apparent that failure is a real threat.

There are many well-documented instances of the cost of failure, including Prudential's cancellation of its internal "Plato" project, costing the company an estimated £40 million. Other failures cannot be expressed in financial terms, when the failures cost human lives.

It is important to consider what specifically is driving any particular change, as the potential exposures differ and will require different techniques to mitigate the related risks. The four main reasons for change can be classified as follows:

- securing existing market share
- expanding market share
- new delivery channels
- new business/new direction.

The driver for change often determines what is changed and how, and therefore the risks will be different for different drivers.

The following sections will look at the risks that organisations are exposed to depending on the reason behind the change.

## 3.1 Securing Market Share

Projects geared to securing market share often involve making subtle changes to existing applications. They are intended to consolidate the current user and product base, by securing current applications and making them more robust and reliable.

Of all the reasons for change this is probably the one that attracts the lowest risk, and probably the smallest financial growth, and as such the testing required is the least extensive.

Such a project would be deemed a failure should the user or revenue base contract. It is therefore vital that testing ensures that current levels of service and functionality are not compromised.

The primary testing technique to be deployed in this instance to address the risk of a degraded service is *regression testing*. The British Computer Society defines a regression test as:

Retesting of a previously tested programme following modification to ensure that faults have not been introduced or uncovered as a result of the changes made. [Glos]

A regression test is a measure of the status of the application before and after the change has been applied and will assess the difference between the baselines. People often regard regression testing exclusively as a test based around the functionality of an application, but there are other facets that could potentially regress as a result of change, particularly performance.

The scope of the functional regression test suite can be further defined or prioritised by understanding the risk of failure of each of the business processes supported by the application. The greater the risk and cost of failure, the higher the priority that should be assigned to the tests.

Similar consideration must be given to the performance aspects of the application. Different performance requirements/expectations for different processes in the application will exist. The relative priority of each process will need to be considered when planning and preparing the performance regression tests. The testing of performance can be made even more pragmatic by measuring a small number of processes, three for example, that encompass the basic data functions of creating, reading, updating/deleting. Such a suite can be created and executed on a much shorter timescale than one that reflects user and usage profiles. These latter extensive tests, while significant when launching a service, need not be used as the primary approach for an established application.

This section has covered only basic functional and performance regression. Obviously, there are a number of others that need to be considered, such a compatibility regression for e-commerce, Web-based applications, but the same principles apply.

When running regression tests you should always be prepared to explore a further level of detail should there be a high rate of unexpected failures: the *diagnostic* tests should be used to gain a better understanding of the root cause of the problem and reduce the problem resolution time.

## 3.2 Expanding Market Share

For the purposes of this chapter expanding market share is considered as extending existing applications and systems to deliver new products or services, to the marketplace; subsequent sections will look at the introduction of new delivery channels.

The changes being made will have an impact on existing software and the services it supports, so once more there is a significant risk that these changes will have a detrimental impact on existing services, etc. Regression testing is an important technique at your disposal to help reduce the potential impact of that risk. Again regression testing provides the foundation for any risk-based testing strategy, this extends to the regression testing of the performance of the application.

In addition, there is a need to ensure that the new services/products being introduced meet the expectations of the marketing and user departments. Testing of the new features needs to be extensive enough to cover the risks of the product. For example, if the new feature has any legal or regulatory requirements or constraints imposed on it, tests need to be carried out to ensure that the organisation could not be subject to any litigation if the product or content of the product is in contravention of any regulations or guidelines, all relevant disclaimers will need to be validated. The content of the product will need to be tested to ensure that there are no inaccuracies in the detail.

It is also important to ensure that the company brand is not impacted by the introduction of the new product or service. Does the new product or feature offer a consistent look and feel to all current offerings and services?

Any new product or service will also have an impact on how the application is operationally supported, from both a technical and a business perspective. There is a risk that the technical effort to support the delivery of the new service may place an additional burden on the team responsible, and therefore impair the success of the project.

To help mitigate this risk involve Operations personnel in the testing of the new product or service from their perspective, and help them ensure that once the service is launched, they can support it within the parameters of their current working practice. Similarly, the back-office staff should also be involved to ensure that they can manage the anticipated additional workload that will accompany the introduction of a new product or service.

## 3.3 New Delivery Channels

So far in this chapter, we have examined only changes that impact existing technologies. The introduction of new delivery channels means that technology new to the organisation will have to be used. This adds another flavour to the risks that will confront the project. Many of the risks described in the previous sections are still applicable. These are supplemented by a type of risk that we have not explored so far – technical risk.

The most common new delivery channel that is being introduced these days is the Internet. For the two reasons stated in the introduction to this chapter, many of the large, well-established household names in many industry sectors waited until after the threats presented by the Year 2000 problem had passed before they started to plan for the introduction of their presence on the World Wide Web as a delivery channel. Whilst these organisations were focused on this problem smaller start-up companies started to establish their own presence on the Internet: these latter organisations were new, and as such did not have the burden of "brand image" to worry about. Therefore they could take risks that more established organisations could not afford to take. Many of the problems that impacted these organisations were well publicised and gave the blue-chip organisations an insight into the pitfalls that lay ahead.

Technical risk potentially impacts a number of areas of an organisation, and there are a number of techniques that can be used to help mitigate that risk.

Technical support staff may not be familiar with the infrastructure components that are needed to support the new delivery channel. There is a risk that if or when things go wrong in the live environment, they may not be able to recover the service in a timely manner and, as a result, the users will give up and seek out alternative suppliers. Remember, in the new world of the Internet, the competition is only a click away! How do you address this issue? One large organisation in the UK addressed this issue by seconding two members of the technical support team onto the project team and charged them with the responsibility of building and supporting the various testing environments that were required by the project team. This provided a valuable resource to the testing function. When these two people return to their home team they will take invaluable knowledge with them that can be passed on to their colleagues. Should failures occur during live operation the team responsible for ensuring the smooth running of the operation, have extensive experience and the service should be recovered with a minimum of disruption to the users.

The expansion in the number of delivery channels will mean that, potentially, a wider user base will be using the service. This raises a number of new risks that we have not addressed so far in this chapter. Let's look at a few of these.

### 3.3.1 What if the Users Cannot Use the Service?

The service is available, but your end-users find it too complex and confusing to use, so they give up and take their business elsewhere.

It is hard to predefine what the user base of the service will be, and what level of experience they will have of using the Internet to transact their business. Someone who is an IT professional or has used PCs on a regular basis will have a different perception of what is intuitive from that of someone who is new to the game. If the users needs and expectations are not catered for, there is a large proportion of the marketplace that will resort to other means and probably other companies to carry out their business, potentially costing you a significant amount of lost revenue.

One technique to use to counter this risk is to bring in what is considered to be a reasonable cross-section of the target user community and ask them to simply try to use the service; they should be observed during this and asked to record their impressions. The notes from the observers and the feelings of the target user group should be collated and passed back to the designers to allow them to improve the service from a usability perspective.

### 3.3.2 What if it Cannot Run on all Operating Systems and Browsers that are Available?

In the general marketplace of the Internet there is a vast choice of operating systems and browsers available to consumers; there is also a variety of versions of each of these components available to the general public. Often service providers develop on a small subset of these as a means of reducing the cost of development. However there is no quantifiable way of knowing what the target user group will have installed on their own PCs. Organisations need to make sure that their online services are available to as wide an audience as possible.

To help mitigate this risk, testing of a subset of the processes supported will need to be carried out on a range of combinations of operating systems and browsers. This type of testing has been called *compatibility testing*.

The problem is further compounded by the fact that it is not possible or practical to know what other software packages and applications any one individual may be running on their machine at any one time. You may elect to simulate the applications your potential users may be running and build this into your test planning, or you may decide to run the tests on completely clean builds of PCs. The first option is a closer simulation to real usage, whereas the second option gives a cleaner base and it is easier to state that any problems that arise are down to "incompatibilities".

## 4 Resourcing Testing Teams

In the preceding sections we have looked at the new expanded role of a test team that uses a risk management approach to help define its testing strategy.

In the days before the Web and client/server, testing teams were, on the whole, organised simply with testing team leaders and a number of testing or quality assurance analysts working on the team.

When client/server architectures entered the fray, testing became a more complex affair, and the testing teams were supplemented with additional technical resources.

At about this time, the use of automated testing tools began to take off, and Automated Test Scripters also become key members of the testing teams.

And so the growth continued, to the point we are at today, where a testing team contains a multitude of skills: Test Leaders, Test Analysts, Automated Testers, Technical Testers, User Testers etc.

Throughout the growth of IT, the testing teams have provided the link between the technical and the user communities, and to reflect this a testing team is in effect a microcosm of the two communities involved in any programme. As a wider range of skills is required in support of any programme in the development, implementation and deployment arenas to help manage the risk of the project, so too has the testing team grown its skill base to help manage the risk of the programme.

## 5 Summary

The preceding list is by no means a comprehensive set of challenges that may confront your project, but it does give some indication of the risks you may be faced with.

The main lesson to be learnt is that pragmatic testing strategies need to take into account the risks that a project is likely to be confronted with.

As Brezier suggests in his maturity model, the industry is moving forward in terms of maturity, while in parallel the user community is becoming more widespread, not only geographically but also in terms of their levels of maturity and what they will tolerate and accept as a "quality" product. We testers need to accept and appreciate these facts and also bear in mind the economic climate in which we work. The drive to reduce costs and increase returns suggest that testing more to address the increased demands of the users is not necessarily the way forward. We have to be cleverer in the way we approach testing. risk based testing can help with this. It does not mean that we are reinventing testing as such; most of the old accepted techniques are still appropriate and applicable. We are however, looking at using risk based-testing to define the objectives of the testing to be carried out and therefore setting the scope of that testing.

Risk-based testing also looks to expanding the catchment area for testers. Traditional sources and team structures, while still having roles to play, no longer provide the full picture. In the days of mainframe-based applications, and to an extent client/server applications, a team of testers and traditional quality assurance analysts with a team leader served to complement the project team and bring into play skills not available elsewhere in the project team. Nowadays the testing team is more likely to be a microcosm of the organisation that will be in place to support the product once it has been launched to the public, and also have in it other skills that reflect the technical advances that have been made in testing, such as the introduction of test automation for functional, regression, load and performance testing.

These days, a testing team, while still likely to be built around a team leader and test analysts, will also have technical testers available to it; it is also likely that infrastructure experts will be on board, as well as support personnel and business unit representatives.

Risk-based testing looks at the "what if's" of the project and aims to address them by using a mixture of testing techniques and a mix of personnel. It targets testing at the things that are important to the organisation, and goes beyond the current textbook of testing.

# Software Reengineering for Mission-Critical Applications – Minimizing Business Risks and Reducing Maintenance Costs

JOACHIM SCHMUCK
*T-Systems GEI GmbH (Germany)*

**Abstract:** This article describes the risk potential of outmoded software systems for business processes. The relevance for the financial service sector is a result of the exceptionally high dependence of the business processes on the underlying data-processing systems. The reason for software aging, the processes involved in aging and the resultant risks are outlined. Software reengineering is introduced as a business solution to this problem.

A discussion of the main success factors facilitates the selection of a useful reengineering approach. Special attention is paid to the sustainability of the effects realized. In addition to risk prevention, the aspect of maintenance cost reduction is elaborated. A case study illustrates how the structural rejuvenation of data processing systems succeeds even under the massive pressure of functional evolution. Special emphasis is placed on the classic combination of COBOL applications and IBM mainframe computers, often found in banking and insurance.

**Keywords:** Legacy software, Reverse engineering, Software lifecycle, Software maintenance, Software reengineering

## 1 Risk Factor Data Processing

Data processing is an integral part of business processes in many economic sectors. Meanwhile, optimal-data processing support of business processes is a deciding competitive factor in the dynamic service sector. The introduction of new services requires flexibility and speedy reactions. Globalization is changing the macroeconomic environment. Mergers and acquisitions produce integration projects. Technological developments trigger alterations, such as the conversion from host-based to client/server processing.

Data-processing systems that do not anticipate these changes in time can rapidly become serious risk factors. This could lead to delays in the introduction of new products or services. Short-term adjustments of the price and rate models in reaction to new competitive conditions may be impeded. Reduced product and service quality may lead to customer migration. Even legal problems are possible, leading, for example, to the rejection of auditor certification owing to a lack of system transparency.

Even if all necessary adjustments are made in time, they can lead to a cumulative deterioration of the software status in the course of time. This is known as software aging and describes a phenomenon that distinguishes software from other products.

Software is not subject to classical material fatigue. However, constant adjustments over a given time period lead to a loss of the original design clarity, a reduction in program code structuring and deviations from guidelines and standards. Deadline constraints cause program documentation to be neglected, and errors are corrected only during implementation and are not updated in the technical design. Maintenance personnel fluctuations introduce different programming styles and problem-solving approaches into the program code. The consequences of all this are that

- The costs and the results of the modifications become increasingly difficult to assess.
- Scheduling is difficult during implementation.
- It is no longer possible to react flexibly and rapidly to new requirements.
- The productivity of the maintenance programmer is lowered, meaning maintenance costs increase.
- Error rates increase and operational stability decreases.

When these aging effects exceed a critical stage, the resultant deterioration of business processes cannot be compensated any longer. Users then generally feel that the data-processing system is no longer useful. Because of their close involvement in operational processes, data processing systems are under constant pressure to change, resulting in a dilemma: constant modifications are vital for survival, but each adaptation leads to software aging and makes future adjustments more risky and expensive.

In many cases, this dilemma is solved by replacing the old system with a new development from scratch. However, taking this step always overlooks the following points:

- The problem will almost certainly recur when the new system reaches a certain age.
- The development of a new software system is a very complex task, which is usually not done without mistakes in the first run. Subsequent corrections have to be made over an extended period of time.
- It is always easier to rework something familiar, than to create something new.
- Approximately 80% of the problems are concentrated in 20% of the program code of the old application, which means that, usually, 80% of the application is still useful to the business. This represents a considerable level of business knowledge and investment (see Figure 1).
- Consequently, an evolutionary solution of the problems within the old system requires only 20% of the costs of a new development.

The discussion of the software lifecycle in the next section illustrates the consequences of this procedure: the development of a new system is more expensive than calculated and results in an initial product that is unstable and contains errors. This results in deadline delays and user dissatisfaction. In addition, only a few years after the stabilization of the system, the new system will start aging and will finally reach the same stage as that in which the old application was before.

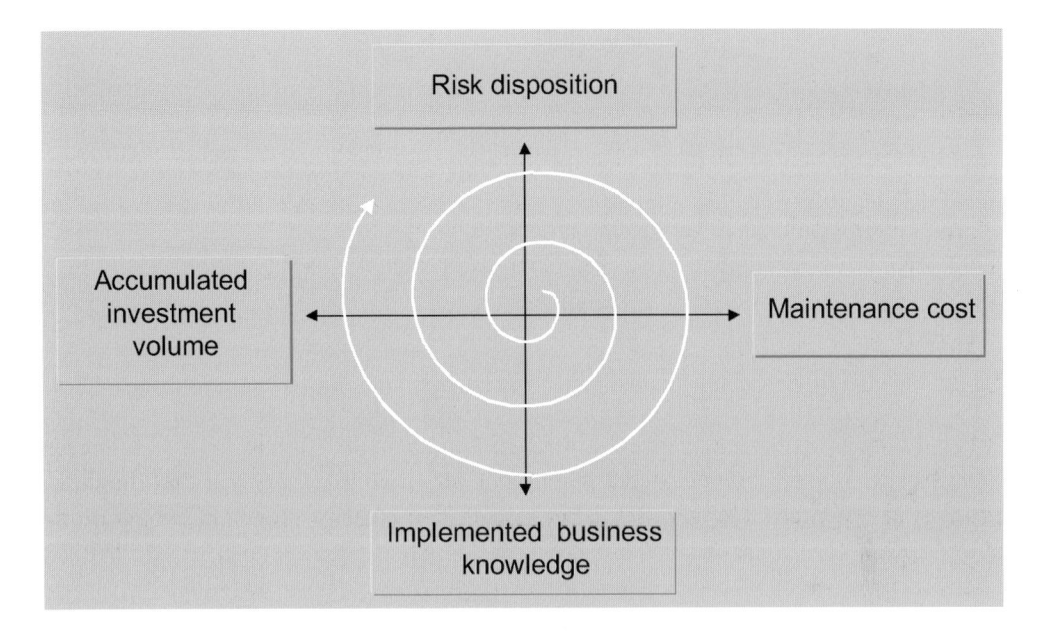

Figure 1: Cycles of development of an aging data-processing system

The economically best method for solving this software maintenance problem is an evolutionary approach, which systematically elevates the software to a level where efficient, safe and economical maintenance is possible again. The maxim "evolution instead of revolution" characterizes this approach. The maintenance process must include principles and techniques aimed at upholding the level reached.

This basis enables even the most complex technical tasks to be carried out, such as the conversion of a COBOL application to an object technique, the decentralization of a host application to a client/server architecture or the inclusion of Java front ends in host applications.

The following sections describe the essential features of this approach. Section 2 examines the aging process and outlines the resultant risks.

# 2 The Lifecycle of Data-Processing Applications

We have seen that software ages, and that aged software is a risk for operational processes and increases software maintenance costs. In order to understand how software reengineering can help in this situation an in-depth understanding of the aging process is necessary. For this, we shall now look at the various development stages of a data-processing application.

## 2.1 Development

This phase includes all processes before start-up. The need to increase the efficiency of a business process using a computer system and the decision to develop a corresponding data-processing system stand at the beginning of this phase.

Developing a software system is a very complex task, which even today, after four decades of experience in this field, fails completely in one in seven or eight cases [Brös00]. In order to master the complexities of this task, a stepwise approach for developing a useful system from the statement of requirements has become established. At each stage, specialists are usually involved in transforming the system description to a more concrete level. This results in the further differentiation of the system.

Complexities become controllable by this procedure. However, there is a certain price to pay. Each transformation step loses information and the translation of the requirements becomes faulty. This loss of information is caused by two factors:

- A faultless transformation demands unrestricted understanding of the system description of the preceding stage. This requires a degree of perceptiveness that is not always available.
- A faultless translation to the next abstraction level is the second prerequisite. However, humans make mistakes, they do not control the necessary methods completely, they do not use tools correctly or they are simply negligent.

The procedure models for software development are supplemented with feedback mechanisms and variants to counteract this problem. Although progress has been made, software development remains a complex task.

## 2.2 Maturation

From the previous section, it is clear that a data processing application is usually not perfect at the start up moment. The main problem at this stage is not the detailed functional correctness, but the basic usability. The problems in this category must be solved, before dealing with the functional deficits. These problems cannot always be traced back to mistakes made during the creation process, but often arise from mistakes made during the requirement description phase. Users frequently do not specify their requirements exactly, unless they have seen the results of their previous specifications. At this stage of the lifecycle, this results in a number of functional corrections. By the end of this phase, the software finally attains functional correctness as well as technical stability.

## 2.3 Maturity

Now the software reflects user requirements well and the system works reliably. This is the ideal state – but it will only last for a short time. Entrepreneurial demands on the operative systems, especially in companies operating in dynamic markets, change all the time. Additionally, information technology is constantly evolving. The adaptation to these factors triggers two opposing developments. On the one hand, the entrepreneurial value of the data processing system increases progressively. This can be measured by the total investments made and the implemented business knowledge. On the other hand, the condition of the application deteriorates as a result of the factors described in section 1.

## 2.4 Age

The negative effects of the problems described above finally assume critical dimensions. The following attributes are no longer fully available:

- *Appropriateness* (of the data-processing solution to the operational task)
- *Usefulness* (of the extensive business knowledge implemented in the data-processing system)
- *Ability to assess* (the effects of modification requirements or error correction)
- *Flexibility* (in modifications required at short notice)
- *Adherence to schedules* (when creating a new release date)
- *Cost efficiency* (of operation and/or maintenance)
- *Staff independence* (from individual maintenance programmers because of undocumented knowledge)
- *Legal firmness* (towards auditor requirements – where appropriate).

Negative effects on business become apparent. Compensatory measures are increasingly necessary. These aggravate the situation even more by using up resources that are required for stabilizing the data processing system. Technically obsolete and with functionalities no longer adapted to user requirements, the system is either mothballed or replaced by a new development from scratch or perhaps a standard product, if appropriate.

## 3 Software Reengineering as a Fountain of Youth

The previous sections examined the cause of software aging and the effects of this problem. This section will deal with a suitable approach to the solution, called "software reengineering". In terms of cost-effectiveness as well as risk minimization, this approach is usually preferable over the alternative of "new development".

Software reengineering is the planned technical improvement of software, including the documentation, without changing the functional behavior of the system. It is carried out by taking an engineering approach; it is sometimes also known as "software remediation". The aim of this approach is to make obsolete software more reliable and increase the cost-effectiveness of maintenance.

In this context, maintenance is defined as the subsequent modification (subsequent to start-up) of the functional behavior of the system. This is differentiated into corrective maintenance, meaning the correction of errors, and adaptive maintenance, meaning value-increasing development in response to new or changed requirements. Maintenance may also include occasional improvements to the program code. However, if systematic approach is not evident, this process must not be confused with reengineering.

In simple terms, reengineering means improving without changing the functionality, and maintenance means changing the functionality without improvement.

### 3.1 Operating Mode

Software reengineering is a targeted approach to rejuvenating obsolete applications. The clock is turned back in the lifecycle of the data-processing system. A state is (re)established that is equivalent to a mature but not obsolete application. Since rejuvenation takes place in small, manageable steps on a familiar object, it can be controlled reliably, the effects are predictable and the costs can be evaluated. All disadvantages of a new development are eliminated while preserving proven aspects of the system.

In contrast to organisms, software-aging processes can be stopped and even reversed. The desired ideal condition is marked by the end of maturation. At this point, the software is functionally mature, in good technical condition, and practically free of errors, and it can be maintained cost-effectively with minimum risk. The software provides the ideal support for business processes. Software reengineering transforms obsolete systems into this state and keeps them there permanently.

## 3.2 Approach

The current situation dictates the reengineering measures applicable to the software system and the documentation. A reengineering project must begin with an inventory of the state of the program code, the program documentation, the design documentation and the functional specifications. The reengineering strategy is derived from this information. The strategy is the result of a combination of so-called "Re-techniques" in a suitable temporal sequence. In some cases, different subsystems may require different Re-techniques.

Re-techniques come in two categories (see Figure 2). Category one is called Reverse Engineering and means the systematic reconstruction of the specification from the data-processing system. This inverts the individual phases of software development (Forward Engineering). The aim is to reconstruct the intermediate products of the

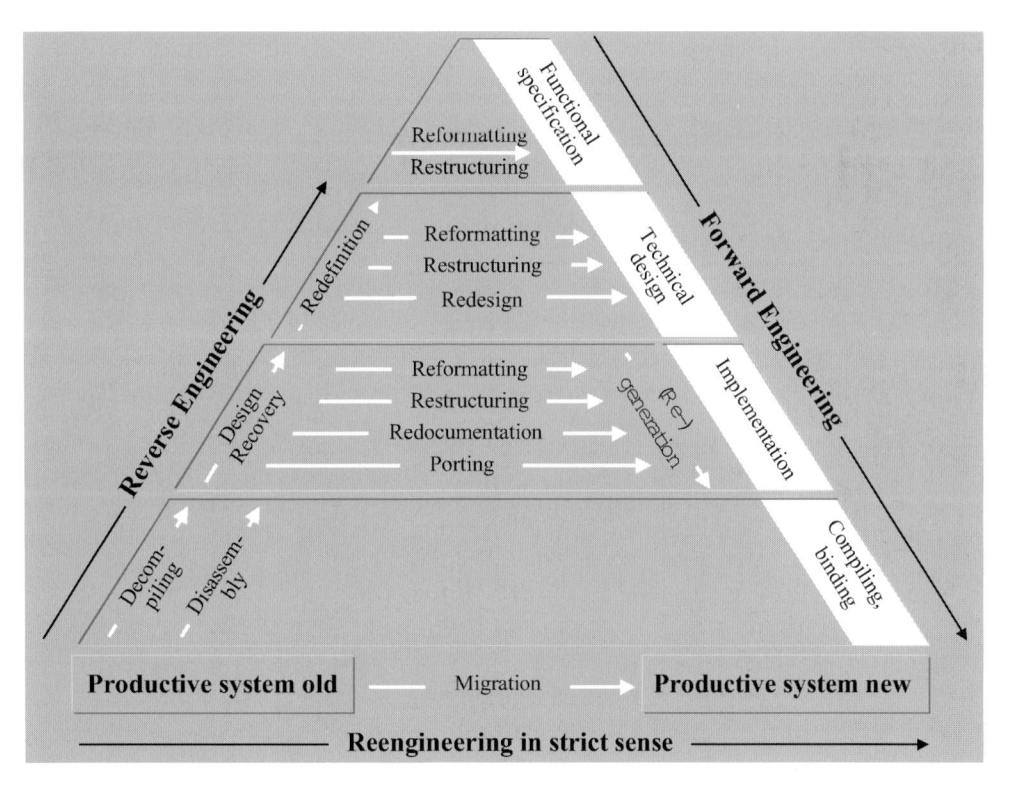

Figure 2: Terminology and relationship of Re-techniques

development process in order to establish the starting point for the revision of the contents. Revision is the object of reengineering in the strictest sense and forms category two. A terminological uncertainty is apparent at this stage, since the term reengineering is also applied to the approach as a whole. Reengineering, in the strictest sense, includes all activities involved in modifying software and its documentation, and in its implementation in a new and easily maintainable form. In combination with classic Forward Engineering procedures, Re-techniques lead finally to a renovated, usable system.

## 3.3 Re-Techniques

The following table gives detailed descriptions of the Re-techniques:

| Re-Technique | Description | Application fields |
|---|---|---|
| Disassembly, decompiling | Recovery of the program codes (assembler or higher programming language) from the machine code by automatic translation | Non-existent or incomplete program sources |
| Design recovery | Recovery of the technical design specifications by tool-supported derivation from the program code | Missing or incomplete design specification. Also if deviations in the translation are suspected |
| Redefinition | Reconstruction of the functional concept on the basis of expert interviews and system and technical-design analysis | Missing or incomplete functional specification. This is an absolutely necessary step for understanding the data-processing system |
| Redesign | Modification of the technical design while preserving professional functionality | Failed technical design (module slice, database design, layer architecture etc.) |
| Reformatting | Preparation to improve readability, taking account of visual appearance. In principle applicable to all types of results. Tool support is possible | Unreadable and therefore incomprehensible program code or documentation |
| Restructuring | Improving technical quality within the program modules by rewriting the program code. In principle, this may also apply to badly structured documents. | Unnecessary data access, redundant code, direct jump instructions, variables used inconsistently, mixture of technical and functional coding, non-normalized database system, etc. |

| Re-Technique | Description | Application fields |
|---|---|---|
| Redocumentation | Recovery of implementation description for users, operators and maintenance programmers | Incomplete, faulty or inadequate program description |
| Porting | Changing the technological platform: hardware, operating system, database management system or programming language. May require additional activities such as redesigning for the change from mainframe to client/server architecture | When the manufacturer no longer supports platform, when maintenance contracts end or because of IT-related strategic decisions. Examples: hardware architecture from mainframe to client/server; programming language from COBOL to C++; user interface from Windows to HTML and Java |
| (Re-)Generation | Automatic creation of system components from the technical specification. Normally part of Forward Engineering, if carried out in time. In view of its central importance for achieving reengineering goals, it is included here as a Re-technique. | If carried out manually before |
| Migration | Replacement of the old productive system while taking account of user requirements for system availability. Not a Re-technique in the real sense but completes the list of necessary steps. | To activate the modifications that have been made. Especially important following modifications of the information structure |

# 4 Principles and Main Success Factors

The previous section introduced us to Re-techniques, which form the building blocks of a reengineering project. Their use in a procedure model follows fundamental principles and considers critical success factors. This section describes both these aspects.

## 4.1 Integrating Maintenance

Conventional reengineering approaches usually assume a single remediation effort. They monopolize the program code during the revision period and return the revised version for implementation after a couple of months. This makes such approaches useless for all applications that interweave with business processes and are subject to frequent demands for functional modifications. The latter often appear unexpectedly and with great urgency. This should not be a hindrance for a reengineering project. It should be possible to interrupt Re-activities at any time without the loss of the results achieved. Once the functional demands have been carried out, Re-activities can resume.

Reengineering activities and maintenance must be freely combinable and it must be possible to replan them at short notice according to demand. This makes reengineering a continuous process, in which functional evolution is embedded. The intensity of reengineering can be adapted flexibly to the available resources, thus optimizing staff workloads and available budgets.

This combined approach requires the use of similar methods, tools and standards for both tasks. There is no differentiation between maintenance programmers and specialist "Re-engineers". Both activities fuse into a single task, presenting an opportunity for enhancing maintenance tasks, which are often seen as second-rate. To achieve this, an additional component must be established in the planning and controlling process, the microcycle.

## 4.2 Microcycles

Segmenting the development process into short sections allows a flexible combination of reengineering and maintenance activities, as well as short-term switching between tasks. Each of these segments incorporates a complete development cycle on a small scale: the specification of a few reengineering activities or a functional demand, followed by translation and testing. Therefore, these segments are known as microcycles. A defined state is reached after the test (including necessary error correction); this forms the basis of the next microcycle, which may consist of reengineering activities or a previously specified functional requirement. Alternatively, this microcycle may also incorporate the translation of an unplanned requirement that has turned up in the meantime. This microcycle is also verified by a test before the next one is initiated; this next microcycle may, for example, be to eliminate operational errors at short notice. Microcycles are a detailed control mechanism, which always includes the same steps irrespective of the type of modification:

- detailed specification of the modification (if required)
- implementation
- test and error correction
- saving the status achieved.

## 4.3 Integrated Testing

Traditionally, software is tested at the end of the development cycle. This approach is risky, since fundamental errors or misunderstandings are detected late. This immediately results in a delay in the date of deployment and may have a negative effect on the budget. Modern test methods must be designed to test at the end only those aspects of the system, which could not be tested before, such as the performance of the system under real-life conditions. All other aspects, especially functional correctness, can be tested within the relevant microcycle.

This requires a graded, differentiated test method that provides the relevant test activities for functional demands, correction of operative faults and reengineering activities. These are carried out within the framework of a microcycle and are supplemented with the required comprehensive tests (for example, integration and performance tests).

Large software systems may need a great number of test cases in order to verify the correctness of the software fully. The test cases of legacy systems may be incomplete, not adequate or not supported by the corresponding test data. In this case, the reengineering efforts must include a sort of reengineering of the test cases and data. This aspect could easily be a subject for a whole article in itself, so the discussion has to stop at this point.

## 4.4 Configuration Management

In a typical reengineering project, a great number of programs and additional system components are affected by a great number of microcycles. Each of these modifications must be based on a defined status and must result in a defined status. If a modification leads to a blind alley, it must be possible to reset the system to the previous status. Finally, the large number of modular and interdependent modifications must be put into operation.

This is guaranteed by the rigorous use of configuration management (CM). CM is also indispensable for the reliable execution of classical development projects, especially those carried out by incremental procedures. However, CM attains special significance in reengineering projects, where the revision intensity is immense.

## 4.5 Maximum Automation

A large part of the program code can be generated from a formal specification, which means it can be created automatically. By generating the program code and other system components, automation replaces transformation processes during the software development process, thus eliminating possible sources of errors. This also results in cost reductions through rationalizing effects. The automatically generated components do not age, and can be converted centrally when technologies are changed. If, for example, all database access is realized by use of generated components, the database management system can be replaced with very little expense. Individual programming is limited to the functional logic, which usually covers about a third of the software.

Making use of the automation potential in obsolete software increases stability but can also mean a quantum leap in the productivity of the developer. This releases resources that are then available for financing parts of the reengineering activities, if the necessary funds are not available to the required extent.

## 4.6 Management of Knowledge

Reliable, efficient modification of software demands technological and functional knowledge about the application. The importance of this knowledge cannot be overestimated. However, long-term maintenance projects are often characterized by personnel fluctuations. This always leads to knowledge fluctuation. Deadline constraints and lack of prioritization can, even in the case of personnel stability, lead to a neglect of documenting (knowledge-storing) tasks. Furthermore, these tasks are traditionally unpopular with programmers.

Knowledge management frees entrepreneurial knowledge from the individual and makes it available for others. As a management concept, it is universally understood and will not be elaborated further here. However, it forms the framework for reconstructing and permanently storing knowledge using a data-processing system.

Three principal results of the work done in the classic development process represent different views that together allow a better understanding of the data-processing system and therefore must be the subject of reconstruction activities (Reverse Engineering):

- the functional description (functional specification, ...)
- the technical design (technical specification, ...)
- the documentation of the program code.

The reconstruction must be followed by the preservation and continual updating of the recovered knowledge by constructively confronting the obstacles mentioned above:

- The storage of functional and technical knowledge in a repository with an appropriate structure is the basis of the program generators. Since only error-free information entries lead to error-free building blocks, need for timeliness and correctness in accordance with the garbage-in-garbage-out principle.
- The generators represent technical knowledge in the same way that a production robot "knows" how the parts of a car body must be welded together. This knowledge does not fluctuate or age.

- The description of the application logic, which cannot be generated from the repository, is carried out in a structure that unites the program code with its appropriate documentation in a common structure. The physical proximity of this so-called "unisource" to the coding facilitates its description.

## 4.7 Maintenance Team

The principles described above must be considered in determining the structure of the assignments of the maintenance team, so that they can be translated adequately. This spawns a number of tasks that must be delegated to experienced coworkers:

- configuration management
- test management
- building block-administration
- quality assurance
- support of the development environment.

The detailed control, in the form of microcycles, must be delegated to the management level. The team leader will carry out this task in small maintenance projects. In large projects, the subproject managers should be in charge of these activities.

The increase in centrally organized tasks is counterbalanced by a decrease in classical maintenance work such as manually modifying the program code (and the corresponding documentation). At the same time, maintenance tasks are enhanced by the Re-activities. This job-enrichment should increase the motivation of the coworkers, since software maintenance often has an (undeserved) low standing in companies.

In addition to this, success depends on the extent of the understanding and acceptance of reengineering principles and methods by the team. Understanding can be promoted by special courses. Encouraging acceptance is an executive duty, which must take account of the self-conception of the developers. The extensive provision of deployable building blocks can disturb the well-maintained picture of programming as an "artistic" activity.

# 5 Cost/Benefit Analysis

The discussion of the subject matter related to software reengineering will end at this point. Given the space, many aspects could be elaborated on:

- metric procedures for quantifying the condition of the data-processing system
- the portrayal of a complete reengineering procedure model

- CARE (Computer-Aided Reengineering) and the reengineering environment
- reengineering test cases and test data
- enterprise-wide reengineering and a reengineering factory

Instead, some attention will now be paid to the financial aspects. An investment in software reengineering must be economically viable. From the details described in the previous sections, we can not only deduce the risk-minimizing effects but also make the first qualitative estimates of the maintenance costs (Figure 3).

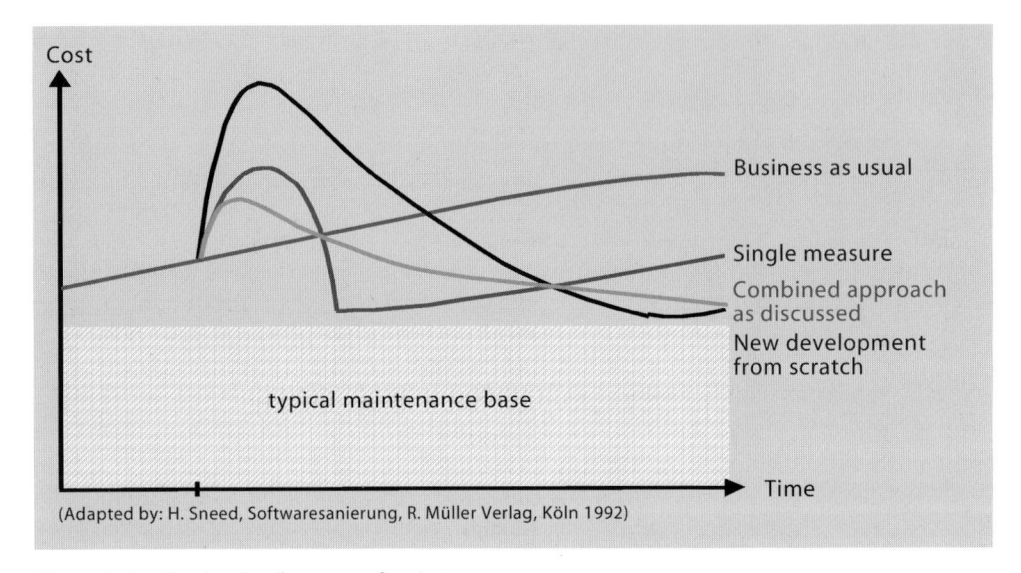

Figure 3: Qualitative development of maintenance costs

An extensive cost/benefit analysis with detailed quantitative statements is not yet possible on this basis. This requires an appropriate instrument, as well as extensive experience. However, a first estimate can be made using universal empirical values [Balz00]:

1. As a rule, reengineering is always useful if
- the data-processing system is older than 5 years
- the remaining service life is more than 3 years
- it is vitally important for business
- the information structure remains the same.
2. In comparison with reengineering, a new development is
- 2 or 3 times riskier
- 4 times as expensive.

3. Reengineering amortizes itself within 2 to 3 years in comparison with the "business as usual" alternative.

If a decision cannot be made on this basis, a detailed cost/benefit analysis must be carried out. Indices such as Payback Period, Net Cash Flow, Discounted Cash Flow or Internal Rate of Return are determined using the cost blocks and use potentials in the following table. These are the basis of the decision-making process.

| Area | Cost blocks | Use potentials | Notes |
| --- | --- | --- | --- |
| Development environment | • Hardware<br>• System software<br>• Tools<br>• Integration<br>• Installation<br>• Administration | • Ergonomics<br>• Efficiency | Only the additional costs in comparison with the available development environment are relevant. |
| System implementation | • Re-activities<br>• KM, TM and QS expenses<br>• Building-block administration<br>• Detailed control | • Maintenance costs<br>• Error correction<br>• Speed of reaction<br>• Adherence to schedule<br>• Achievability of very complex requirements | Only the additional costs in comparison with previous KM, TM and QS expenses are relevant. |
| IT Personnel | • Tool course<br>• Methods course | • Motivation<br>• Fluctuation<br>• Lost hours<br>• Personnel independence | |
| Operation | • None | • System crashes<br>• Lost hours<br>• Correct workmanship<br>• Cost of errors | |
| User | • None | • Satisfaction<br>• Prospective willingness for investment | |
| IT Organization | • None | • Process quality<br>• Solution competence<br>• Service sense<br>• Image | |
| Company strategy | • None | • Customer satisfaction<br>• Competitive advantages<br>• Cost advantages<br>• Market share | |

# 6 Case Study

The starting point that we use here for illustrating the previous explanations is a legacy system, created in the early days of data processing and further developed over decades. We begin our observations in the first half of the 1990s and follow them through to the present date.

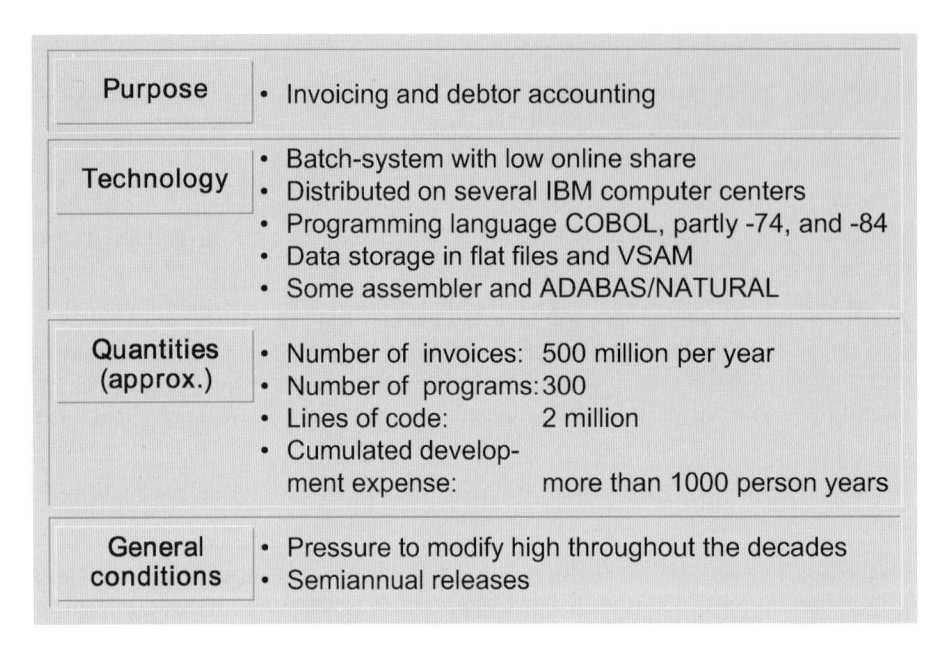

| | |
|---|---|
| **Purpose** | • Invoicing and debtor accounting |
| **Technology** | • Batch-system with low online share<br>• Distributed on several IBM computer centers<br>• Programming language COBOL, partly -74, and -84<br>• Data storage in flat files and VSAM<br>• Some assembler and ADABAS/NATURAL |
| **Quantities (approx.)** | • Number of invoices: 500 million per year<br>• Number of programs: 300<br>• Lines of code: 2 million<br>• Cumulated development expense: more than 1000 person years |
| **General conditions** | • Pressure to modify high throughout the decades<br>• Semiannual releases |

Figure 4: Description of system in case study

## 6.1 History

A great number of programmers with different programming styles have left their fingerprints over a period of 20 years. After an initial phase of following the philosophy of standardized programming, the approach of structured programming was used. The extent of the system increased greatly during this period. The implementation was shaped by times where storage space and CPU time were limited. As a result of the extreme quantity structures, processing emphasized performance suitability. Programs with more than 1000 GOTO commands were created. As a result of occasional experiments with new technologies, a younger program complex was realized with ADABAS.

Everything was fine for a long period of time. But finally, a dramatic situation occurred. The privatization of the company and deregulation of the market created a new competitive situation. A continually increasing competitive pressure was predicted for the following years. The introduction of new products to the market in increasingly shorter times would also increase the invoicing workload. This initiated an effort to reorganize the complete product and tariff structure, which was accompanied by a drastic migration of experienced coworkers.

## 6.2 Procedure

In response to this situation, a large-scale reengineering project was started under the motto "Restoration of maintainability". The main target of this long-term project was to bring the system into a condition to cope with the enormous upcoming changes with minimum risk. The cost aspect played a minor role at this stage. The deciding factor was the ability to implement new or modified functionalities in a regular six-month release cycle, parallel to the reengineering activities.

The combined Re-approach outlined above was applied to the first critical part of the system, and a proof of concept was arranged. The extent was expanded from release to release, until the complete application was integrated – in various stages – into the reengineering. Each part of the application was treated according to the same pattern: the individual Re-techniques used are summarized in the following table. Figure 5 and 6 illustrate the main tasks in the initial processing phase and the following phases.

| Step | Description |
| --- | --- |
| Disassembly, decompiling | Was not necessary. |
| Design recovery | Tool–supported registration of jobs, programs and files as design objects in a repository tool. By use of generators, the potential for automating these objects was realized rapidly. Additional objects followed. |
| Redefinition | The functional view was stored only in verbal descriptions and not in the form of concepts. These descriptions were stored as delta documents, containing descriptions of the changes in relation to the previous release only. A description of the functional volume as a whole was not available. A combination of interviews and delta documents enabled the reconstruction of the functional specification. This was then stored using the SA/DT (Structured Analysis/System Design) method. Additionally, overview documents were created. |
| Redesign | Successive central routines were conceived for sequence control, I/O handling, data access, error handling, and parameter transfer and processing. From these routines, building blocks for incorporation into the programs were automatically created, using the repository entries as parameters (see "(Re)generating") |

| Step | Description |
|---|---|
| Reformatting | Reformatting activities were mostly carried out by the developers and were not subject to systematic planning. |
| Restructuring | After the Redesign activities had clarified the picture of the actual application logic in the programs, these were restructured according to the "basic principles of good programming". |
| Redocumentation | A large part of the necessary documentation for users, operators and maintenance engineers was generated automatically from the filled repository. This placed problems of correctness, completeness and timeliness firmly in the past. Adding information on the application logic (which was not suitable for storing in the repository) completed the generated documents. These were stored in and automatically extracted from the program code as comments, in accordance with the unisource principle outlined previously. |
| (Re-)generating | The unisources consisted of extensive instructions for the generators, which translated these into three types of results:<br>• Executable programs<br>• Program documentation<br>• Metrics and log files.<br>These instructions were described by metacodes in order to distinguish these from the actual program code. The metacode controlled the integration of the generated program building blocks.<br>Because the program documentation was created automatically, it showed a high level of standardization. The uniformity of structure, visible appearance and depiction of the contents significantly simplified understanding and use of the objects.<br>Log files and metrics were used to control the Re-process. The translation of the metacode was verified using the log files. Metrics detailed the grade of automation and reconstruction. They were an important aid for the programmers on the one hand and for detailed control of the the microcycles on the other. |
| Migration | The analysis of requirements, technical design and implementation and the reconstruction of the relevant documentation were the prime targets in the initial phase of the reengineering project. In view of this, migration of the productive system did not play a role (see Figure 5). This changed in the subsequent processing phases (Figure 6). The increasing conversion to a generated code, as well as the functional extensions, made migrations in a 6-month cycle necessary. This step required little restructuring, since a suitable procedure already existed. |

A 17-point plan for the detailed control was presented. This consisted of the reengineering activities carried out by the developers, such as the integration of the building blocks for data access or error handling. These 17 activities were managed according to priority, and planned and controlled according to their relevance, for all program modules.

## 6.3 Results

- The use of the generated building blocks cut the proportion of individually programmed functional logic by more than half.
- The reengineering activities on the programs continued for approximately four releases on average, meaning two years.
- 20–25% of developer work hours was spent on reengineering, the rest was taken up by functional evolution.
- In total, reengineering activities were spread over a four year time period.
- 12 releases, including some with huge modification volumes, were implemented on schedule and reliably, before system shutdown.

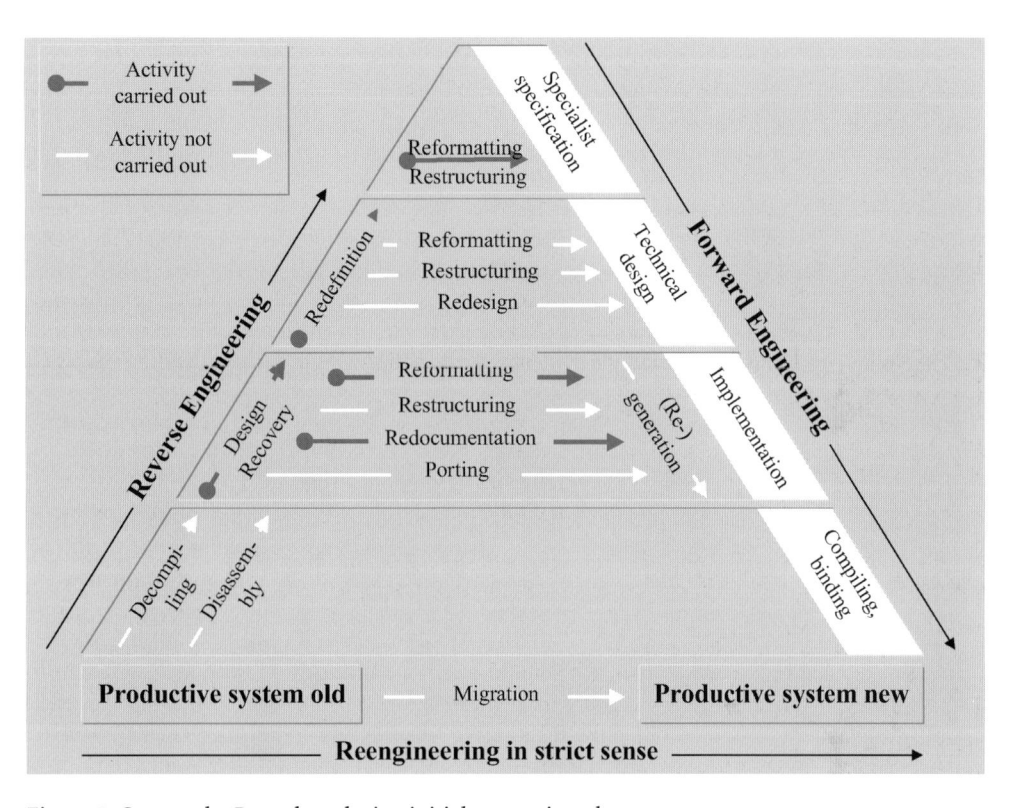

Figure 5: Case study: Procedure during initial processing phase

## 6.4 Part Two of the Story

While these developments were occurring, IT-strategic considerations led to the acquisition of follow-up systems. Standard software for debtor accounting and the configurable billing system of another company were to bring the IT landscape in this area up to date. It was decided that the old system did not provide enough flexibility for the entrepreneurial requirements of the 21st century, despite the positive reengineering experiences. The decision not to carry out a year 2000 conversion marked the end of the old system.

However, before their deployment, both of the new systems required an enormous adaptation effort over several years. This was necessary, on the one hand, because business processes and products were not depicted sufficiently and, on the other hand, because of a lack of suitability for a larger amount of business activity. Only a great effort could increase the number of services that could be paid for through this system. In consequence, the migration of customers from the old system took a long time. Functional modifications had to be realized in both worlds during this period.

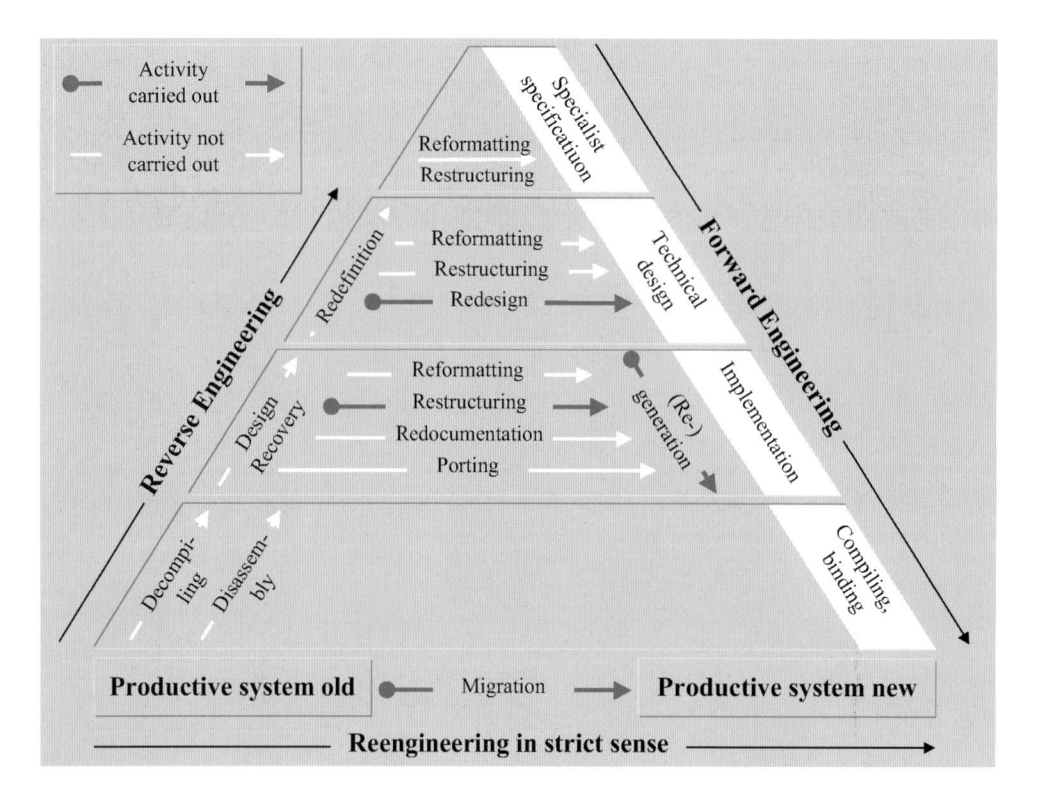

Figure 6: Case study: Procedures during subsequent processing phases

In time for the end of the millennium, the functional scope of the new billing system was fully realized, all customers had migrated, and the old system could be shut down. However, by now the new billing system had become a case for remediation.

As a result, flexibility and sustainability are limited, which prevents the company from making plans to extend the billing process chain to a company-wide billing service. Enormous maintenance costs push the process costs over the relevant benchmarks. Because of this situation, a reengineering measure is being considered again.

# 7 Summary

- Resist all temptations to let old systems die prematurely.
- Resist all temptations to underestimate the extent of the implemented. business knowledge
- Resist all temptations to underestimate the costs and risks of a new development from scratch.
- Resist all temptations (just kidding).
- Resist all temptations to overestimate the flexibility and the economic advantages of ready-made solutions
- Resist all temptations to underestimate the remaining useful life of a data-processing system.
- Resist all temptations to see software maintenance as second-class work.

# References and Links

| | |
|---|---|
| [AIRM] | Association of Insurance and Risk Managers: Web link http://www.airmic.com |
| [Anno92] | BAKRED: Announcement, October 16, 1992, Sections 3, 9; Web link http://www.bakred.de |
| [Balz00] | Balzert H.: *Lehrbuch der Softwaretechnik*, Spektrum Akademischer Verlag, Heidelberg, 2000 |
| [BASE] | Basel Committee: Home page, Web link http://www.bus.irg/bcbs/index.htm |
| [Base98] | Basel Committee on Banking Supervision: *Framework for Internal Control System in Banking Organisations*, September 1998, Web link http://www.bis.org |
| [BBA] | British Bankers' Association: *Operational Risk Management Survey*, Chapters 1–3, Web link http://www.bba.org.uk/pdf |
| [BCI] | The Business Continuity Institute: Home page, Web link http://www.thebci.org |
| [BGCM] | Business Guide to Continuity Management, Web link http://www.bgcm.co.uk/index.htm |
| [BIS] | Bank of International Settlement: Home page, Web link http://www.bis.org |
| [Blan98] | Bland M.: *Communicating Out of a Crisis*, Macmillan Press Ltd, Houndsmills, Basingstoke, Hants RG21 6XS, England, 1998; Web link http://www.compuware.com |
| [Boeh88] | Boehm B.: "A spiral model of software development and enhancement", IEEE Computer, May 1988, pp. 61–72 |
| [Boeh89] | Boehm B.: *Software Risk Management*, IEEE Computer Society Press, New York, 1989 |
| [Boeh98] | Boehm B.: *Software Risk Management*, CS577, University of Southern California, Center for Software Engineering, 1998 |
| [Brau86] | Braudel F.: *Sozialgeschichte des 15.-18.Jahrhunderts, Der Handel*, Kindler, Munich, 1986 |
| [Broc96] | *Brockhaus-Enzyklopädie*, Brockhaus, Leipzig, 1996 |
| [Brös00] | Brössler P., Siedersleben J.: *Softwaretechnik – Praxiswissen für Softwareingenieure*, Carl Hanser, New York, Chichester, Brisbane, Toronto, Singapore, Weinheim, 2000 |
| [BSL] | Banking Services Luxembourg S.A.: Web link http://www.bankingservices.lu |
| [Carr93] | Carr M.J., Konda S.L., Monarch I.A., Ulrich F.C., Walker, C.F.: *Taxonomy-Based Risk Management Identification*, SEI Technical Report SEI-93-TR-006, Software Engineering Institute, Pittsburgh, 1993 |
| [Char89] | Charette R.N.: *Software Engineering Risk Analysis and Management*, McGraw-Hill, New York, 1989 |

| | |
|---|---|
| [Chic98] | Chicken J.C., Posner T.: *The Philosophy of Risk*, Thomas Telford, London, 1998 |
| [Cial97] | Cialdini R.R.: *Die Psychologie des Überzeugens*, Huber, Göttingen, 1997 |
| [Cir101] | Commission de Surveillance du Secteur Financiere: *Implementing Regulations on the Legal Tasks of Auditors*, Circular 01/27, March 23, 2001, Section 3.4, Web link http://www.cssf.lu |
| [Cir201] | Federal Banking Supervisory Office: *Outsourcing to Another Company According to Art. 25a II 2 KWG*, Circular 11/2001, I3-272-2/98, August 17, 2001, no. 39ff |
| [Circ99] | *Outsourcing*, Circular 2/99, August 26, 1999, pp. 29ff; Web link http://www.ebk.ch |
| [Comp] | Computer and Software Services Association: Web link http://www.cssa.co.uk |
| [Cont] | ContinuityPlanner.com: *An Online Resource for Business Continuity Planners*, Web link http://www.continuityplanner.com |
| [Cour99] | Courtney H., Kirkland J., Viguerie P: *Strategy under uncertainty*, in series Harvard Business Review Paperbacks, "On Managing Uncertainty", Harvard Business School Publishing, Boston, MA 02163, USA, 1999 |
| [Deut99] | Deutsche Bundesbank: "Electronic banking from a banking supervisory point of view", Monthly Report, December 1999, pp. 43ff; Web link http://www.bundesbank.de |
| [Disa] | Disaster Recovery Institute International: Web link http://www.drii.org |
| [Doro96] | Dorofee A.J., Walker J.A., Alberts C.F., Higuera R.P., Murray T.J., Williams R.J.: *Continuous Risk Management Guidebook*, Software Engineering Institute, Pittsburgh, 1996 |
| [DTT] | Deloitte Touche Tohmatsu: Web link http://www.deloitte.co.uk |
| [E&Y] | Ernst & Young: Web link http://www.ernstyoung.co.uk |
| [Effe99] | European Central Bank: *Effects of Technology on the EU Banking System*, July 1999, Web link http://www.ecb.int |
| [FAZ101] | Frankfurter Allgemeine Zeitung: "In China kein Zugang zum Netz", February 10, 2001 |
| [FAZ201] | Frankfurter Allgemeine Zeitung: "Druck auf den falschen Knopf sendet Börse auf Talfahrt", May 16, 2001 |
| [FFIE] | Federal Financial Institutions Examination Council: *Information Systems, Examination Handbook*; Web link http://www.ncua.gov/ref/ffiec/ffiec_handbook.html |
| [FSA01] | Financial Services Authority: *The Interim Prudential Sourcebook for Banks*, FSA, London, 2001, Section 4.3 |
| [GARP] | Global Association of Risk Professionals: Web link http://www.garp.com |
| [Glob] | The Global Portal for Business Risk and Continuity Planning: Web link http://www.globalcontinuity.com |
| [Glos] | British Computer Society Special Interest Group in Software Testing: *The Glossary of Terms Used in Testing*, Version 6.2; Web link http://www.sigist.org.uk |
| [GoBS95] | Federal Department of Finance, Germany: Letter of November 7, 1995, to the supreme tax authorities of the federal states, Section 5 |

| | |
|---|---|
| [Guid99] | British Financial Services Authority: *Guide to Banking Supervisory Policy*, Volume 2, OS (outsourcing), Section 4, June 30, 1999 |
| [Hall98] | Hall E.M.: *Managing Risks: Methods for Software Systems Development*, Addison-Wesley, Massachusets, 1998 |
| [Heat98] | Heath R.: *Crisis Management for Managers and Executives*, Financial Times/Pitman, Harlow, 1998 |
| [Hein] | Heine & Partner GmbH: Home page, Web link http://www.heine-partner.de |
| [Holt01] | Holthöfer N.: "Mit App-Mining Business-Code ausgraben", Computerwoche 23/2001 |
| [IDW01] | IDW: EPS 330, July 2001, Section 3.4.5 |
| [IDWd01] | IDW: *Principles of Proper Accounting for the Use of Information Technology*, March 2001, Draft IDW Accounting Principle (Draft IDW AcP FAIT 1), pp. 82ff [this draft will partially supersede the "old" FAMA 1/1987]; Web link http://www.idw.de |
| [Info] | Info AG: Web link http://www.info-ag.de/de/home.html |
| [IRF] | Interactive Risk Forum: Web link http://www.riskforum.com |
| [IRMG] | Institute of Risk Management: Web link http://www.irmgt.co.uk |
| [ISO00] | ISO: *Information Technology – Code of Practice for Information Security Management*, ISO 17799, 1st edition, January 2000; Web link http://www.iso.org |
| [JCCM] | Journal of Contingencies and Crisis Management; Web link http://www.blackwell-publishers.co.uk |
| [Jone94] | Jones T.C.: *Assessment and Control of Software Risks*, PTR Prentice-Hall, Burlington, MA, 0-13-741406-4, 1994 |
| [KaBr95] | Kaminske G.F., Brauer J.-P.: *Qualitätsmanagement von A-Z – Erläuterungen moderner Begriffe des Qualitätsmanagements*, 2nd edition, Hanser, Munich, Vienna, 1995 |
| [Kend98] | Kendall R.: *Risk Management for Executives*, Pearson Education, Harlow, 1998 |
| [Kont97] | Kontio J.: *The Riskit Method for Software Risk Management*, version 1.00, Computer Science Technical Report CS-TR-3782/UMIACS-TR-97-38, University of Maryland, 1997 |
| [KPMG] | KPMG: Web link http://www.kpmg.co.uk |
| [Laga93] | Lagadec P: *Preventing Chaos in a Crisis*, McGraw-Hill Book Company Europe, Shoppenhangers Road, Maidenhead, Berks SL6 2AL, England, 1993 |
| [Masi88] | Peters O.H., Meyna A.: "Sicherheitstechnik", in *Handbuch der Qualitätssicherung*, 2nd edition, Hanser, Munich, Vienna, 1988, pp. 301ff |
| [Mill98] | Miller H.W.: *Reengineering Legacy Software Systems*, Digital Press, Boston, Oxford, Johannesburg, Melbourne, New Delhi, Singapore, 1998 |
| [NIST01] | National Institute of Standards and Technology: *Information Security Management, Code of Practice for Information Security Management*, International Standard ISO/IEC 17799:2000, Frequently asked questions, Web link http://csrc.nist.gov/publications/secpubs/otherpubs/reviso-faq.pdf |
| [NIST1] | National Institute of Standards and Technology: *An Introduction to Computer Security: The NIST Handbook*, Special Publication 800-12, 1995, Chapter 11; Web link http://csrc.nist.gov/publications/nistpubs/index.html |

| | |
|---|---|
| [NIST2] | National Institute of Standards and Technology: Special Publications, Web link http://csrc.nist.gov/publications/nistpubs/index.html |
| [NIST95] | National Institute of Standards and Technology: *An Introduction to Computer Security: The NIST Handbook*, Special Publication 800-12, 1995; Web link http://csrc.nist.gov/publications/nistpubs/index.html |
| [OCC] | OCC: Web link http://www.occ.treas.gov/netbank/ebguide.htm |
| [OECD92] | OECD: *Guidelines for the Security of Information Systems*, 26 November 1992, Chapter 3, Definitions |
| [Perr99] | Perrow C.: *Normal Accidents*, Princeton University Press, Chichester, 1999 |
| [Prac] | Practical Risk Management Inc.: *PRM Online*, Web link http://www.pracrisk.com |
| [PWC] | PriceWaterhouseCoopers: Web link http://www.pwcglobal.com.uk |
| [Rada99] | Rada R.: *Reengineering Software*, Glenlake, 1999 |
| [Risk01] | Bank for International Settlements: *Risk Management Principles for Electronic Banking*, May 2001, Web link http://www.bis.org |
| [Risk99] | Standards Australia: *Risk Management*, AS/NZS 4360:1999, 1999; Web link http://www.standards.com.au |
| [RML] | PMI Risk Management Specific Interest Group: *Risk Management Lexicon*, Web link http://www.risksig.com/lexicon.htm |
| [RMR] | Risk Management Reports: Web link http://www.riskreports.com |
| [Rowe88] | Rowe W.D.: *An Anatomy of Risks*, Robert E. Krieger Publishing Co., Malabar, FL, 1988 |
| [RWG] | Risk Waters Group: Search engine for books, Web link http://www.riskbook.com |
| [Sch197] | Schmidt M.J.: *What's a Business Case? and Other Frequently Asked Questions*, White Paper, Solution Matrix, Boston, 1997–1999 |
| [Sch297] | Schmidt M.J.: *The IT Business Case: Keys to Accuracy and Credibility*, White Paper, Solution Matrix, Boston, 1997–1999 |
| [Sch397] | Schmidt M.J.: *Business Case Essentials: A Guide to Structure and Content*, White Paper, Solution Matrix, Boston, 1997–1999 |
| [Surv] | Survive Business Continuity Group: Web link http://www.survive.com |
| [TUEs95] | Technische Universität Esslingen: *Software-Entwicklung – Methoden, Werkzeuge, Erfahrungen*, 6th Colloquium, 1995 |
| [USRI] | US Risk and Insurance Management Group: Web links http://www.rims.org; http://www.rmisweb.com; http://www.riskinfo.com |
| [Wall99] | Wallmüller E.: *Riskmanagementprozess*, Produktbeschreibung V1.9, Qualität & Informatik, Eigenverlag, Zürich, 1999 |
| [Webs81] | *Webster's Third New International Dictionary*, Merriam, Springfield, MA, 1981 |
| [WiBa87] | Wix B., Balzert H.: *Softwarewartung*, BI Wissenschaftsverlag, Zürich, 1987 |
| [WiMe01] | Wieczorek M., Meyerhoff D.: *Software Quality – State of the Art in Management, Testing, and Tools*, Springer, Berlin, Heidelberg, 2001 |